EMIKO DAVIES

ACQUACOTTA

**RECIPES AND STORIES
FROM TUSCANY'S SECRET
SILVER COAST**

Hardie Grant
BOOKS

FOREWORD
STEPHANIE ALEXANDER

My contribution and participation in social media is a bit hit and miss, but it was through Instagram that I first made contact with the remarkable Emiko Davies. In 2016 I read her first book, *Florentine*, and was enchanted. Emiko seemed to share my interest in foodways first of all, then in art, and in recording and noting how life was lived and enjoyed in that wonderful city. I was planning a short holiday to Florence, where Emiko was living at the time. I bravely made contact and am now pleased to report that we met, shared a meal or two and have since become good friends, despite the distance.

Many years before we met, I had visited the remote and less well-known Tuscan region of the Maremma and was amazed at its wild beauty. In 2017, Emiko had just written and published *Acquacotta* and after reading it I knew that part of my next holiday would have to be in that part of Tuscany. And so I did and visited many of the places she describes in *Acquacotta*. I also went to Giglio Island, a story for another day, and found it an unforgettable experience that involved overcoming my fears and successfully climbing many rocky and uneven steps and disembarking from a small boat directly onto rocks. Scary but exhilarating.

So I am pleased to have been asked to write a foreword for this new edition of *Acquacotta*.

Emiko is not just a good cook; she is also a brilliant photographer and a thorough researcher. Just as the Maremma, or the Silver Coast as it is known, is an interesting mix of mountain and rocky landscapes and charming small towns teeming with life, so too does this book allow the serious reader to know so much of the history of Tuscany. It includes dishes from the past that are still cooked today, together with very accessible and simple combinations that feature the best local ingredients. There could be no better commentator and interpreter of the landscape and its close connection to what one eats. Emiko notices and notes down, and takes wonderful photos and follows up to find out more.

In this book there are recipes that require skill and lots of time, and there are others that are immediate. Australian readers may have to make some substitutes for harder to locate ingredients like fresh and salt-packed anchovies, live eel and mantis shrimp, and wild boar, and not every cook will be prepared to make their own artichokes *sott'olio* or *sott'aceti* (page 135), but there are so many other possibilities. You could start with the book's titular soup, Acquacotta (page 14), or the crostini featuring polenta and mushrooms (page 25), and move onto the delicious fish and shellfish dishes (pages 93, 106, 110), the tagliolini with chickpeas (page 187), the tomato and celery leaf salad from Giglio Island (page 164), the ricotta-filled pastries (pages 223, 228), the melon granita (page 246) and dozens more dishes. I am already planning a party so I can cook a large piece of venison in place of wild boar using Emiko's reproduction of *cinghiale in dolce-forte* (page 55), an ancient dish that includes candied citron, chocolate and pine nuts.

This is a beautiful book and turning the pages and enjoying Emiko's outstanding location shots will have you planning a new holiday while you discover a delicious dish for dinner.

INTRODUCTION / 9

FROM THE WOODS
DAL BOSCO / 19

FROM THE SEA AND THE LAGOON
DAL MARE E DALLA LAGUNA / 59

FROM THE VEGETABLE PATCH
DALL'ORTO / 127

FROM THE FARMHOUSE
DALLA FATTORIA / 171

SWEETS
DOLCI / 205

REFERENCES / 260
INDEX / 262
GRAZIE / 269
ABOUT THE AUTHOR / 271

INTRODUCTION

This book is an ode to a beautiful sliver of the Maremma, in the southernmost part of Tuscany, where I lived for six months in 2015 with my daughter and my Tuscan husband, Marco, while he was working as Head Sommelier of Il Pellicano's renowned restaurant. We made our home in the pretty little fishing village of Porto Ercole, the smaller but more ancient of the two towns on the rugged, island-like promontory of Monte Argentario. A few kilometres away is Orbetello, with its lagoon and its strong Spanish history. The island of Giglio is a short ferry ride away. And a quick drive down the road is the beautiful town of Capalbio, the last Tuscan town on the border of Lazio.

It's a little corner of paradise known locally as *la Costa d'Argento*, the Silver Coast, supposedly named for the silvery shimmer of the salt and pepper sand that you find in these parts, along the Tyrrhenian Sea. A little further inland are the towns of Saturnia, with its pummelling natural hot springs; and Pitigliano, a stunning and ancient town seemingly carved out of the tuff rock it sits on, with a long and significant Jewish heritage.

This is a region of wide open spaces, swaying wheat fields, hills polka-dotted with olive trees, rambling vineyards bearing native grapes, overgrown fig trees and rampant prickly pears, long beaches and wild animals. Little villages sit perched, relatively undisturbed, on their hilltops with views of the sea – their roots stretching back to the most ancient of all Tuscans (the Etruscans). Closer to Rome than Florence, this stunning corner of the Maremma has a cuisine influenced largely by fishermen, hunters, farmers and *butteri* (cowboys). Straightforward, thrifty and fully dependent upon its landscape of sea and hills, it's rich with history and flavour. And it is unlike any other in Tuscany.

One-pot dishes are a preferred way of cooking in the area, and whether it's a seafood or lamb stew or a soup of vegetables and a poached egg, it is food that I love to eat and love to cook – comforting, low-maintenance and easy to prepare. Much of it is born out of poverty, which means there also happens to be a surprising selection of vegan and gluten-free dishes (see the vegan and gluten-free index entries at the back of the book to find these quickly). It's also food that calls for sharing with friends or family, gathered around a big table with plenty of local wine and good conversation, perhaps finishing with a homemade digestif made from foraged herbs. Like most peasant cuisine, it's about getting the best out of a few ingredients and providing a belly-filling and nutritious meal that not only doesn't cost the earth but is simply delicious.

THE RECIPES

The recipes in this book are ones that I enjoy preparing, sharing and eating, much of it according to the seasons. In the long, hot and humid summer months in southern coastal Tuscany, the oven is off-limits and so is most cooking, except for a quick boil of some pasta here or there or some toasted bread, rubbed with tomato and doused in olive oil. I could live on cold dishes made with just-hauled-in seafood, such as lemon-cured sole or marinated fried mackerel. Come late summer and early autumn, you find any way possible to eat wild mushrooms – fried, on *crostini*, in pasta with thick, silky handmade *pappardelle* and in soup – while white grapes and plump green figs pile high in the shops, just asking to be cooked into jam. As soon as the temperature becomes remotely reasonable to begin cooking long and slow again, one of the things I crave most is *acquacotta*, a stew of tomato and onions with a poached egg on top.

The chapters are organised by themes that I think are particularly Maremman in nature. *Dal Bosco* (literally 'from the woods') includes recipes from the mountains and scrub-covered areas where hunting for game and foraging for mushrooms, chestnuts, wild flowers and herbs, once activities born from necessity, have now become favourite local pastimes. A guide to the local mushrooms is included.

Dal Mare e Dalla Laguna ('from the sea and the lagoon') includes some of the many ancient seafood dishes of this corner of Tuscany, in particular from the fishing towns of Monte Argentario and the lagoon of Orbetello. It's still one of the most important fishing areas in Tuscany and there is a wealth of seafood found here. To navigate it all, I have included a guide to some of the most commonly found seafood in this area.

Working through this cookbook, I realised that many of the recipes happen to be vegetarian, even vegan, and others barely have any red meat – just some lamb and the hunted wild boar. This is in stark contrast to the 'typical Tuscan food' most think of when dining, for example, in Florence, where *bistecca* reigns. It's interesting, but simply a reflection of the poverty of the area. In contrast to the bigger cities, many kept their own vegetable gardens on the Silver Coast, even growing their own grains and beans, foraged the nearby woods, and perhaps raised small animals for consumption (*da cortile*, or 'courtyard animals'), such as rabbits, poultry and pigs. The *Orto and Fattoria* chapters ('from the vegetable patch' and 'from the farmhouse', respectively) are inspired by this.

Finally, there's *Dolci* ('sweets') to finish things off, with things like *biscotti* for dunking into wine, ricotta tarts and chestnut cake. This chapter includes many of the most traditional preparations, namely biscuits and homely tarts and cakes, as well as preserves and granita inspired by the favourite local summer fruit.

PRACTICALITIES

Recipes were tested on a standard gas cooktop. When I say 'low heat', I mean as low and gentle as you can get. You may need to adjust cooking times for induction or electric cooktops.

Baking recipes were tested in a conventional oven. If using a fan-forced (convection) oven, you may need to adjust the temperature by lowering slightly.

When a recipe calls for eggs, particularly a pasta or baking recipe, use free-range eggs roughly weighing 55–60 g (2 oz).

Forgetting to add salt to the water when boiling pasta or under-seasoning it will result in very bland pasta, something that cannot be corrected later, no matter how tasty the sauce. Italians are very quick to point out under-seasoned pasta (just as much as over-cooked pasta), and I admit that although it took me several years of eating pasta almost daily, I finally now fully understand why. To cook perfectly seasoned pasta, you'll need to add about a teaspoon of salt per litre of water and approximately a litre of water per 100 g (1½ oz) of pasta.

I always measure recipe ingredients by metric weight (with the occasional handful or pinch by eye, by feel or by taste). It is the way Italians cook and it is the most reliable way to measure out ingredients in a recipe. I thoroughly suggest doing the same for best results, particularly for pasta and baked goods. The conversions listed here indicate Australian (metric) cups and tablespoons, not US cups and tablespoons. Note that they are slightly different: 1 metric cup is 250 ml (8½ fl oz) and a tablespoon is 20 ml (¾ fl oz), but in the US 1 cup is 237 ml (8 oz) and a tablespoon is 15 ml (½ fl oz). So American cooks can be a little generous with their cup and tablespoon measurements.

SOME OTHER HANDY TIPS
Deep frying – page 24
Tips for foraging flowers – page 35
Cleaning anchovies – page 75
Cleaning calamari – page 80
Cleaning octopus – page 87
Purging clams – page 95
Cooking polenta – page 109
Preparing raw fish – page 124
Sterilising and sealing jars – page 137
Making pastry in hot weather – page 225
Bringing eggs and butter to room temperature quickly – page 230

WHAT IS ACQUACOTTA?

There is a well-known European folktale known as 'The Stone Soup', or *zuppa di sasso* in Italy. I first heard it through my friend Giulia Scarpaleggia, who recounted it in the context of a Tuscan soup, known as *acquacotta*. As the story moves from one side of Europe to the other, it changes slightly, from country to country and storyteller to storyteller. Sometimes the moral emphasises the soup-maker's ability to trick his host into giving him a free feed, and sometimes it highlights the sense of community and working together.

My favourite version is one my daughter has in a beautifully illustrated picture book by Anaïs Vaugelade, where the protagonist is depicted as an old, starving wolf, who approaches a village of wary but curious animals with a sack containing a stone. He asks the hen if he can make a stone soup over her fireplace. One by one the neighbouring animals suggest it might be better, more flavourful, with one of their favourite ingredients – a celery stalk, some leek, a zucchini (courgette). In the end, the animals pull up chairs around the fireplace with steaming bowls of delicious soup, wobbling glasses of wine and conversation.

It's my favourite version because it is, to me, so much about what Italian food is all about: conviviality. And also a bit of that, 'I like to put such and such ingredient in that dish' or 'My mother or grandmother always did this but she would put two cloves of garlic', which so often influences how recipes are learned, passed on and cooked. The folktale's stone soup actually exists in Tuscany – *brodo di sasso* or 'rock broth' is a soup from Livorno, where stones from the sea are placed in a pot of boiling water to give a hint of the flavour of the sea, even when you have nothing much else to put in it.

I think so many recipes born out of Tuscan *cucina povera* came about this way – from having very little and needing to feed the family with whatever is at hand. A piece of stale bread, some weeds from the field outside, some water and, with luck, an egg from the chicken coop. This is, essentially, the recipe for *acquacotta*. Like the folktale's stone soup, there are many, many versions of *acquacotta*, changing depending on which town you are in, what you can scrounge around for and how hungry you are.

Acquacotta literally means 'cooked water' or, better, 'cooked in water' and it describes the basic process of the meal – boiling vegetables in water. It is arguably the most famous dish of the Maremma, a dish I like very much but also a concept that evokes so much more than just the dish itself.

An ancient soup, it was once a travelling meal for the many Maremman occupations that took people far from their homes – a meal that was thrown together outdoors, over a campfire, with a pot of boiling water, made by cowboys, shepherds or fishermen, wherever they happened to be. Along with the water, the other ingredients included some dried, stale bread (even bread that was specifically dried to be easily portable for travelling and keeping well), garlic and wild herbs and jagged-edged greens that were foraged from around the fields during the spring and autumn. Fishermen would add some small fish from their catch, the sort of thing that you couldn't sell at the

market. At home, onions, potatoes or tomatoes from the vegetable patch were added.

Sometimes it's more solid and chunky, letting the bread soak up any liquid. In other places it's a watery broth, with plenty of vegetables floating through it. Often, an egg for each person is cracked into the simmering soup to poach, or they are beaten together with a handful of pecorino cheese and poured over the top of the bubbling soup. The addition of eggs in *acquacotta*, something that makes it unique among Tuscan soups, is an ancient one, according to Florentine gastronome Paolo Petroni in his cookbook, *Il Grande Libro della Vera Cucina Toscana* (1996).

In *Cucina Maremmana* (1991) Aldo Santini wrote, *'In Maremma tutto si assomiglia e niente si ripete'* (In Maremma, everything is similar but nothing is repeated.) He was referring to the preparation of wild boar (see page 50) but it's relevant for *acquacotta*, too. Every town has its own version and each is decidedly different from the other, even though they all share the same name and the same story.

MAREMMA AMARA

Known for its wild natural beauty, the idyllic coastline of the Tyrrhenian Sea and winding (often crumbling) hilltop villages, Maremma is an area marked by an invisible border of Etruscan history squeezed between the geographical borders of the sea and the mountains. Almost a region within a region, it runs the length of the Tuscan coastline from Cecina, in the southern part of the province of Livorno, to Lazio's province of Viterbo. Making up about a quarter of Tuscany's surface area, it has the town of Grosseto and its province, more or less, at its heart.

Dante Alighieri helped define Maremma's area in the *Inferno* of the *Divine Comedy*, where he describes the Maremma of the 1300s as a rugged, harsh land inhabited only by wild animals:

*'Non han sì aspri sterpi né sì folti
quelle fiere selvagge che 'n odio hanno
tra Cecina e Corneto i luoghi cólti.'*

Even its name, Maremma, comes from a description of its landscape – from the Latin *maritima* (of the sea) and from the Castilian word *marisma* (marsh or wetland).

It is this wetland that plagued the Maremma with deadly malaria from Dante's time until the early twentieth century, resulting in poverty, isolation and abandonment for centuries. In the 1700s and early

1800s, improvements to the Maremman wetlands and the soil were attempted by the Grand Dukes of Tuscany, notably Ferdinand III (who ironically caught malaria there and died in the summer of 1824), and then his son, Leopold II. The idea was to repopulate this part of Tuscany by draining the marshes and making the soil fertile enough to cultivate. But it wasn't until the 1920s that the marshes were drained and the area successfully repopulated under the Fascist government.

In part, the delay in ridding the Maremma of malaria and its devastating effects has to do with the fact that it wasn't until 1898 when the cause of malaria was finally discovered and proven as a mosquito-borne infectious disease. Although even the ancient Romans realised that malaria occurred in areas where stagnant water was found, they didn't know it was because it was the preferred breeding ground of mosquitoes. Before the discovery of the cause of malaria, it was thought that stagnant and dirty water created a sort of miasma that made the air toxic and unhealthy and that this, as well as poor quality or badly-kept food, was the cause of malaria – which comes from the Italian words, mal aria, literally, 'bad air'.

The words of a famous nineteenth-century folk song, called Maremma Amara, is sung in a beautiful but melancholy and mournful tone. With its eerie and extremely sad undertone, it can be likened to Portuguese Fado. It's a song that speaks of the real pain, suffering, longing and isolation caused by the malaria-stricken lands.

'Tutti mi dicon Maremma, Maremma
ma a me mi pare una Maremma amara.
L'uccello che ci va perde la penna
io c'ho perduto una persona cara.
Sia maledetta Maremma Maremma
sia maledetta Maremma e chi l'ama.
Sempre mi trema il cor quando ci vai
perchè ho paura che non torni mai.'

'Everyone tells me Maremma, Maremma
but it seems to me a miserable Maremma.
The bird that goes there perishes
I have lost there a loved one.
Damned Maremma Maremma
damned Maremma and those who love it.
Still my heart trembles when you go there
because I'm afraid you'll never come back.'

The few Maremmans who remained steadfast, such as the butteri (the cowboys who raised long-horn cattle) became icons who symbolised the tough and hard-working lifestyle of this unique part of Tuscany. The many centuries of malaria, poverty and isolation may have been the Maremma's curse, but today they also seem to be its blessing. Everything that you see now has been shaped by it, from the unspoilt landscape to the culture and its important connection to the land and its wonderful food, with its rich traditions.

FROM THE WOODS

DAL BOSCO

MUSHROOM FORAGING ON MONTE ARGENTARIO

By the end of summer I'm ready for a change. Don't get me wrong. I love nothing more than being barefoot. I love eating fresh peaches and melons for lunch, jammy figs or gelato as snacks, and I adore ripe, squidgy tomatoes with olive oil for dinner. But after a particularly hot summer, I'm ready for a chill in the air, for wearing scarves and hats, and indulging in a warming cup of tea in the afternoon. Seeing mushrooms is the hint that that's all soon to come.

By August, mushroom gatherers have already got a plan to andare a funghi in the chestnut and oak woods looking for late-summer funghi, which will then be used in soup (page 28), tossed with pappardelle (page 30) or layered on top of crostini (page 25).

Umberto, a friend who lives in Porto Ercole, is a hairdresser by trade but moonlights as a mushroom forager and fisherman – like many Maremmans. He shows me the photographs of his latest mushroom haul – what looks like hundreds of porcini spread out over and filling the top of a large table. He doesn't even like porcini, but his friends do, so he picks them, bags them and freezes them or gives them away.

When I ask him how he learned how to identify and know where to find wild mushrooms, he looks at me as if I just asked him how he learned to walk and talk. He shrugs, but then responds that it's from going foraging with his family as a child, and then later while going hunting with friends – you'd spot the mushrooms as you were walking through the forest.

He doesn't have to go far to find them; they are everywhere if you know how and where to look for them. Sometimes Umberto spots mushrooms on the way to his daughter's preschool and will return with bags of them on the back of the motorino.

Monte Argentario is full of rich, serene and unique Mediterranean forest and scrub. Not only do the wild boars love it, but the mushrooms do too – in the right season, they're prolific, especially when the right amount of rain follows the summer. Once an ancient island, now joined to the mainland by the sandy, pine-covered dunes of Feniglia and Giannella, Argentario has a unique mixture of plant life, which Umberto is convinced makes the mushrooms more delicious and more aromatic than anything he has ever tasted on the mainland. Here, he collects mushrooms under cork trees, corbezzolo (Irish strawberry trees) and erica (heather), rather than the more commonplace oaks of inland Maremma, and there's no doubt this rich combination of plant life contributes to beautifully fragrant and tasty mushrooms.

Before going mushroom picking you should not only be armed with a good, illustrated book on local mushrooms, but if you are a novice, make sure you have an expert with you as well. An illustrated book is not the only way to help you choose the right mushrooms; note that toxic mushrooms will often let you know by sight and smell that they are not for eating. There are some types of boletus (porcini-related) that you cannot mistake for being poisonous, thanks to their unusual colours: they have red stems and when you cut into them the flesh of the mushrooms turn blue. Similarly, the fairytale bright red, white-spotted mushrooms are to be avoided. Often a toxic mushroom also has an unpleasant, harsh smell – the kind of smell that you don't want to put in your mouth. Nature has its way of telling you. Good mushrooms should smell wonderful: earthy, nutty, but more specifically like almonds or amaretti, sometimes like flour, uncooked bread dough, butter, aniseed or even honey. In Tuscany, if you are not a resident in the area where you are foraging, you need to obtain a permit. You will also need clothes that cover arms and legs, gloves and a basket (not a plastic bag – the spores of the mushrooms should be able to fall through the cracks in the basket, to help the continuity of mushrooms growing in the area).

CAESAR'S MUSHROOMS

Ovoli (*Amanita caesarea*) These beautiful mushrooms start out looking like round, bright vermillion-orange eggs (hence their Italian name, which means 'egg'). But then they grow with a long thin stem holding up a deep-orange umbrella-like top with lemon-yellow gills. They like to grow in the shade of oak and chestnut trees, and do particularly well after a very hot summer. The best way to eat the young, egg-shaped ones is raw, thinly sliced, with olive oil. When cooked, these rusty-orange capped mushrooms give out a beautiful yolk-coloured sauce, looking almost like it is spiced with saffron. Ancient Romans were as fond of these as their modern counterparts, hence their name in English. It is even thought that the Roman armies helped distribute this native Italian mushroom north of the peninsula as they are still found along ancient Roman routes. Although it's not hard to see the difference, note that there is a related mushroom that is toxic (it is not deadly but will cause highly unpleasant results if you eat it). *Amanita muscaria* looks in all ways similar except for the colour – deep red caps with little white or beige spots just like a fairy toadstool. The most deadly of all mushrooms, the aptly named 'Death Cap' (*Amanita phalloides*) is a common mushroom with a similar form but, again, colour will help you distinguish them (these have a greenish-tinted cap). They are rarely found in mountains, but do like to grow near oak and cork trees.

CHANTERELLE MUSHROOMS

Galletti (*Cantharellus cibarius*) Pretty, yolk-yellow chanterelle mushrooms are sweet and delicate – and excellent prepared with calamari (page 80) or with pasta (page 30). These mushrooms take on different characteristics depending on the trees you find them under.

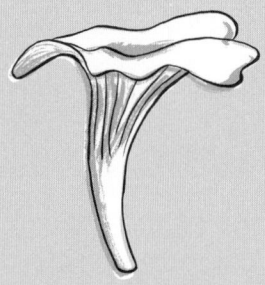

MONK'S HEAD

Ordinali (*Clitocybe geotropa* or *Infundibulicybe geotropa*) These are highly prized mushrooms that go by many a name. In English they're known as trooping funnel or monk's head. In Argentario they're also known as *cardarelle*, named after the shape of its cap, which opens up to the sky like the traditional buckets used by *muratori* (builders). They also go by *funghi di san Martino* or *cimballo* (for their cymbal-like shape) and even Maremmano, which is self-explanatory. Cream-coloured with a sturdy stem, they grow in rings ('fairy rings' as we say; Italians call them 'witches circles') in fields, where their presence makes the grass greener. Look for young ones, which have an intense, nutty aroma. Some say you can cook these in place of truffles, such is their strong, pleasant scent. They're good for roasting, stewing (Umberto likes adding them to a sugo) or preserving in oil.

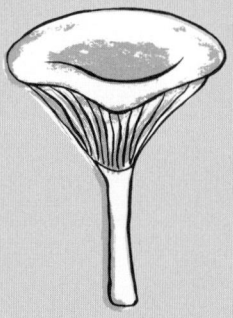

PARASOL MUSHROOM

Bubbola or *Mazza di tamburo* (*Macrolepiota procera* or *Lepiota procera*) These mushrooms have a delicate flavour and slender stems bearing a shaggy parasol top that can grow to the size of a dinner plate. When you find them with the top still closed, much like an umbrella shut tight, these are particularly good roasted (cook them well; they are slightly toxic in their raw state). A very similar mushroom known as the shaggy parasol (*Lepiota rhacodes* or *Chlorophyllum rhacodes*) is like a miniature version of the *bubbola* that grows in beds of fallen needles from fir trees. Note that this mushroom is very similar to a number of toxic ones: *lepiota cristata*, or *false mazza di tamburo* and, in North America, *Chlorophyllum molybdites* (the 'false parasol').

PORCINI

(*Boletus edulis*) The king of mushrooms barely needs an introduction; they are the most prized, of course, and the most used in traditional dishes. With a unique aroma and flavour, these are found mostly in autumn in pine forests but *Porcini estivi* (*Boletus aestivalis*) can be found (as their name hints) in summer, growing under chestnuts, oak and beech trees. Like the *galletti*, they're wonderful prepared with calamari (page 80).

WEEPING BOLETE

Pinaioli/Pinaroli (*Boletus granulatus* or *Suillus granulatus*) Named for their special attachment to pine trees, under which they grow, these mushrooms have a shiny cap, which is sticky when wet and pale-yellow, sweet flesh. Remove the stalks and peel the cap before eating and then try them sliced and deep-fried (see page 24) or preserved in oil as in *Carciofini Sott'olio* (page 135).

FROM THE WOODS

FUNGHI FRITTI
FRIED MUSHROOMS

The end of summer is synonymous with mushrooms – and when mushrooms are mentioned in Tuscany, they're usually talking about porcini. This is a delicious and straightforward way to enjoy these particularly meaty and earthy mushrooms – simply cut into thick slices, dusted with flour and thrown into a pan of bubbling oil.

Nineteenth-century gastronome Pellegrino Artusi has a recipe for *funghi fritti* among his 790 recipes in *Science in the Kitchen and the Art of Eating Well* (1891). It doesn't include any measurements but offers good advice on how to choose and prepare the best mushrooms for frying. Medium-sized porcini are best, he says, as large ones will be too soft and spongy, while small ones too hard. Cut the stalks where they touch the earth and wash them whole, quickly – but do not soak them or you'll lose part of their unique aroma. His fat of choice for frying mushrooms is olive oil and he thinks dipping the mushrooms in egg is 'superfluous' – here I disagree, as I am rather partial to the light, crisp, bubbly coating that the egg adds. If you want to keep these simple, omit the egg and simply dust the mushrooms in flour, Artusi's way.

SERVES 4

Rinse the whole mushrooms quickly under water, drain, then thoroughly pat dry with a clean tea towel. Slice into 1 cm (½ in) thick slices.

Arrange the flour in a shallow bowl. Beat the egg (if using) in a separate shallow bowl and place in the fridge until needed. Dust the slices of mushroom first in the flour, coating well and evenly. Shake off the excess and place on a wire rack until all the slices are coated in flour.

Pour enough olive oil into a medium saucepan so that the slices of mushrooms can float – at least 2–3 cm (¾–1¼ in) deep – and place the pan over medium–high heat. When the oil temperature reaches about 170°C (340°F), begin frying in batches (see 'Tips for a good fry'). If using the egg, dip the floured mushroom slices in the chilled egg to coat on both sides, just before placing immediately in the hot oil. Fry each batch for about 90 seconds, until the outside is crisp and golden and the inside is soft and cooked.

Remove slices from the oil and drain on paper towel, then serve hot, sprinkled with salt. Serve immediately.

400 g (14 oz) fresh porcini mushrooms
plain (all-purpose) flour, for dusting
1 egg, chilled (optional)
olive oil, for frying

NOTE
If you can't get fresh porcini mushrooms, replace with sturdy, meaty mushrooms like king brown or portobello.

TIPS FOR A GOOD FRY
Use chilled eggs for ultimate crispness.

The olive oil should be hot enough to cook the mushrooms through, but not too hot that it burns the outside and leaves the inside raw – ideally, it should be about 170°C (340°F). If you don't have a sugar thermometer to measure the temperature, do it the old-fashioned way and test by placing the end of a wooden spoon in the oil. Tiny little bubbles should immediately appear around the edges.

Fry in batches and don't overcrowd the pan or you'll reduce the temperature of the oil too much, resulting in soggy batter.

CROSTINI DI POLENTA CON I FUNGHI
POLENTA CROSTINI WITH MUSHROOMS

The hard work goes into preparing this firm polenta, but once it is cooked and set (which can be done well in advance) you only need to slice it, then grill, bake or fry the polenta slices to crisp them up. Polenta, or ground cornmeal, is naturally free of gluten so these make a wonderful *crostini* alternative with just about any kind of topping – but they are particularly good with something juicy like ragu (see *Sugo Maremmano*, page 194) or this mushroom topping.

In Italy, polenta generally comes in three different types: *bramata*, which has a coarse grain, and is good for making a firmer polenta; *fioretto*, a fine-grain cornmeal, ideal for soft, creamy polenta or for baking cakes or biscuits; and instant polenta. The instant variety is partially cooked, then dried again, and takes just minutes to prepare. What you make up for in time, however, you'll lose in flavour and texture (much like quick cooking rice). I find it's only really useful for baking into cakes if you can't get the finer ground *fioretto*.

MAKES ABOUT 18 CROSTINI

To prepare the polenta crostini, cook the polenta in 1 litre (34 fl oz/ 4 cups) of water and a good pinch of salt in a large non-stick saucepan over the lowest heat for about 30–40 minutes to create a very dense, very thick polenta. Use a wooden spoon to stir regularly – not constantly, but you want to give it a good mix every couple of minutes. It may help to have another pair of hands to take over when your arms get tired. If big bubbles start emerging in the polenta, remove it from the heat for a minute, then continue. When you think the polenta is ready, taste it – it should not taste floury or feel grainy. It should have a soft and creamy texture.

Take out a baking tray or a shallow casserole dish, about 21 x 30 cm (8¼ x 12 in). Line it with baking paper or grease it with olive oil. When the polenta has cooked, transfer it to the baking tray. Quickly (as it sets fast), press the polenta down with a silicone spatula – or with damp hands if it's not too hot – spreading it out as you go, until it is about 1.5 cm (½ in) thick, and smooth and even on top. Put the tray in the fridge if you have space, but the benchtop is fine if you don't. Once completely cool and set, cut the polenta into rectangular slices approximately 5 x 7 cm (2 x 2¾ in). This can all be done in advance.

When ready to serve, there are many ways to prepare the polenta slices – ideally you want them golden, crisp and crunchy outside and warm and soft inside. To bake, place the polenta slices on a baking tray lined with baking paper, drizzle with a little olive oil and bake for approximately

300 g (10½ oz/2 cups) coarse-ground polenta (such as *bramata*)
olive oil for greasing and/or drizzling (optional)

MUSHROOM TOPPING
500 g (1 lb 2 oz) mushrooms
2 garlic cloves
2 tablespoons extra-virgin olive oil
1 handful herbs, such as calamint or thyme
salt and pepper

SUBSTITUTIONS
Use any mushroom you like for this; a mixture of different types is even better than just one kind. Calamint (Nepitella in Italian) is a wild herb that likes to grow in cracks along less-travelled paths or in tufts, hidden in the grass, only revealing itself with a strong, sweet, minty perfume when trodden on. It's the favourite herb to partner with mushrooms in Tuscany. If you can't find it, you can use a mixture of marjoram or oregano and mint or just substitute it completely with thyme, which is also very nice with mushrooms.

Pictured overleaf >

20 minutes at 200°C (400°F) until they are golden. Alternatively, you can brush them with a bit of olive oil and then grill, sear or even barbecue them until golden, or deep-fry them in hot oil (see page 24 for tips on frying in oil).

In the meantime, prepare the mushroom topping. Cut off the ends of the stems, clean the caps gently of any dirt with some paper towel and slice thinly. Flatten the garlic cloves with the back of a knife and place in a frying pan with the olive oil over medium heat. Let the olive oil infuse with the garlic for 2 minutes, then add the mushrooms and cook until soft. The type of mushrooms you use will dictate how long this takes, but most will be ready in under 5 minutes. Remove the garlic cloves, add the fresh herbs and season with salt and pepper.

Top the hot crostini with the warm mushroom mixture and serve immediately.

VARIATION

Leftover polenta can be cut into bite-sized pieces or gnocchetti (little gnocchi). They're placed on a greased ovenproof dish with Sugo Maremmano (page 194) over the top and baked at 180°C (350°F) for 10–15 minutes.

ZUPPA DI FUNGHI
WILD MUSHROOM SOUP

The first time I had this classic Maremman soup was in a well-lit football field during a late-summer *sagra* (see page 202), where we feasted on wild boar and other local specialities while mosquitoes feasted on us. Pasta dressed in wild mushrooms (see page 30) is often *in bianco* (which means 'white' or without tomato), in a simple preparation that showcases the flavour of the mushrooms. However, in this soup, meaty wild mushrooms are cooked in a rich tomato base that makes a sturdy partner and lends a pleasant acidity to nutty, creamy porcini. (See page 22 for information on specific wild mushrooms foraged on Monte Argentario.) If you like a bit of heat, the chilli in this soup is an absolute must.

SERVES 4

In a large pot, cook the onion and garlic over low heat in olive oil for approximately 10 minutes, or until the onion softens but doesn't colour.

If using dried porcini, put them in a small bowl and pour just-boiled water over the top to cover. Let the mushrooms soften in the water for about 15 minutes. Remove the mushrooms carefully (they will be hot!), straining the liquid through a fine-meshed sieve lined with a coffee filter or a couple of sheets of paper towel. Chop the reconstituted mushrooms roughly.

Add the fresh and reconstituted mushrooms to the onion and garlic, season with a pinch of salt, and then pour over the white wine. Turn the heat up to medium–high and simmer for 10 minutes. Add the tomato passata, along with 125 ml (4 fl oz/½ cup) of water, season with another pinch of salt and add the chilli, if using (or freshly ground black pepper instead). Continue cooking for another 15–20 minutes until the mushrooms are tender and the soup reduces slightly and thickens. Remove from the heat and add the herbs.

Grill (broil) or toast the bread slices. Rub the warm toast just once with a peeled, raw clove of garlic for extra flavour. Put the toast in the bottom of four bowls and pour the soup over the top.

1 brown (yellow) onion, finely chopped
2 garlic cloves, finely chopped, plus 1 extra for rubbing bread if desired
2–3 tablespoons extra-virgin olive oil
20 g (¾ oz) dried porcini (if using)
450 g (1 lb) mixed fresh mushrooms (including fresh porcini if possible), roughly chopped
125 ml (4 fl oz/½ cup) white wine
400 g (14 oz) tomato passata (puréed tomatoes)
chilli flakes or chopped fresh red chilli (optional) or freshly ground black pepper
1 handful calamint (or marjoram or oregano and mint)
4 slices white crusty bread

SUBSTITUTIONS

If you don't have access to fresh porcini or other wild mushrooms, you can make this soup with dried porcini and a mixture of available fresh mushrooms (such as Swiss brown, button, oyster and Japanese shimeji mushrooms). The important thing in any case is to use a variety for depth of flavour and texture.

ON SOUP

> 'It is impossible to think of any good meal, no matter how plain or elegant, without soup or bread in it.'
> – M.F.K. Fisher

Soup is loved in the Maremma. So you will find here, too, many soup recipes. I say 'soup' but really they are much more than that. Italians have a way with words, especially when it comes to describing their food, but in English, we have rather limited descriptions. As *Oxford Companion to Italian Food* author Gillian Riley says, 'Soup and stew are easy-going, almost interchangeable words in English, used to describe many recipes, anything from a thick to a runny dish.'

In Italian, however, there are words that describe many different types of soup that we would have to use adjectives with in English. These include *crema* or *vellutata* (which comes from *velluto*, meaning velvet or smooth), a thick, creamy soup that has usually been blended, but is slightly different from passata (a thin vegetable or legume purée that has literally been 'passed' through a food mill to get its texture).

Minestra is a liquid-based soup, often with vegetables and/or meat, while minestrone is like *minestra* but heartier or bigger, perhaps with the addition of beans or pasta or both. These last two soups come from the Latin word *minestrare*, which describes the act of ladling soup out to the family and shares the same root word as *somministrare* (to distribute or hand out), as you would with soup to the homeless in a shelter.

Meanwhile, *zuppa* – a word that dates to the Renaissance – comes from *inzuppare* ('to sop' in English). The action of sopping up the juices with bread is a part of eating the *zuppa*. It usually describes a thick soup with seafood, meat or vegetables and is served with bread, of course, usually stale or toasted to withstand being submerged and soaked in liquid.

In Tuscany, soups take on their own unique names, too. *Pappa al pomodoro* is named for its texture, lent to it by thickened bread, whereas *pappa* (a mush made from bread) comes from the word *pappare* ('to gobble'), as does *pappardelle*. *Ribollita*, the hearty bread and vegetable soup, is literally 'reboiled'. Then you have soups unique to Tuscany's Maremma: *Acquacotta* (page 42), or 'cooked in water'; and *Caldaro* (page 110), a seafood soup of Argentario, named after the cauldron in which it was traditionally cooked.

PAPPARDELLE SUI FUNGHI

PAPPARDELLE PASTA WITH WILD MUSHROOMS

This is my favourite way to prepare any wild mushroom – that is, extremely simply, letting the mushrooms speak for themselves. I like to use a mixture of mushrooms whenever possible. I find porcini on their own incredibly strong, so I like to add a handful of sunny chanterelles or Caesar's mushrooms, which not only add depth of flavour but they brighten up the plate, too. Once you've taken the time to clean the mushrooms of their forest floor dirt, this sauce is very quick to prepare. It goes best with fresh pasta, but in a pinch, dried pasta makes this a very quick meal indeed. Don't go overboard with the cheese (in fact, you could easily leave it off entirely) as you don't want to mask the flavour of the mushrooms.

Marco's nonna Lina was superstitious in the kitchen (you could never lay a loaf of bread upside-down or let the salt spill around her) and she used to prepare freshly picked mushrooms with *nepitella* (calamint) and an obligatory garlic clove. They used to say that the garlic would turn black to warn you if any of the foraged mushrooms were poisonous impostors (there are several varieties of mushroom that look very similar to Caesar's mushrooms but are actually deadly). I like to think this old wives' tale is just a way to remember that garlic goes really, really well with wild mushrooms.

SERVES 4

PAPPARDELLE PASTA

200 g (7 oz/¼ cup) semola rimacinata (fine semolina), plus plenty more for dusting

200 g (7 oz/1⅓ cups) plain (all-purpose) flour

4 eggs

SAUCE

300 g (10½ oz) mushrooms (about 2 medium-sized porcini, plus a handful of chanterelles, button or Caesar's mushrooms)

3 tablespoons extra-virgin olive oil

1–2 garlic cloves, squashed with the flat edge of a kitchen knife

125 ml (4 fl oz/½ cup) dry white wine

1 handful calamint (or marjoram or oregano and mint)

grated pecorino cheese to serve (optional)

To make the pasta, combine the flours together in a bowl. Make a well in the centre of the flours and crack the eggs into it. Begin mixing with a fork, from the centre outwards, slowly incorporating the flour. Eventually you will need to use your hands instead of the fork; keep combining the flour until you have a nice, soft dough. On a clean surface, well dusted with flour or semolina, knead the dough for about 10 minutes or until it is elastic and no longer sticky. Let the dough rest for at least 30 minutes, covered.

Divide the dough into 2–3 portions. With a pasta machine or on a work surface dusted with flour, roll out each portion into a thin sheet about 1 mm thick. I highly recommend a pasta machine for this job (though by hand it's not impossible); if using one, start with the widest setting and roll the dough through. Dust with semolina. Change the setting to the next consecutive number and roll the dough through again. Dust with semolina. Continue this way until you have a thin sheet about 1 mm thick – this is usually the second last setting on the pasta machine. You may find the sheet gets so long that it's difficult to handle – a second pair of hands is enormously helpful. You can also cut the sheet into manageable lengths.

Cut the pasta sheet lengthways into strips with a pastry wheel cutter about 2–2.5 cm (¾–1 in) wide for long, flat *pappardelle*. Or, for a quicker method, dust the pasta sheet generously with semolina, fold the pasta sheet several times over itself (dusting each fold with flour so it doesn't stick) and cut with a sharp knife or pastry wheel cutter into strips. Note that a fluted pastry wheel cutter gives a ruffled edge, which is nice for holding sauce. Unroll the noodles, dust generously with semolina and lay in a single layer on baking paper, or you can shape into little nest-like bundles of equal portions. If using soon, cover with a tea towel (dish towel) until the rest of the pasta is ready. If using the next day, you can let them 'air dry' and, in this case, it's better to lay them flat in a single layer.

In the meantime, prepare the mushrooms by cleaning them of any dirt gently with a damp cloth. Cut off the ends of their stems and slice the rest thinly or cut into dice. In a wide frying pan, heat the olive oil, add the garlic and cook over low–medium heat to 'infuse' the oil for 2–3 minutes, or until the garlic begins to colour. Add the mushrooms, season with salt and pepper, and cook for a further 5 minutes. Add the white wine and let the liquid cook down a little, for approximately 5 minutes. Turn off the heat, add the herbs and check for seasoning. Set aside.

Put the pasta in a large pot of boiling, well-salted water – ideally, use 1 teaspoon of salt per 1 litre (34 fl oz/4 cups) of water. Cook until silky and al dente, about 3–5 minutes. Drain, saving some of the cooking water, and toss the *pappardelle* with the mushrooms. If it is a bit dry, add the reserved pasta water. Serve with grated pecorino cheese, if desired.

NOTE
Use eggs that weigh 55–60 g (2 oz). Larger eggs will result in a stickier dough and you may need more flour to correct it. If using dried pasta, you'll need to cook 320 g (11½ oz), or 80 g (2¾ oz) per serve.

Pictured overleaf >

FIORI DI ACACIA FRITTI
FRIED ACACIA (BLACK LOCUST) BLOSSOMS

For a short couple of weeks in late spring, maybe even less, the country roads of the Maremma are lined with thin trees bearing bunches of pretty white flowers. Hanging down like miniature chandeliers, they have a heavy intoxicating perfume, quite like jasmine or orange blossom. You can't miss them. Known as Black Locust trees (or False Acacia, *Robinia pseudoacacia*) in English, they are native to North America, and were brought to Europe in the early 1600s. In Italy they go by the name *acacia* (pictured opposite and overleaf).

You can serve fried blossoms as an afternoon snack or as part of an antipasto. The result is similar to fried zucchini flowers (courgette or squash blossoms), which are really just a vehicle for eating deliciously crisp, fried batter – but with black locust blossoms, you have a delicate flavour of nectar and spice mingling with that perfume reminiscent of orange blossom. They can be sprinkled with sea salt, dusted in icing (confectioners') sugar or – my favourite – drizzled with locust honey (also known as *acacia* honey), a pale, delicate and fragrant honey.

You can use this same batter for frying sage leaves, zucchini flowers and heads of blooming, fragrant elderflower (*Sambucus nigra*), which overlaps the black locust season in southern Tuscany – together they make an impressive platter of fried flowers and herbs to serve as antipasto. If you're using the amount of batter in this recipe, it's plenty to fry about four of each type of flower.

SERVES 4

150 g (5½ oz/1 cup) plain (all-purpose) flour
12 large bunches of acacia (black locust) blossoms
vegetable oil, for frying
sea salt flakes or 1 tablespoon honey

Whisk the flour and 250 ml (8½ fl oz/1 cup) of water together in a large bowl until smooth. Let it rest and chill in the refrigerator for at least 30 minutes. The batter should be smooth and fairly runny – it should run off a spoon quickly. You may find after the resting time that you need to add a little more water.

In the meantime, prepare the flower bunches by trimming off any leaves and cutting into separate bunches. Leave the stem a good 4–5 cm (1½–2 in) long – it's handy for dipping and pulling the bunch out of the oil. Do not wash them (see Tips, opposite).

Pour the oil into a medium saucepan until it's about 4–5 cm (1½–2 in) deep – enough oil for the flowers to float in. Place the pan over medium-high heat and bring the oil to a temperature of about 160°C (320°F). You can use a sugar thermometer or test with the end of a wooden spoon – the spoon should be surrounded immediately by lots of tiny bubbles as soon as it hits the oil. If the oil starts smoking, it's too hot – turn down the heat or remove from the heat to cool it down for a moment.

Fry in batches of 3–4 so that you don't overcrowd the pan. Dip a bunch of flowers into the batter and turn to coat evenly. Holding the bunch by the stem, let the excess batter run off the flowers for a moment. Still holding the stem (tongs can do this if you're not game with fingers), place in the hot oil, shaking a little for the first few seconds so that the flowers separate from each other. Cook, turning as needed, for about 30–60 seconds or until the batter is crisp and evenly pale golden.

Drain on paper towel and continue dipping and frying with the rest of the bunches. Serve the warm fried flowers with either a sprinkling of sea salt flakes or a drizzle of honey.

TIPS FOR FORAGING AND PREPARING FLOWERS

Take a pair of pruning shears and a basket for the flowers.

Avoid polluted areas such as roadsides.

Go in the morning when flowers are freshest.

Smell before you pick. Keep only the best-smelling flowers, as these will also be the best-tasting ones. Avoid wilted or old flowers and don't pick flowers right after the rain.

Eat only the flowers and not the stems or leaves, which in some cases are toxic, but for ease of preparing, cut the flowers with stems intact.

Don't wash the flowers, as they can lose their fragrant pollen. However, do check for insects.

TORTA SALATA CON ASPARAGI SELVATICI
WILD ASPARAGUS TART

Any sort of savoury tart can be made with this recipe, but if you are lucky enough to be in possession of some peppery, foraged wild asparagus and herbs, this is possibly one of the nicest ways to make a meal of them. A wonderfully versatile tart, it can be served in thin slices as part of an antipasto, as a light lunch with some salad, bread and a glass of wine, or packed in a picnic or brought along to a friend's barbecue.

This pastry is quick and easy to pull together. It's a very basic shortcrust dough adapted from an Artusi recipe (one for *pasticci* or savoury pies). You can also use a store-bought roll of plain shortcrust pastry or puff pastry if you're short on time (start the recipe at the blind baking stage) – but honestly, this doesn't take long to make. The pastry can be prepared (and blind baked) the night before and the tart simply all put together right before you need it.

SERVES 4

To make the pastry, rub the chopped cold butter into the flour until there are no more large pieces of butter left. Add the salt and the milk (or water) a bit at a time until the dough just comes together (you may not need it all). Don't overwork it – stop as soon as it looks smooth and is neither sticky nor dry. If you're doing this in a food processor, it's even easier – blitz the butter and flour together and add the liquid in pulses until it comes together and is a smooth consistency. Chill in the fridge for 30 minutes, covered.

On a work surface dusted with flour, roll the pastry out to 3–4 mm (¼ in) thickness. Carefully transfer it to a pie dish approximately 24–26 cm (9½–10¼ in) in diameter, and gently press it down into the grooves of the dish. Trim the top edge with a sharp knife. Prick the base of the pastry all over with a fork. If making this ahead of time, at this point you can keep the raw pastry crust in the fridge overnight, covered, or keep in the freezer for another time.

When ready to use the pastry crust, heat the oven to 180°C (350°F).

Blind bake the pastry crust (this goes for store-bought pastry too) by setting baking paper over the top of the crust and filling the entire pastry case with baking beads. This will help the pastry to bake evenly. If you don't have baking beads, you can use some dried rice or beans. These are re-usable for this purpose; I keep mine in a jar labelled 'For blind baking' so I don't mix them up with the rest of the rice or beans.

SHORTCRUST PASTRY

70 g (2½ oz) chilled butter, chopped
250 g (9 oz/1⅔ cups) plain (all-purpose) flour
¼ teaspoon salt
80 ml (2½ fl oz/⅓ cup) chilled milk (or water)

FILLING

1 handful wild herbs (see variations)
350 g (12½ oz) wild asparagus
1 small brown (yellow) onion, thinly sliced
3–4 tablespoons extra-virgin olive oil
60 ml (2 fl oz/¼ cup) dry white wine (or water)
6 eggs
30 g (1 oz) finely grated parmesan or pecorino cheese

VARIATIONS

You can use any herbs here. Wild ones common to southern Tuscany would be wild fennel fronds, calamint, wild garlic, nettle and dandelion greens – a mixture of them adds fragrance and zingy character. But otherwise, a mixture of common fresh herbs such as thyme, marjoram, chives, mint and basil would be the next best thing. You can use regular asparagus here too, but try to get the thinnest ones possible. You can even skip the pastry crust completely and have this as a sort of baked frittata.

Bake for approximately 10–15 minutes, or until the edges of the pastry begin to turn golden. Remove from the oven and remove the baking beads and baking paper carefully. Return the crust back to the oven to 'dry' out the base for no more than 5 minutes. Set aside to cool.

Meanwhile, wash and pick through the herbs and asparagus, cutting off any tough parts of the stalk and chopping the rest roughly. I like to leave the asparagus long (if using regular asparagus, cut in half lengthways).

Put the onion in a large pan with half the olive oil and a pinch of salt. Cook gently over low heat for 5–10 minutes, stirring occasionally, so the onions sweat and soften without browning. You may need to add a splash of water to keep the mixture moist and so it doesn't stick. Add the asparagus and the wine (or water), and season with salt and freshly ground black pepper. Cook, stirring, over low–medium heat for approximately 7–10 minutes, or until tender. Set aside to cool.

Beat the eggs together gently with a fork. Season with salt and freshly ground black pepper. Add the cooled asparagus mixture, along with the chopped herbs and cheese, to the eggs. Pour the mixture over the pastry and bake in the oven for approximately 20–25 minutes, until the top is puffed and golden.

WILD ASPARAGUS

In Italy wild asparagus (Asparagus acutifolius) *looks just like cultivated asparagus but a very thin version that's usually dark green verging on purple. It shouldn't be confused with* Ornithogalum pyrenaicum, *also known as Prussian or Bath asparagus, which has a long, thin stem with a top of young flower shoots that resembles the tips of cultivated asparagus.*

If you are foraging for the asparagus yourself, there is some good advice in Patience Gray's classic book Honey from a Weed *(1986). She says that the long shoots are only tender at the top, so it's best to break them off at a length of 8 cm (3¼ in), which also allows the plant to continue developing shoots.*

Pictured overleaf >

L'ACQUACOTTA VITERBESE
VITERBO-STYLE ACQUACOTTA

This version of *acquacotta* comes from Viterbo, an ancient Etruscan town of Lazio, halfway between Capalbio (on the border of Tuscany) and Rome. The star ingredient here is the wild chicory, which lends an irreplaceable flavour to this dish — one of very pleasant bitterness (which sounds like an oxymoron but once you taste it, you'll see what I mean). It grows in curly mounds of jagged-edged weeds and can be collected around the surrounding countryside in the spring before they flower, often together with other wild vegetables and greens, such as stinging nettles, dandelions, sow thistle, wild beet, wild fennel and wild asparagus.

The characteristic of this Viterbo-style *acquacotta* is that the vegetables and aromatics are cooked entirely in water, not sizzled in olive oil. It's a wonderfully simple dish of clean flavours, where tufts of strong, bitter wild chicory sing out in contrast to the creamy, mellow egg yolk and fruity raw olive oil. I think it's perfect as is, but a traditional variation is to add pork sausage, crumbled into the soup after removing the casing.

To serve the *acquacotta*, the vegetables and accompanying broth are spooned over a slice of stale bread, which soaks up any liquid like a sponge. If you haven't got stale bread handy, dry out some slices of fresh crusty bread in a low oven. Choose a delicious, well-structured bread — it makes all the difference here. Remember that the dish should not be at all 'soupy'. In fact, any liquid that has not been soaked up by the bread should be removed, as it would interfere with the final touch: some extra-virgin olive oil, drizzled over the top.

SERVES 4

200 g (7 oz) wild chicory or silverbeet (Swiss chard), about 2 large bunches
2 whole, unpeeled garlic cloves
2 small potatoes, peeled and thinly sliced
300 g (10½ oz) tomatoes, chopped
4 slices stale bread (use a good, dense, wood-fired country loaf)
4 eggs
extra-virgin olive oil, to serve
1 handful chopped wild fennel and calamint, to serve

SUBSTITUTIONS
If you don't have wild chicory, you could use silverbeet (Swiss chard), though it won't have that same characteristic flavour. Other substitutes include watercress, dandelion greens and English spinach. If you don't have fresh wild herbs like wild fennel and calamint, try feathery fennel tops (instead of the wild fennel) and oregano, marjoram, thyme or mint (instead of the calamint).

Carefully wash the wild greens several times over or until all the dirt has been removed (if particularly dirty you can leave them to soak in a bowl of cold water first). Wild chicory should have its root stubs scraped well or cut off and any wilting leaves picked off. If they are particularly tough or large, you may need to chop roughly and give them some extra cooking time by blanching them first until tender. If they are young and small, then just use them as they are, in their tufts.

Put the garlic cloves, potatoes, tomatoes and wild greens in a large saucepan and pour in 1 litre (34 fl oz/4 cups) of cold water. Season with a good pinch of salt and place over low–medium heat. Bring to a simmer, stirring occasionally to distribute the vegetables evenly (the greens will wilt down soon enough). Cook for approximately 10–12 minutes, or until the vegetables are tender. Taste the broth to check for seasoning and add salt and pepper as needed.

In the meantime, prepare the bread slices – if using fresh bread, dry the slices out in a low oven until dry to the touch but not coloured (this is just like toasting but you want them to still be pale, so as not to affect the taste).

Crack the eggs into the simmering soup and cover with a lid until the whites are cooked but the yolks are still runny, about 2 minutes. Remove from the heat.

Place a slice of bread in each shallow bowl and ladle over some soup topped with one egg. Let it rest for a minute before serving so that the bread can soak up the broth. Ideally, the bread should soak everything up and there should be no liquid in the bowl. If the bread is still dry in places, ladle over some extra broth from the pot. there is any extra liquid present in the bowl, remove it with a spoon or some paper towel. Finish with a drizzle of very good olive oil and a generous handful of chopped wild fennel and calamint.

< Pictured on previous spread

LIQUORE ALL'ALLORO E ROSMARINO
BAY LEAF AND ROSEMARY LIQUEUR

Although homemade liqueurs require quite a bit of patience and waiting time before you can finally have a taste, they make a wonderful addition to the dinner table. It's the ultimate gesture of Italian hospitality to offer guests a strong and aromatic *digestivo* (usually a herbal-based liqueur) at the end of the meal. As the name suggests, *digestivi* or digestifs are thought to aid digestion.

This fragrant liqueur is inspired by some of the herbs of the Mediterranean scrub that you can find growing rampant along the Maremman coastline: bay laurel and a hint of rosemary. Not by chance, *rosmarino* in Italian references the sea (*marino*, or marine), which it commonly grows near.

A nice addition to this liqueur would be a couple of tablespoons of *mirto* – berries from the myrtle plant, which are also used in the not-far-away islands of Sardinia and Corsica for traditional liqueurs. The berries' flavour profile is sometimes likened to a mixture of rosemary and juniper (which you can also find among the Maremman scrub). Sage leaves are a nice addition, too.

MAKES 500 ML (17 FL OZ/2 CUPS) LIQUEUR

16 fresh bay leaves
2 rosemary sprigs
1 x 5 cm (2 in) strip of orange peel
250 ml (8½ fl oz/1 cup) neutral spirit at 150° proof (75% alcohol)
100 g (3½ oz/½ cup) sugar

Add herbs and orange peel (make sure there is no white pith as it is too bitter) to the alcohol in a glass bottle or jar and leave to infuse in the fridge for 1 week, agitating once a day. You will notice it looks fluorescent green – I love this colour that the liqueur draws out of the bay leaves, but unfortunately it turns darker as it ages.

Make a simple sugar syrup by combining the sugar and 150 ml (5 fl oz) of water in a saucepan and bringing to the boil. Let it simmer for 10 minutes, then allow it to cool completely. Add the cooled syrup to the alcohol and herb mixture. Leave to infuse for 1 more week, then filter the alcohol through a fine sieve lined with muslin (cheesecloth).

Pour into a glass bottle and let it age in a cool, dark place for 3–4 weeks before serving for the first time. If it is still a little cloudy, you can filter again if you wish. If you leave it cloudy, just remember to shake the bottle a little before serving.

Serve chilled and neat in small glasses to sip after a meal.

NOTE
Choose a spirit that is neutral in both flavour and fragrance, and preferably perfectly clear, too. In Italy, you can easily buy 190° proof (95% alcohol) in the supermarket for the purpose of making homemade liqueurs, but this isn't available in many other countries. If using a 190° proof alcohol, you should make slightly more syrup to dilute the liqueur sufficiently – use 200 ml (7 fl oz) of water and 150 g (5½ oz) of sugar. The resulting liqueur should be around 37–40% alcohol, which is as strong as you would want a drink like this! This is less successful with lower proof alcohol, but you could do an infusion of grappa or vodka, where the herbs lend the alcohol their flavour (not so much the colour). You don't need to dilute the alcohol, so rather than use syrup simply add 2 tablespoons of sugar along with the bay leaves. Filter after 2 weeks and serve.

THE ROBIN HOOD OF MAREMMA

There is a liqueur made in Capalbio, flavoured with local herbs, bitter orange and caramel and named after Domenico Tiburzi, a nineteenth-century Maremman outlaw. His criminal career began when he was caught collecting the leftover ears of wheat from a field belonging to the Marchese Guglielmi. Imprisoned and ordered to pay an unreasonable fine, Tiburzi murdered the Marchese's guard and escaped into the thick Maremman forest. Bandits were common in Maremma during this time and Tiburzi was revered as a 'good' bandit, murdering the dangerous ones and protecting nearby farmers and their families for about thirty years. When authorities finally caught and executed him in Capalbio in 1896, the townspeople insisted their hero be buried in the cemetery against the church's will. They compromised, and Tiburzi was buried halfway in and halfway out.

ZUPPA DI CECI E CASTAGNE
CHICKPEA AND CHESTNUT SOUP

Foraged chestnuts traditionally were a delicious, free and readily available ingredient that kept well for months over long winters and filled up hungry bellies. During times of great poverty in Italy, they say that polenta saved the north and fish saved the south, while chestnuts saved central Italy. This particular dish was a frugal way to stretch the chickpeas in a meal, a very literal illustration of the saying that a poor person *deve contare anche i ceci* (must count even his chickpeas).

Traditionally, dried chickpeas are used in this soup. If you have these, soak them in cool water for 12 hours before boiling them until soft with a rosemary sprig and a clove of garlic. Dried or freshly collected chestnuts can also be used; both need to be boiled until tender, the latter scored with a deep cross before heading for the pot and peeled after boiling. Don't throw away the liquid used to cook any of these ingredients; it can become the broth for the soup.

For convenience sake, this version uses pre-cooked chickpeas and chestnuts, which means this soup can be made in less than 15 minutes. It will feed four as part of a multiple-course meal, or two very hungry people if it's the only dish served. It's a humble, comforting soup, just the thing for a cosy night in with a glass of robust red wine.

SERVES 4 AS A FIRST COURSE OR LIGHT MEAL

Put the garlic in a large stockpot with the olive oil, rosemary and sage. Cook gently over low heat to infuse the oil, about 3–5 minutes. When the garlic is soft, add the white wine to the pot, turn the heat up to medium and cook for 30 seconds, then add the cooked chickpeas, season with salt and cover with water (if you have cooked the chickpeas yourself, you can use the cooking water here).

Bring to a simmer, then blend about half of the chickpeas until smooth. A stick blender is handy for this, but otherwise, transfer the chickpeas and some of the water to a blender and blend, then return the mixture to the pan. Add the chestnuts, which you can keep whole, roughly halve or crumble in your hands as you put them in (I prefer the latter). Continue simmering, uncovered, for approximately 10 minutes or until the liquid has reduced slightly and is creamy. Taste for seasoning.

Serve the soup in bowls with a drizzle of extra-virgin olive oil and freshly cracked black pepper. Some warm, crunchy, just-grilled bread rubbed with a garlic clove and drowned in some good extra-virgin olive oil goes well with this soup, too.

2 garlic cloves, squashed with the flat edge of a kitchen knife
3 tablespoons extra-virgin olive oil, plus extra to serve
1 rosemary sprig, leaves picked
4 sage leaves
80 ml (2½ fl oz/⅓ cup) dry white wine
400 g (14 oz) pre-cooked chickpeas, drained
200 g (7 oz) cooked and peeled chestnuts

VARIATIONS

For a richer flavour, you can use unsalted chicken stock instead of water. If you prefer a brothy soup, leave the chickpeas whole rather than partially blended – this is especially nice if you have cooked dried chickpeas and you have the cooking water as the base of the soup. The chestnuts are usually kept whole or crumbled into pieces, as puréed chestnuts become extremely thick. You can also use other legumes in place of the chickpeas, such as borlotti or cannellini beans. Some recipes also add some tomato passata (puréed tomatoes) to the soup as well. Although I like this mellow, sweet and creamy soup as is, you could add a hint of warmth with some chilli added to the garlic at the beginning.

GNOCCHI DI CASTAGNE
CHESTNUT GNOCCHI

A staple in Tuscany's peasant cuisine for centuries, the chestnut is a hearty, versatile autumn ingredient that could easily be foraged in the woods. It can be found fresh, dried or in flour form, and is used often for stuffing roast meat or poultry, and for making desserts like *Castagnaccio* (page 216). In Saturnia, you can find boiled mashed chestnuts as a hearty filling for tortelli (as square ravioli are known in Maremma), dressed in melted butter infused with wild fennel seeds. They're also enjoyed all on their own, boiled or roasted over a fire and then dipped in red wine as an end to an autumn or winter dinner.

Here, chestnut flour made from dried and ground chestnuts, is used in place of wheat flour to make these plump gnocchi, and an extra egg is added to help bind the mixture. They can be served simply with some melted butter and chopped sage leaves, or with a *Sugo Maremmano* (page 194). They are also excellent with the sauce used as a topping for *Crostini Maremmani* (page 172), which is a ragu made of half chicken liver, half minced (ground) meat. As chestnuts and their flour are naturally quite sweet, you can be heavy-handed on the cheese here.

SERVES 4

Rinse the potatoes, place them whole in their skins in a large saucepan and cover with cold water. Bring to the boil and cook over medium heat until they are completely soft and a fork slips easily into their centres. Drain the potatoes and, while still hot, peel them – use a fork to 'hold' the potato in one hand while you peel the skin with a sharp knife with the other hand. Immediately mash them, spreading them out over a chopping board or a tray to allow the steam to escape as quickly as possible.

When you have fluffy and cool mashed potato, combine the eggs and salt, beating well into the potato until you have a smooth, creamy mixture. Add the chestnut flour, bit by bit, incorporating with each addition until you have an easy-to-handle dough that rolls nicely without sticking (depending on the quality of the chestnut flour, you may or may not need all of the flour). Because these gnocchi have no gluten in them, you don't need to worry about overworking the dough as with regular gnocchi, but it should be a pretty fast procedure.

On a work surface, lightly dusted with chestnut flour, cut the dough into four portions. Work with one piece at a time. Roll the dough into a long log about 2 cm (¾ in) thick, then cut into pieces 2.5 cm (1 in) long. Place the finished gnocchi in a single layer on a tray lined with baking paper. Continue until the dough is finished.

- 1 kg (2 lb 3 oz) whole potatoes – use starchy varieties such as dutch creams, king edwards or russets (idahos)
- 2 eggs, beaten
- 1 teaspoon salt
- 200 g (7 oz/2 cups) chestnut flour, plus extra for dusting

NOTE
Try to use potatoes of similar size for even cooking. Use eggs that weigh 55–60 g (2 oz) in the shell each.

Continued overleaf >

Cook the gnocchi in a large saucepan filled with gently simmering, salted water – ideally, use 1 teaspoon of salt per 1 litre (34 fl oz/4 cups) of water. Once the water comes back to a simmer and the gnocchi are floating, let them cook for a further 1–2 minutes. Remove gently with a slotted spoon and place them directly into serving bowls. Pour over your preferred warm sauce (as these don't have gluten in them, they are a little too delicate to toss through the pan with the sauce). Serve immediately.

VARIATION

You can also serve the gnocchi baked – this is a good solution if you would like to prepare these gnocchi in advance. Boil them as described, then lift them out of the pan with a slotted spoon and place in an ovenproof dish in a single layer. They can be kept like this, the dish covered overnight or for 24 hours. Then, the next day, drizzle 1–2 tablespoons of extra-virgin olive oil or melted butter over the top, followed by your preferred sauce. Sprinkle a generous handful of grated pecorino or parmesan cheese over the top and place in a hot oven – 200°C (400°F) – until the cheese has melted and the sauce is bubbling, about 15 minutes.

WILD BOAR – SYMBOL OF THE MAREMMA

'Do your neighbours have pet wild boars?', an alarmed visitor once asked me after admiring the view of Porto Ercole from the terrace to see some young boars – cute little things with their slightly faded beige and brown striped coats – foraging around the back of our palazzo. 'No, they're just... wild boars.' They would travel down the hills of forest and scrub and through the olive groves that reach right into town, where they must have found something very interesting as their snorting and rummaging could be heard from our terrace every evening and most early mornings.

Il Cinghiale (or *il cignale* as they say, with a silent 'g', in a southern Tuscan accent) is the symbol of Maremma. It's a strong, courageous and resilient animal, like the inhabitants who share this place and its rugged, thick forest-covered hills. As hunting and foraging are a traditional pastime, wild boar is also one of the most prized items on the menu. Towns such as Capalbio are well known for wild boar – just take a look at any of the restaurant menus and you'll find it in every form imaginable. And in summer, there's the *sagra del cinghiale*, a fifty-year-old food festival dedicated to the animal.

When it comes to the home kitchen, many *nonne* (and therefore their children and grandchildren) will tell you that *cinghiale* needs to be marinated overnight, or even longer, in a mixture of wine, vinegar, herbs and often onions. It's a traditional, even ancient technique, born before the time of refrigeration, with the purpose of helping tenderise, preserve and conserve meat so that it could be eaten over a period of time without putrefying. In *L'art du Cuisinier* by the great French restaurateur, Antoine Beauvillier (published in 1814 just before his death), he places wild boar in a marinade of half water, half vinegar for five days. Prepared this way, he notes the meat can be conserved for six months.

The *nonne* will tell you that the purpose of marinating is to 'take away the wildness of the meat', but surely this wildness is the point of eating game? Many food writers, chefs and gastronomes, from Pellegrino Artusi to Aldo Santini, point out that marinating disguises the boar's true flavour and is completely unnecessary except in tenderising the meat of more mature animals. So, in the question of whether or not to follow tradition and marinate wild boar, I suggest skipping it. If you can possibly find out the provenance of the meat, choose a younger animal. If you know you are working with a more mature animal, you may need a little more cooking time. Very mature wild boars are tough as old boots, so steer clear.

A CHANCE ENCOUNTER

One extremely hot summer's day, while taking some friends out to visit nearby Capalbio, we spotted a shack-like roadside fruit and vegetable stall. 'Go there!' was the unanimous cry from the back of the hot car. We were greeted with a small paradise: ice-cold quarters of watermelon, bunches of fresh basil, baskets of purple and yellow plums, round and lavender-striped eggplants (aubergine), fragrant rockmelon (cantaloupe), traffic light–coloured capsicums (peppers) and cucumbers twisted in all manner of shapes.

We filled a bag to the brim. After a bit of chit chat with Gianni the shopkeeper on what to do with serpent beans and whether he had a good recipe for acquacotta (Maremma's most famous and beloved dish), he decided to introduce us to his neighbour, Ilena Donati, an elderly but spritely woman who was, for most of her working life, the cook in a restaurant in Capalbio.

I don't know what was better: the photogenic fruit and vegetable stand like an oasis along the dusty via Aurelia, biting into refreshing homegrown watermelon after a sweaty car ride from Argentario, or sitting in the dark but airy kitchen of Ilena hearing her talk enthusiastically about her recipes and watching her blue eyes light up as she talked about food and dishes she has been making for decades.

She was generous with her advice – 'let acquacotta cook slowly, slowly. That goes for wild boar, too. The farro soup is good cold with a drizzle of olive oil'. And, my favourite – 'buy yourself a big, black pan'. She meant a cast-iron one (enamelled cast-iron is the safest bet for slow cooking of acidic ingredients like tomatoes). 'I can't tell you if these dishes will come out well with a non-stick pan. But in a cast-iron pan, they're wonderful.' She even (eventually) revealed her secret recipe for cherry leaf liqueur, which I feel I should keep secret for her.

But the one I have immortalised in my memory from that moment is her recipe for wild boar (see page 52). Cinghiale. 'In pieces, with the bone, of course, as it's more flavourful.'

Much of that conversation with Ilena ended up in this cookbook, even if she only mentioned a dish or a recipe for a brief moment, even one line. Just the idea of roast rabbit filled with fried potatoes or adding copious amounts of herbs and chilli to the *Scottiglia* (page 198) were inspired by something she said.

CINGHIALE IN UMIDO
WILD BOAR STEW

Don't marinate it, said Ilena Donati, firmly, referring to the common practice that everyone's *nonna* advocates of marinating game in wine for 24 hours before cooking it. *It disguises the true flavour of the meat. Besides, the wild boars today aren't like the ones they once were.*

And especially not in Capalbio, where there is plenty of farmed boar, more 'polite', tender and delicate, as gastronome Aldo Santini says.

Lots of bay leaf. Lots of rosemary. Whole. A pinch of chilli. Not everyone likes it, but it's good. She said it in a way that means the chilli really belongs there.

And brown the meat. Brown it really well. Add a splash of vinegar. When that evaporates, add vino nero – she means red wine, but calling it 'black wine' is an old-fashioned expression that makes me smile.

And then tomatoes, broken down with your hands – she gestures with her hands as if holding them above the pan and I'm imagining the feel of peeled tomatoes being squashed between my fingers – *and cook it, slowly, slowly.* This last treasured piece of advice for cooking like a Maremman, *piano, piano,* is the key to this very special stew. See page 51 for more on Ilena, the inspiration behind this dish.

SERVES 4

In a large casserole pot, brown the meat in the olive oil in batches over high heat until seared evenly on all sides. Don't worry if the meat sticks – that wonderful brown crust on the bottom of the pot will just add flavour later. Once well-browned (about 10–15 minutes per batch), return all the meat to the pot, season with salt and freshly ground black pepper, add the garlic and let it colour a little, about 2 minutes.

Pour over the vinegar to deglaze the pot and stir, scraping at the brown crust, with a wooden spoon. Let the liquid evaporate almost completely, about 5 minutes, then add the herbs, wine and tomato. Add chilli, if using.

Once the liquid comes back to the boil, turn the heat down to a low simmer and cook, uncovered, until the meat is tender and falling off the bone – about 2 hours. Top up with water as necessary to keep the meat covered with liquid.

Serve the stew as it is with something starchy to mop up the juices, such as good crusty bread or soft polenta. It is often served with a side dish like the Sformato di Cipollotti (page 168). Alternatively, toss it through some pasta like tagliatelle or pappardelle and serve it like the Pappardelle sulla Lepre (page 56).

1 kg (2 lb 3 oz) wild boar, cut into large chunks (on the bone)
2 tablespoons extra-virgin olive oil
4–5 garlic cloves, whole
60 ml (2 fl oz/¼ cup) red wine vinegar
4 rosemary sprigs
4 bay leaves
1 litre (34 fl oz/4 cups) dry red wine
400 g (14 oz) tinned peeled tomatoes
chilli flakes or chopped fresh red chilli (optional)
good crusty bread or soft polenta, to serve

NOTE
You can source wild boar from game meat suppliers, speciality butchers and even online. (Local wild boar is easily available in the US, UK and Australia.) However, this recipe works with any wild game, including venison, hare and even duck.

CAPALBIO

The medieval hilltop hamlet of Capalbio, Tuscany's southernmost town on the border of Lazio, is a picturesque tangle of enclosed piazzas and winding alleyways of little shops selling locally made liqueurs and jams or traditional gear for *butteri* (Maremman cowboys), and *trattorie* specialising in wild boar and porcini mushrooms. You can climb up to and walk the castle-like ramparts that circle (and once protected) the entire town – from here there is a stunning and seemingly endless view of Maremma, with its hills polka-dotted with olive trees, fields of sunflowers following the sun, and the sea, a blue haze in the distance.

A short walk from the town, heading down the hill towards the sea, you arrive through the scrub of juniper and rosemary at the long, flat sandy beaches of Capalbio. The aptly named *l'Ultima Spiaggia* (the last beach), known for its soft sand and shimmery, silvery toned water, is literally the last beach of Tuscany, with the old customs house – now housing a fashionable restaurant – separating it from the border of Lazio.

CINGHIALE IN DOLCE-FORTE
WILD BOAR IN CHOCOLATE SAUCE

A truly age-old Maremman dish, this is one of Tuscany's most famous. One bite of this luscious, dark, sweet and sour stew and there is no mistaking that it was plucked out of the Renaissance, mostly unchanged. Some say that it crept into the province of Grosseto from the border of the province of Siena, where the sweet and peppery Christmas treat *panforte* is well known. In fact, the lingering sweet flavours of this dish are reminiscent of those of *panforte*.

This recipe, which is inspired by Pellegrino Artusi's, begins with a very simple stew, where the wild boar simmers, softening, for a couple of hours. Right before serving, the 'dolce-forte' is added to the pot, completely transforming it: a mixture of sultanas, pine nuts, candied fruit peel, sugar, vinegar and the darkest chocolate you can find. Like *Cinghiale in Umido* (page 52), you can serve this with something starchy: mashed potatoes, soft polenta or a nice crusty loaf of Tuscan bread to mop up the sauce. The *Sformato di Cipollotti* (page 168) would be a nice side dish, too.

SERVES 4

Pour the olive oil in a casserole pot and cook the onion, carrot, celery and bay leaves over low–medium heat until the vegetables are softened but not coloured, about 10 minutes. Add the meat to the vegetables, season with salt and pepper, and let it colour on all sides evenly, a further 10 minutes.

Add the flour and toss through the mixture. Let it cook for 2 minutes, then add the red wine, turn the heat up to medium–high and let it reduce until the sauce begins to thicken, about 10–15 minutes. Add stock (or water) to cover and bring the stew to a boil. Turn the heat down to low and let it simmer, uncovered, until the meat is tender, about 2 hours (but it could take up to 3 hours depending on the meat). Check occasionally, and top up with water as needed.

In the meantime, prepare the 'dolce-forte' sauce. Mix the sultanas, pine nuts, candied peel, sugar, chocolate and red wine vinegar in a small saucepan and put over medium heat until the chocolate is melted and the mixture well combined. Remove from the heat and set aside (it is good to do this at least 1 hour before you need it).

When the meat is tender, turn the heat up to medium to reduce the sauce until it is thick (if it isn't already). Add the dolce-forte sauce and combine, letting the stew come back to the boil. Remove from the heat and serve.

3 tablespoons extra-virgin olive oil
1 brown (yellow) onion, finely chopped
1 carrot, finely chopped
½ celery stalk, finely chopped
2–3 bay leaves
1 kg (2 lb 3 oz) wild boar, cut into 4 cm (1½ in) cubes
2 teaspoons plain (all-purpose) flour
250 ml (8½ fl oz/1 cup) red wine
1 litre (34 fl oz/4 cups) beef stock (or water)
40 g (1½ oz/⅓ cup) sultanas (golden raisins)
30 g (1 oz) pine nuts
30 g (1 oz) candied fruit peel (orange or citron)
40 g (1½ oz) sugar
40 g (1½ oz/¼ cup) dark chocolate, chopped (80% cocoa)
60 ml (2 fl oz/¼ cup) red wine vinegar

NOTE
Because this thick and silky stew has such a rich flavour, you could halve this recipe to easily serve four smaller portions, especially if you plan on eating it as a main following several other dishes in a long, drawn-out special occasion meal. If it's the only dish, make the whole thing. If there are leftovers, that's good news – they will probably taste better than the original dish. It freezes well, too.

VARIATIONS
You can make this with wild hare or venison instead of wild boar.

PAPPARDELLE SULLA LEPRE
PAPPARDELLE WITH HARE SAUCE

Though not as common as it used to be in the Maremma, this dish is still a local favourite. Pellegrino Artusi includes two recipes for *pappardelle* with hare in his 1891 cookbook. He points out that hare can be a dry, flavourless meat, so it needs to be rescued with a rich, hearty sauce. Pancetta is an obligatory addition to the sauce as it adds that fattiness (and flavour) that is missing from this lean meat. You could prepare any game this way, including venison or wild rabbit. For a pasta sauce with wild boar, see page 52.

As this dish is normally made with a whole hare, the recipe for the stew makes enough for about six to eight people, so keep this in mind when measuring out the pasta for the number of guests you would like to serve. However, leftover sauce is always a good thing, so if you're only serving four, simply keep the leftovers for dinner the following night – you can serve as a stew over creamy polenta (see *Vongole e Polenta* for creamy polenta recipe, page 106). Leftover sauces are often tastier. In fact, you may want to make it a day ahead and reheat it slowly back to a simmer before tossing through pasta just for this reason. This sauce will also freeze well.

SERVES 6–8

Put half of the olive oil in a large casserole pot over high heat. Brown a single layer of the meat in batches for about 5–7 minutes, turning to sear all sides. Set aside.

In the same dish, add the carrot, celery, onion, garlic and pancetta with the rest of the olive oil and turn the heat down to low. Cook gently for about 15 minutes, or until the chopped vegetables are softened but not coloured and the pancetta's fat has rendered and become transparent.

Season with a good pinch of salt, add the chilli, tomato paste and herbs, and continue cooking for 5 minutes, then return the meat to the pan. Add the wine, along with enough water to cover – roughly 1 litre (34 fl oz/4 cups). Bring to the boil, then turn the heat down to a simmer and let the sauce cook, uncovered, for 1 hour or until the meat is tender but not falling apart too much. Also, do not stir too often, as you'll risk 'shredding' the meat too much.

Remove from the heat and carefully transfer the chunks of meat to a plate and let them cool. When cool enough to handle, remove and discard the bones from the meat, leaving it in good-sized chunks if possible, and return the meat to the sauce.

1 hare, about 1.5–2 kg (3 lb 5 oz–4 lb 6 oz), cleaned and jointed into large pieces
80 ml (2½ fl oz/⅓ cup) extra-virgin olive oil
1 small carrot, finely chopped
½ celery stalk, finely chopped
1 medium brown (yellow) onion, finely chopped
4 garlic cloves, whole
170 g (6 oz) pancetta, finely chopped
good pinch of dried chilli flakes (optional)
1 tablespoon tomato paste (concentrated purée)
1 rosemary sprig
4 sage leaves
2 bay leaves
750 ml (25½ fl oz/3 cups) red wine
400 g (14 oz) tomato passata (puréed tomatoes) or tinned peeled tomatoes
½ teaspoon freshly grated nutmeg
fresh pappardelle pasta (see *Pappardelle sui Funghi*, page 30)
finely grated parmesan or pecorino cheese, to serve

Add the tomato, along with 500 ml (17 fl oz/2 cups) of water. Continue to simmer until the sauce is thick and reduced but not too much – you want to easily coat the pasta in this sauce. Finally, add the nutmeg, taste for seasoning and adjust with salt and freshly ground black pepper. If you find you have simmered too long and it's too thick, you can always loosen it with some of the pasta cooking water just before tossing the pasta in the sauce. You will only need about half of this amount to serve four people, so the rest can be frozen or kept in the fridge for the next day.

When you are ready to eat, put the pasta in a large saucepan of boiling, well-salted water (see page 13). Cook until al dente, about 3–5 minutes. Drain the pasta (reserving some of the cooking water to loosen the sauce, if necessary) and add it to the sauce. Serve with freshly grated parmesan or pecorino cheese.

NOTE
You can source hare from game meat suppliers, speciality butchers and even online. Wild rabbit can also be used here (not farmed rabbit, which is more like chicken).

FROM THE SEA AND THE LAGOON

DAL MARE E DALLA LAGUNA

SEAFOOD IN THE MAREMMA

AMBERJACK
(see Horse Mackerel, page 62)

ANCHOVY
Known as *acciuga* (*acciughe* plural) or *alice* (*alici* plural) in Italian (*Engraulis encrasicolus*), the anchovy is one of the most plentiful, cheap and important fish in the traditional cuisine of Argentario and the Tuscan archipelago. This rich, nutritious fish belongs to the family of sardines, pilchards, shad and herrings and, together with mackerel and bonito, is collectively known as *pesce azzuro* (oily fish). Fresh anchovies are versatile in a Tuscan kitchen – fried (as in *Alici Dorate*, page 74), part of a *frittura* (page 115), baked in gratin (page 68) or cooked in sauces to coat pasta. You can also buy preserved anchovies, packed in salt or oil. Tinned sardines are wonderful for turning into a quick salad, such as *Insalata di Pesce* (page 72).

BONITO
Palamita (*Sarda sarda*) is a relative of the mackerel or *scombridae* family. With its meaty flesh, in many ways it resembles tuna (and can be used much like tuna). Versatile and tasty, this Mediterranean fish can be prepared in brine and preserved in oil (page 69) or fried and marinated in vinegar as in *Scaveccio* (page 82). It was popular, even in ancient Roman times.

CALAMARI
(see Squid, page 65)

CLAMS
Known as *arselle* in Tuscany, *telline* in Italian, or wedge clams in English, these small, flat bivalves (*Donax trunculus*) have a white to grey to lavender (usually inside) hue. They are normally around 2 cm (¾ in) wide but can grow to 3½ cm (1½ in). They're similar to Australian pippies or pipis (*plebidonax deltoides* or sometimes known as *donax deltoides*). *Vongole verace* (*ruditapes decussatus* or *venerupis decussata*), or carpet-shells, are native to the Mediterranean Sea and found in the North Sea and British Isles. They are one of Italy's most famous and beloved shellfish.

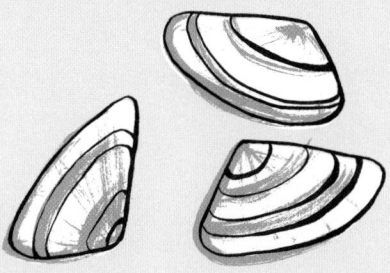

COD
Nasello, merluzzo (*Merluccius merluccius*) or hake refers to fresh cod, but Italians more often than not eat a version of dried cod – *stoccafisso* (which is air dried) or *baccalà* (salted and dried). In Argentario there is a speciality known as *stocchetto*, a dried and salted fish (similar to baccalà) known as *ficamaschia*, the local term for *melù* or blue whiting (*Micromesistius poutassou*), which is part of the cod family. It's a rather plain-tasting fish that is either crumbed, fried like the *Alici Dorate* (page 74) or used in a rich tomato stew with pine nuts and olives (page 114). Haddock is a good substitute.

CUTTLEFISH
Known as *seppia* (*Sepia officinalis*) in Italian, this large creature is often found covered in its own black ink in piles at the fish markets. Deliciously tender when slow cooked, cuttlefish can be used just like octopus or calamari in recipes such as *Polpo e Patate* (page 86) or *Calamari e Funghi* (page 80). See also Octopus (page 63) and Squid (page 65).

DOGFISH

Also known as catshark (*Scyliorhinus canicula*) and by a number of other names, in Italian it is *gattuccio*, from 'gatto' for cat. This small ground shark, boneless and delicate, is often used in fish soups like *Caldaro* (page 110). It is common in British waters and was often found in fish and chip shops under various other names, including rock salmon, rock eel, huss and sweet william – the equivalent to flake in Australia.

EEL

European eel (*Anguilla anguilla*) is simply known as *anguilla* in Italian and is generally considered an endangered species in Europe. Orbetello's lagoon has long been an important place for the eels (which travel for miles through freshwater rivers, saltwater lagoons and the open sea during their lifetime). As a result, they're part of the traditional cuisine. Traditionally, smaller eels are used for the centuries-old speciality *Scaveccio* (page 82). *Tòrta* or *pantanina* is the name local fishermen use to describe the pale, silvery 'blond' colour that the eels take on at a certain stage of their life (in English, fishermen call them 'silver eel'). They're exceptionally tasty, with a delicate skin and are caught during the spring and autumn while travelling towards the sea from the lagoon. In contrast, moray eels (*Muraena helena*) and conger eels (*Conger conger*) – known respectively as *murena* and *gronco* in Italian – live purely in the sea and are used in traditional fish soups like *Caldaro* (page 110).

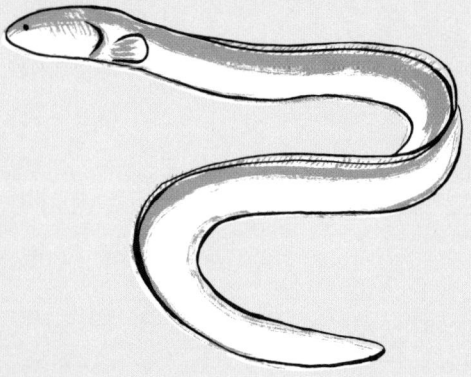

GURNARD, TUB

Known as *Gallinella* or *capone* (*Chelidonichthys lucerne*) in Italy, this is a pretty but unusual-looking fish with an enormous head and a duck-like face. Also known as a sea robin, it feeds off crustaceans and is much appreciated in Italian kitchens for its firm white flesh. It's particularly loved in soup, such as *Caldaro* (page 110).

HORSE MACKEREL

Despite its English name, *Sugarello* is from the *Carangidae* family (which include jacks and amberjack, or *ricciola* in Italian), not the mackerel family. It's excellent for frying and marinating, as in *Scaveccio* (page 82).

JOHN DORY

Pesce San Pietro (*Zeus faber*) can be cooked the same way as sole. Little ones are used in fish soup like *Caldaro* (page 110).

LIMPET

Patella in Italian (*Patella caerulea*) or *lampatella*, as they are known in Monte Argentario, these are small sea snails hiding in conical shells that sit on rocks on the shore. They give *Caldaro* (page 110) its flavour, which is unique to Argentario.

MACKEREL

Sgombro (*scomber scombrus*) is also known as Atlantic mackerel. This fish, with beautiful shimmery blue and dark navy lines running along its back, is one of my favourites. Like its relative, bonito, it is meaty and has a strong flavour. It is excellent fried and marinated as in *Scaveccio* (page 82) and its tinned version can make a wonderful, quick salad (see page 72).

MANTIS SHRIMP

Spernocchie, *sparnocchie*, *pannocchie*, *cannochie* and *cicale di mare* are just a few of its many names in Italian (*Squilla mantis*). One of its Italian names means 'cicadas of the sea'. It is, indeed, a strange-looking creature, but incomparably delicious (and therefore essential) in fish soups such as the *Caldaro* (page 110). When the females have eggs, even better. Their flavour doesn't compare to other shrimp or prawns, but are perhaps more similar to lobster, a flavour that is highlighted in a simple preparation such as *Spaghetti alle Spernocchie* (page 93).

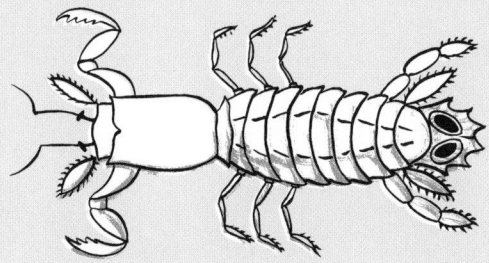

MULLET, GREY

This fish is known as *muggine* or *cefalo* in Italian (*Mugil cephalus*). The intact egg sacs of the females are salted and dried to make bottarga in Italy (mainly in Sardinia and Sicily). In Tuscany, Orbetello's grey mullet is famous (see *Spaghetti alla Bottarga*, page 91), though there are counterparts all over the Mediterranean, from Tunisia to Turkey.

MULLET, RED

Triglie, from the goatfish family, come in two types: *triglia di fango* (*Mullus barbatus*) and *trigilie di scoglio* (*Mullus surmuletus*). They look almost identical, but the latter has shimmery yellow stripes across its red body (in fact, it's known as striped red mullet in English) – it's also the more popular fish, and this is reflected in its price. The ancient Romans were very fond of red mullet and farmed them to try to grow them into huge specimens that would fetch absurd prices. They're usually about 15–20 cm (6–8 in) long, and are still one of the favourite fish in Italy. They have delicate flesh and should be used as fresh as possible. They're excellent for frying.

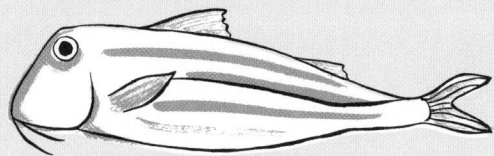

OCTOPUS

In Italy, they're known as *polpo* (*Octopus vulgaris*). Look for the ones that Italians call *polpo di scoglio* (rock octopus), identifiable by the double-row of suction cups on their tentacles. *Moscardini* (*Eledone cirrosa*), identified by its single-row of suction cups, is not as well regarded in Italian kitchens but can be a suitable substitute. Octopus can be extremely tough when cooked, so for centuries many fishermen and cooks have devised different ways to cook it to make it tender. I like to stew it for a long time in its own juices, as in *Polpo e Patate* (page 86).

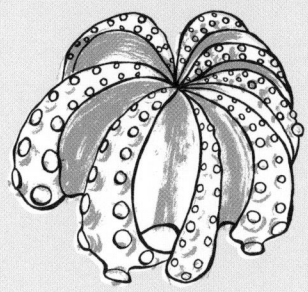

PRAWNS (SHRIMP)

Mazzancolle or *gambero imperiale* (*Penaeus kerathurus*) are similar to caramote prawns (*Melicertus kerathurus*) or tiger prawns (*Penaeus monodon*). They are wonderful simply grilled or cooked briefly in soup (see *Acquacotta del Pescatore*, page 88). Small prawns, such as school prawns, are good for frying whole as part of a *Frittura di Paranza* (page 115). See also Mantis shrimp (opposite) and Scampi (page 64).

SCAMPI

Known also as Dublin Bay prawns, Norway lobster or langoustines (*Nephrops norvegicus*), they are slim, pretty, salmon-pink lobsters that live in the Atlantic Ocean and the Mediterranean Sea. British fishermen once threw them back in the water, but in Italy they are highly regarded for their delicate, sweet flavour. In Argentario they make a delicious soup with them (*Zuppa di Scampi e Patate*, page 103) and it's also common to see them served raw as antipasto, in their shells, with lemon juice and olive oil. They should be prepared very simply, so as not to mask their sweet, lobster-like flavour – you could also prepare them in place of the mantis shrimp in *Spaghetti alle Spernocchie* (page 93).

SCORPION FISH, RED

Known as *scorfano* (*Scorpaena scrofa*) in Italy and *rascasse* in France, this fish is used mainly for soup, where it is usually cooked whole. British food writer and historian Alan Davidson's original cover of his culinary classic *Mediterranean Seafood* (1972) featured this fish. As he says, 'For me at least, a fine large scarlet rascasse serves as the most apt and memorable symbol of Mediterranean fish generally.' He notes its importance because it 'can do something for bouillabaisse which no other fish can do'. And this is true, too, for Italian fish soups like the *Caldaro* (page 110) and *Minestra di Pesce* (page 101).

SEA BASS, EUROPEAN

Branzino or *spigola* is highly prized fish in Italy (*Dicentrarchus labrax*). British food writer Elizabeth David called them 'one of the finest flavoured Mediterranean fishes'. They are farmed in Orbetello's lagoon (sea bass has been farmed in the area since ancient Roman times), along with a regular harvest of sea bream, grey mullet and eels. A delicious firm-fleshed fish with few bones, they are good baked (as in the *Orata al Cartoccio*, page 120), or simply grilled and lovely with pasta as a ragu (see page 99). Sea bass is also known as *ragno* in Tuscany, which is confusing as it means 'spider' in Italian.

SEA BREAM

Orata refers specifically to gilthead sea bream, a delicious, versatile and easy to prepare fish, wonderful baked whole as in the *Orata al Cartoccio* (page 120). In Maremma you can also find *boga* (bogue) and *sparaglione* (annular sea bream), both from the sea bream family. *Orata* are sustainably farmed in Orbetello's lagoon. This family of fish are also known as porgies.

SHRIMP

See Prawns, page 63.

SILVER SCABBARDFISH

Pesce sciabola (*Lepidopus caudatus*) is an impressive, vicious-looking fish that, as its name suggests, looks like a long, silver sword – they can grow to a length of 2 metres (6 ft 6 in). In Argentario, you'll often see it in fish markets and featuring in traditional local dishes. The long shape of its body and smooth skin (they have no scales) is often used to its benefit – it's wonderful prepared as 'involtini', where the fillet is rolled up with a filling inside, secured with a toothpick and baked. It's a delicious fish (and dish) that is also well suited to frying and marinating.

SQUID

Calamari (*Loligo vulgaris*) is easier to handle than huge cuttlefish. Baby ones are known as *calamaretti* and are great for frying, whole, as part of a *Frittura di Paranza* (page 115). They are commonly fished during the cold months of autumn and winter. In spring, you find *totani* (*Todarodes saggittatus*) – 'flying squid', which will glide out of the water as an escape tactic. These are small squid with a mahogany tone that will fit in your hand. You can use these for stewing with mushrooms as in *Calamari e Funghi* (page 80).

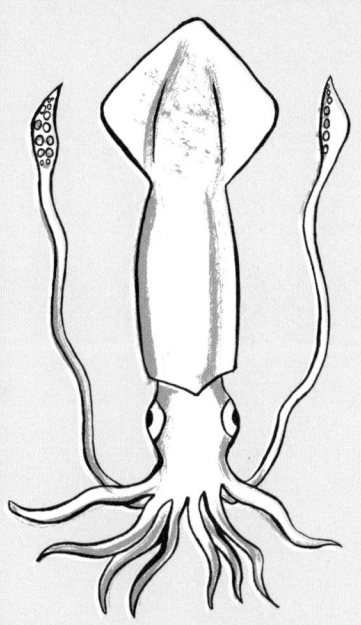

SOLE

Sogliola (*Solea solea*) is a delicate flatfish that is simply delicious prepared in so many ways. I especially like the simple preparation in a lemon juice marinade overnight, to be eaten raw with parsley and olives the next day (see page 123). In Argentario you can also find four-spot megrim (*rombo quattrocchi* in Italian and locally called *suaci*, which is also the name for scaldfish, a kind of flounder); it's part of the turbot family. Small specimens are often part of soup like the *Minestra di Pesce* (page 101) or fried as in *Frittura di Paranza* (page 115). Megrim sole (*Lepidorhombus whiffiagonis*) – also known as sail-fluke or whiff, or *rombo giallo* in Italian – is a similar relative, and all can be used just like common sole.

STARGAZER

Pesce prete ('priest fish', *Uranoscopus scaber*) has eyes permanently set looking upwards, so it's not a beautiful fish, but it is favoured in Tuscan fish soups, such as the *Caldaro* (page 110), the *Minestra di Pesce* (page 101) and Livorno's *cacciucco*. They're not particularly easy to handle – watch out for the poisonous spikes behind their eyes.

WHITING

See Cod, page 61.

ACCIUGHE E CARCIOFI GRATINATI

ANCHOVY AND ARTICHOKE GRATIN

This is inspired by a traditional fisherman recipe from Giglio Island, where the dish is normally made with just anchovies and eaten with a purée of fresh tomatoes. Artichokes grow abundantly in this part of Tuscany and are used in countless ways in the late winter and spring when they fill up the markets crate by crate. Their tangy and fresh flavour pairs wonderfully with this tasty, meaty fish and this is a very simple, quick preparation once you have the anchovy fillets ready.

When artichokes aren't in season, I think this is rather nice with very thin slices of potato (a mandoline would be handy for this).

SERVES 4

The anchovies should be cleaned (interior and heads removed) and butterflied (see how to clean fresh anchovies, page 75). Once you do this, you should have 400 g (14 oz) fresh, cleaned anchovy fillets.

To prepare the artichokes, first fill a large bowl with cold water and squeeze the lemon juice into it – this is to stop the cut and exposed parts of the artichoke from oxidising. Peel the tough outer leaves of the artichokes until you come to very pale and tender leaves. Trim the stalk to about 2 cm (¾ in) and peel. Cut the artichokes in half. Put one half in the lemon water while you work on the other half: remove the fluffy choke with a teaspoon and then slice the artichoke halves finely. Place the slices in the lemon water and continue until you have sliced all the artichokes. Until needed, cover the water with two sheets of paper towel to help protect the top layer of artichokes.

Preheat the oven to 180°C (350°F).

When ready to assemble the dish, drain the artichoke slices. Grease a rectangular casserole dish with 1 tablespoon of the olive oil. Scatter over the chopped garlic and parsley. Place one layer (about half) of the anchovies, skin side down, over the top of the garlic and parsley. Scatter over about half of the artichoke slices in a layer and season with salt and pepper. Repeat a layer of anchovies, then a layer of artichoke slices, salt and pepper.

Sprinkle the white wine over the top, then scatter over the breadcrumbs evenly followed by the rest of the olive oil. Bake in the oven for about 15–20 minutes.

Serve with a nice loaf of crusty bread.

600 g (1 lb 5 oz) whole fresh anchovies
3 artichokes
juice of 1 lemon
3 tablespoons extra-virgin olive oil
1 garlic clove, chopped
3–4 flat-leaf (Italian) parsley sprigs, finely chopped
1½ tablespoons white wine
25 g (1 oz/¼ cup) fine dried breadcrumbs
crusty bread, to serve

NOTE

If you'd prefer to buy the anchovies already prepared, ask your fishmonger for 400 g (14 oz) fresh, cleaned anchovy fillets.

PALAMITA SOTT'OLIO
BONITO PRESERVED IN OIL

Bonito is fished out of the waters of the Tuscan archipelago between spring and summer, and again in early autumn. It's a decent-sized, delicious oily fish, often sold whole in its armour of silver stripes. Though its flesh is rather similar to tuna, it's significantly cheaper – in fact, it's often known as 'poor man's tuna'. Preserving it in flavoured oil is the perfect way to ensure you always have some of this tasty fish on hand to whip up a quick meal.

Essentially tinned tuna but better, bonito in oil is delicious just as it is, served as part of an antipasto platter. But my favourite way to have this is with an impromptu salad dressed in red wine vinegar and olive oil with white cannellini beans and thinly sliced red onion that's had a 10-minute soak in some cold water. It's also great crumbled into some tomato and basil pasta sauce or on a panino with sliced boiled eggs and parsley or fresh tomatoes and lemon zest. And you could use it in place of the tinned mackerel in the following recipe for a fish salad.

This recipe is adapted from a Tuscan recipe book on the cuisine of Elba Island, *Zuppe e Stornelli* (1991), by Alvaro Claudi and Sergio Rossi. I recommend using smaller jars – as opposed to 2 jars of 500 ml (17 fl oz/2 cups) capacity each – so that you can quickly consume the opened jars.

MAKES ROUGHLY 4 JARS OF 250 ML (8½ FL OZ/1 CUP)

1 kg (2 lb 3 oz) whole bonito
600 g (1 lb 5 oz) rock salt
10 whole dried black peppercorns
4 bay leaves
1 red chilli, fresh or dried (optional), chopped
mild-flavoured vegetable oil, such as grapeseed oil, to cover

Remove the entrails, the head and the tail of the bonito and chop the rest into thick steaks, about 5 cm (2 in) wide, bone and skin intact. Avoid cutting pieces from the smaller or narrow sections of the fish, too close to the tail or the gut, as these smaller pieces tend to be too salty. Put the steaks in a bowl of cold water (traditional recipes call for this to be seawater, but regular tap water will suffice) and refrigerate for 2–3 hours. Change the water once or twice during this time. This is to remove any traces of blood.

Put 3 litres (101 fl oz/12 cups) of water in a large stockpot with the salt and bring to a simmer over high heat. Drain the bonito steaks, put in the pot and simmer over low heat, covered, for about 1½–2 hours. They should be firm and cooked through.

Drain and pat the bonito steaks dry. When cool enough to handle, use your fingers to break apart the bonito into a few smaller sections, removing the central bone and skin as you go. Wrap the fish pieces in

Continued overleaf >

a clean tea towel (dish towel) or in layers of paper towel and place on a colander set over a plate. Chill in the fridge for several hours or overnight to drain it well.

Put the drained bonito in sterilised jars (see page 137 on how to sterilise jars) and evenly distribute the peppercorns and bay leaves (and chilli, if using). Pour over the oil, making sure the fish is entirely covered with about 1 cm (½ in) of oil. Tap the jar on the counter to allow any trapped air bubbles to come to the surface and, if you wish, break apart the bonito further to get it to fit nicely. Once the air bubbles are gone and the fish is well covered with oil, put the lid on. If you plan on keeping this for a while, seal as described on page 135 (see *Carciofini Sott'olio*).

Store in a cool, dark place – I keep mine in the fridge. This is best about a month after bottling (if you can wait that long) and will keep for 3 months. Once opened, keep it in the refrigerator and make sure the remaining fish is covered in oil. The fish will keep for 7–10 days.

INSALATA DI PESCE ALLA GROSSETANA
GROSSETO-STYLE FISH SALAD

When it's too hot to cook in summer and you need a handy, fast, filling meal that you can pull together in just minutes, this salad is here to save you. It's also a good make-ahead dish (let the flavours mingle), which is ideal for packing for picnic lunches for the beach. Traditionally made by boiling a variety of *pesce azzuro* (oily fish), such as anchovies, sardines and mackerel, the tinned versions of these fish are perfectly suited (or you can use your own Bonito Preserved in Oil, page 69), making this a quick and tasty meal.

Inspired by a recipe I spotted in Laura Rangoni's Tuscan seafood cookbook *La Cucina Toscana di Mare*, I've adapted it a little to suit my tastes and make it my summer staple. The original recipe calls for 4–5 raw garlic cloves, chopped and muddled through the salad. It's a bit overpowering for me. I prefer to leave them out entirely but garlic lovers might like to add them. You can use capers in brine instead of the salted ones (brined ones don't require soaking) but I always prefer salted capers.

SERVES 4

2 teaspoons salted capers
10–12 green olives in brine
2 fresh tomatoes, chopped
300 g (10½ oz) tinned sardines (or any other tinned fish, such as tuna or mackerel)
juice of 2 lemons
2 tablespoons extra-virgin olive oil
1 handful flat-leaf (Italian) parsley, finely chopped

Rinse the capers of the salt and place in a bowl. Cover with water and let them soak for about 15 minutes. Drain, pat dry, then finely chop.

Pit the olives by flattening them with the side of a large knife and pulling out the pit. Chop roughly.

Combine the capers, olives and tomatoes in a salad bowl. Drain the tinned fish and crumble into the bowl. Toss with the lemon juice, olive oil and parsley to combine well. Taste for seasoning and, if desired, add freshly ground black pepper (between the fish, capers and olives, you've got a lot of flavour going on and you may only need the tiniest pinch of salt, if any).

ALICI DORATE
DEEP-FRIED ANCHOVIES

The best fish shop in Porto Ercole, Da Ledo, is run by Elisa Costagliola, a Sally Field lookalike whose family fishing boat brings its catch right up to the port every evening. The seafood is so fresh that it's often still moving. There are crates of scampi and huge *mazzancolle* – caramote prawns (shrimp), quite similar to tiger prawns – piles of small fish for 'soup' or frying, glistening vermillion-splattered *triglie* (red mullet), funny-faced four-spot megrim and the aptly named *pesce sciabola* (silver scabbardfish), with its long, smooth, sword-like body, wrapped around itself. And there are, of course, anchovies – the fleshiest, freshest, firmest, bright-eyed, silvery anchovies I have ever seen.

Once, when I asked Elisa to describe some of the most typical seafood preparations, she didn't hesitate: *Alici dorate*, 'golden anchovies'. They're a speciality of Porto Ercole and possibly one of my favourite things, ever.

You can always ask your fishmonger to clean anchovies for you, but in Porto Ercole, a fishing village, everyone does it themselves. Once you get into the rhythm of it, it's quite therapeutic, I think.

500–600 g (1 lb 2 oz–1 lb 5 oz) fresh, whole anchovies
2–3 tablespoons plain (all-purpose) flour, for dusting
1 egg, chilled
vegetable oil, for frying

SERVES 4 AS AN ANTIPASTO OR A SNACK

Prepare the anchovies as described (see opposite) and put them on a plate.

Spread the flour in a shallow bowl. Beat the egg in a separate shallow bowl with a pinch of salt and place in the fridge until needed. Dredge the butterflied anchovies in the flour, coating well and evenly. Shake off the excess flour and place on a wire rack until all the anchovies are coated in flour.

On one side of the stove top, prepare a wire rack with a few layers of paper towel for draining the oil off the cooked anchovies. Place the plate of chilled egg on the other side of the stove top. Put a medium saucepan over medium–high heat with enough vegetable oil so that the anchovies can float – at least 3 cm (1¼ in) deep. It's time to cook when the oil reaches about 170°C (340°F) – see 'Tips for a good fry', page 24. Begin frying in batches – depending on the size of the pan and the size of the anchovies, I like to fry about 4–6 at a time.

Dip the floured anchovies into the chilled egg to coat, let the excess egg drip off momentarily, then place in the hot oil. Fry until the outside is crisp and golden and the inside cooked, about 2 minutes (if particularly small, it'll only take 90 seconds). If they are browning and darkening too quickly, turn the heat down slightly.

Remove from the oil and drain on the prepared paper towel. Sprinkle with salt.

Ideally, you want to serve these piping hot, so try to serve them as you fry. Or you can keep the fried anchovies warm, uncovered, in a low oven until you have finished frying them all.

HOW TO CLEAN FRESH ANCHOVIES

Note that very fresh anchovies have firmer flesh, which means that pulling away the spine is harder to do than when they are a couple of days old and seem much more relaxed. But older anchovies also are more delicate to handle as the flesh literally falls away. For the purpose of frying them, use the freshest anchovies you can find as they hold their shape better.

Set up a work space: I like to have a firm chopping board next to a clean kitchen sink (quite a bit of splashing goes on) with a plate or tray lined with paper towel for the cleaned anchovies. You could arm yourself with a small knife if you want to, but I find hands are the very best tool. Maybe you can have a pair of sharp kitchen scissors at the ready if you want to cut off the dorsal fin (as I do). I always like to keep the tails on.

1. Snap off the head from the bottom up towards the spinal cord. Run the nail of your thumb lengthwise along the belly to open and simultaneously remove the guts, which should come away easily. Running water from the sink can be handy to wash this away, though it's not entirely necessary as you can rinse the fish later.

2. Continue running the nail of your thumb down the whole length of the body of the fish to split it in two, lengthways, and open it like a book. You should now see the spinal cord exposed. Pull it out, starting from the head side and snap it off at the tail. Once you get the hang of this, you can do all of this in one swift motion – and head, spine and entrails all come out in a clean, easy sweep.

3. Give it a quick rinse under the tap and place on the paper towel to drain.

CALAMARI E FUNGHI
CALAMARI AND MUSHROOMS

The first time I tasted this saucy dish of squid and mushrooms was at a restaurant that sits directly on a pretty, pebble-covered beach between Porto Ercole and Porto Santo Stefano, and it struck me how perfectly symbolic of Argentario this dish was, with that strange but wonderful combination of *mare e monti*, or 'sea and mountains'. It reminds me of a Japanese saying that my mother taught me to appreciate, that the perfect meal should include something from the sea and something from the mountains. And there are plenty of other wonderful combinations of local sea and mountain dishes in the Maremma – octopus cooked with red wine and chestnuts is another intriguing one.

You would normally prepare this with *seppie* (cuttlefish), which are large, warm-water-loving creatures popular in many cuisines of the Mediterranean, but calamari (squid) and *calamaretti* (baby squid) are similar and easier to find. This is usually served as part of antipasto (with plenty of bread to mop up the juices) but you could double the recipe and serve it as a main, or even use this as a sauce to go with pasta.

SERVES 4 AS AN ANTIPASTO

First, clean the calamari. Cut off the head, and remove the eyes and the beak (you will find this in the middle of the tentacles – you can simply pull it out). Then reach into the body and remove the quill (a glassy strip inside the body that looks like it's made of plastic) and pull out the entrails – do this gently if you want to keep the ink sac intact. You can use this for flavouring risotto or adding to pasta to colour it black. It's also quite wonderful to serve with the Sea Bass Ragu (page 99). Slice the body in half lengthways and cut into thin strips cross-wise, about 1 cm (½ in) wide. The tentacles can be left as they are if small, or cut in half lengthways.

Clean the mushrooms of any dirt, trim the bottom of the stalks and slice or chop. Set aside.

Heat the olive oil in a wide frying pan over high heat and sear the calamari in the pan. Cook for 5–7 minutes or until the calamari is well browned and even begins sticking slightly to the pan.

Add the garlic and the wine. Season with salt and freshly ground black pepper, cover with a lid, and turn the heat down to low. Cook on low for about 30 minutes or until the calamari is extremely tender – the tip of a

400 g (14 oz) calamari
300 g (10½ oz) fresh mushrooms
60 ml (2 fl oz/¼ cup) olive oil
2 garlic cloves, finely chopped
250 ml (8½ fl oz/1 cup) dry white wine
1 handful flat-leaf (Italian) parsley, chopped

NOTE
Use a mixture of fresh mushrooms – poplar, porcini, chanterelles, button, whatever you can get your hands on.

knife should easily slip in, like cutting butter. You may need to top up with water along the way to keep the calamari cooking in plenty of liquid.

Add the mushrooms, along with about 125 ml (4 fl oz/½ cup) of water. Bring back to a simmer and continue cooking a further 7–10 minutes, or until the mushrooms are tender and cooked.

Sprinkle over the chopped parsley and serve warm with slices of firm, crusty bread.

SCAVECCIO DI SGOMBRO
MACKEREL SCAVECCIO

This is a variation of one of Orbetello's most famous dishes, *scaveccio*. Traditionally it's made with eels fished out of the lagoon that are deep-fried, then marinated in vinegar, herbs and chilli. It's not easy to get these eels outside Orbetello, so I make them with mackerel, which mimics the meaty, oily flesh of the eels and reminds me of a dish called *nanbanzuke* that my Japanese mother makes regularly with mackerel. In the Japanese dish, the fish is similarly floured, fried and marinated in rice vinegar, soy sauce, onions, chillies and mirin (though my grandmother used sake).

In that strange way that food can bring together two completely different places and cultures, there is a link here – both Orbetello and Japan were introduced to this technique for preserving fish by the Spanish (who in turn learnt it from the Arabs) in the sixteenth century. For the Orbetellani, the dish dates to the mid-1500s when the city came under Spanish rule – an influence that still resonates in the lagoon-city's civic architecture as well as traditional foods such as bottarga and this dish, *scaveccio*. Its name comes directly from the word *escabesce*, the Spanish method for curing fish under vinegar.

It's a wonderful dish to have in summer, as you can prepare it the night before and have a refreshing, cool, zingy lunch ready for you the next day when you come home from a morning at the beach. Serve it cold or tepid, with boiled potatoes that tame the bite of this robust, spicy, vinegary *scaveccio*.

SERVES 4

The mackerel should be cleaned of entrails, head removed and filleted. If you've never done this before, you could ask your fishmonger for fillets. Cut the fillets into pieces with a width of about 5 cm (2 in). Debone the fillet pieces by plucking the bones out with tweezers. There can be quite a number of them – run your fingers along the fish to feel them.

Dust the fish in the flour.

Pour enough vegetable oil in a small saucepan to cover a depth of about 3–4 cm (1¼–1½ in) and place over medium–high heat to achieve an oil temperature of 170–180°C (340–350°F). If you don't have a sugar thermometer handy to measure this, the old-fashioned test is to stick the end of a wooden spoon into the oil. When ready, it should immediately be surrounded by lots of tiny bubbles. Fry the fish pieces in batches until

1 kg (2 lb 3 oz) whole mackerel, about 4 small fish
2–3 tablespoons plain (all-purpose) flour or cornflour (cornstarch)
vegetable oil, for frying
250 ml (8½ fl oz/1 cup) dry white wine or water
250 ml (8½ fl oz/1 cup) white wine vinegar
1 whole fresh or dried red chilli
2 garlic cloves, whole
1 rosemary sprig
1 bay leaf

VARIATIONS
In Italy, eels are sold live, even from the supermarket, and there is a rather gruesome procedure to quickly kill very slippery live eels. This, I must admit, is the main reason why I like to do scaveccio *with mackerel instead. You could also use pieces of* orata *(gilthead sea bream), or whole fresh sardines or anchovies here. I've seen variations of* scaveccio *made with other local eels and fish such as* gronco *(conger eels),* boga *and* sparaglione *(both from the sea bream family), as well as* sugarello, *a relative of the horse mackerel that you will often find as* nanbanzuke *in Japan. You could also use* palamita *(bonito).*

golden, firm and cooked through (about 2–3 minutes), and drain on paper towel. Sprinkle with salt.

In a separate saucepan, prepare the marinade by bringing the vinegar and wine to the boil. Add the chilli, garlic and herbs and continue cooking for a further 2 minutes.

Place the fried fish in a shallow dish – terracotta is traditional, but a glass ovenproof dish works, too. Pour over the hot marinade and let it sit a few hours before serving. If you've got the time, it tastes even better after marinating overnight, or even a few days. If keeping longer than a day or two, remove it from the marinade as it will become too strong. The vinegar acts as a preserving agent, so it keeps very well in the fridge for 1 week.

ORBETELLO'S EELS

Orbetello's other famous creation, anguilla sfumata, *is a spicy smoked eel dish that was created to conserve an abundance of eel for a long time. The live eels are killed, butterflied, cleaned, then strung up to dry in the sun and wind. They're then brushed with a sauce made of red capsicums (bell peppers), hot chillies, vinegar and salt, and smoked. Herbs from the Mediterranean scrub, such as rosemary and bay leaf, are added to the fire to produce an aromatic smoke that dries out the eels. The flavoursome, spicy, smoked eel can be kept like this for some time. When needed, it's cut into pieces and deep fried before serving.*

Pictured overleaf >

POLPO E PATATE
OCTOPUS AND POTATO BRAISE

The tricky thing about cooking octopus is making sure it's tender. There are many, many ways Italians will tell you to cook octopus. Many have their 'secrets' to getting it meltingly tender – some include boiling with a wine cork, vinegar, sea water or pummelling the beast to break down the fibres before putting in the pot. Others don't boil it in water but let it cook in its own juices. A very wise (and guaranteed) tenderiser is to pop the fresh octopus in the freezer the day before you need it (or use a frozen one to begin with). It's the method I find easiest, and it achieves a beautiful result every time.

The cork tradition is a funny one, with a story that my husband Marco likes to tell. Along the ports of Sicily, it was traditional for freshly caught, whole octopus to be cooked right then and there in enormous, bubbling barrels. To recognise your octopus, a cork was tied to the octopus with a piece of string before going in – the floating cork was also handy for pulling out the right octopus when the time came. Passersby believed the cork in the boiling pots of octopus helped tenderise it, and decided to try the same thing at home. In reality, its usefulness as a tenderiser is a myth (albeit a charming one).

The general rule with octopus is to either cook it for a very brief time (flash searing, for example) or to cook it long enough that it gives way and becomes meltingly soft. You can make this dish with baby octopus too – it is considerably easier to clean and only takes 20 minutes to cook completely. If you have a larger octopus, an hour usually suffices. You can serve this right away, warm, or you can eat it chilled, which is excellent in hot weather.

SERVES 4

1 kg (2 lb 3 oz) octopus
3 garlic cloves, whole
60 ml (2 fl oz/¼ cup) extra-virgin olive oil
125 ml (4 fl oz/½ cup) white wine
500 g (1 lb 2 oz) potatoes, peeled and cut into chunks
1 large handful flat-leaf (Italian) parsley, leaves picked and finely chopped
juice of 1 lemon

Prepare the octopus by first rinsing it under a tap. Feel around the tentacles and make sure they are free of any particles, especially if you have bought it fresh. Remove the eyes and clean the inside of the head thoroughly, but otherwise leave the octopus whole.

Put the garlic in a tall pot with a tight-fitting lid. Pour over 3 tablespoons of olive oil and heat gently to infuse the oil for a few minutes. Add the octopus and turn the heat up to medium; cook for 2 minutes and let it colour all over. Pour over the wine, bring the liquid to a simmer, then cover and cook over low heat for about 45 minutes. Check for tenderness – a fork pierced through the thickest part should find no resistance (another 10–15 minutes of simmering, covered, may be necessary).

In the meantime, put the potatoes in a medium saucepan, fill with cold water to cover and add a good pinch of salt. Bring to the boil and cook over medium heat for 12–15 minutes, or until soft. Drain.

When the octopus is very tender, take it off the heat and leave in the pot until cool enough to handle. Leaving the juices in the pot, drain the octopus on paper towel. If you've got a large octopus, you may need to peel it – the 'skin' should come off very easily, just by rubbing or scraping it gently. Small ones won't need this treatment. Chop it into 5 cm (2 in) pieces. Return the octopus to the juices in the pot, along with the potatoes. Add the parsley and lemon juice plus the rest of the olive oil, and season with salt and freshly ground black pepper. Toss to combine and serve warm or cold with plenty of bread to mop up the sauce.

If planning to serve leftovers cold the next day, drain the stew of its juices and keep them separate in the fridge. When you want to serve the octopus, think of it more as a salad. Some crunchy slices of celery or some black olives make nice additions. Reheat the reserved juices just until they become liquid again and add a spoonful to dress the octopus, along with some olive oil and a little extra lemon juice. Toss together.

< Pictured on previous spread

ACQUACOTTA DEL PESCATORE
FISHERMAN'S ACQUACOTTA

Acquacotta is a true peasant dish. Fishermen of another time may have added a piece of long-lasting baccalà (dried salted cod) or some cheap but tasty fish brought in with the catch – the sort of fish that maybe never makes it to the market. But this is a modern version, using a popular mixture of clams, mussels and prawns – the same mix that you would find in a *spaghetti allo scoglio* – but you could add anything you like.

SERVES 4

See page 95 on how and when to purge clams. Weed out any with crushed shells (a tiny chip or crack is usually fine) or that are open and don't move when touched or squeezed. (Rule of thumb: if they are open *before* cooking, they're dead. If they *don't* open *after* cooking, they're dead. Throw them away). Purge the clams, if necessary, for at least 1 hour. And regardless of whether or not you're purging, do not skimp on step 5.

Scrub the mussels and pull out the beards. I like the prawns whole if they are smaller, but they can be a bit messy to eat, so you can chop them in half lengthways, right down the body, to make it easier to access the meat without getting fingers too messy.

Pour the olive oil in a large casserole pot and warm over gentle heat. Cook the onion and celery, along with a pinch of salt, in the oil until very soft, about 15–20 minutes. The slower the better – do not let the onions colour, so stir them often, keep the heat low and add a splash of water if necessary. Add one of the garlic cloves and the chilli, cook for 1 minute, then add the tomato and 500 ml (17 fl oz/2 cups) of water. Season with salt and bring to a simmer. Cook gently for about 40 minutes, topping up with water if it begins to look too thick.

In the meantime, prepare the bread – stale bread is best as it soaks up the liquid without becoming soggy. If it is not stale, you can dry it out in a low oven until crisp. Rub the bread once with the remaining garlic clove.

Add the prawns, mussels and clams to the simmering liquid. Cover and let them cook for about 2 minutes, or until the shells have opened and the prawns are just cooked.

Remove from the heat and stir through the parsley. Place the stale bread in the bottom of the serving bowls and scoop the *acquacotta* over the top of them, distributing the seafood evenly.

---

500 g (1 lb 2 oz) clams and mussels

4 large mazzancolle prawns (or tiger prawns)

60 ml (2 fl oz/¼ cup) extra-virgin olive oil

2 brown (yellow) onions, finely sliced

1 celery stalk, finely sliced

2 garlic cloves, whole

1 small red chilli, chopped (optional)

700 g (1 lb 9 oz) tomato passata (puréed tomato)

4 thick slices of stale Tuscan bread (or crusty white loaf)

1 handful flat-leaf (Italian) parsley, chopped

VARIATIONS

In a seafood cookbook called La Cucina Toscana di Mare, *by prolific Italian food writer Laura Rangoni, there are two enticing seafood* acquacotta *recipes. One features fresh and salted anchovies and silverbeet (Swiss chard) together with the tomato-based soup. Instead of poaching the eggs in the soup, Rangoni beats the eggs with a handful of grated pecorino cheese and pours this over the top. The other is an acquacotta with chickpeas and wedge clams, which are first cooked so the clam meat can be plucked out, then added to the soup without their shells. She sprinkles grated pecorino cheese on the bread first, then pours the acquacotta on top.*

ORBETELLO

Approaching Orbetello from Monte Argentario, the southern Tuscan town seems to rise straight out of the lagoon, a little reminiscent of Venice. It's a unique sight in Tuscany.

The lagoon characterises and defines the city, and is created by two sand bars, the beautiful, long, soft-sanded beaches of Feniglia and Giannella, which connect Monte Argentario to the Tuscan mainland. The historical centre of Orbetello is finger-shaped and juts out into the lagoon so that the town is surrounded almost completely by water. Being in Orbetello, you live and breathe the humidity, the tiny, persistent mosquitoes, the horizontal wind that this unique body of water brings – it is as much a part of the city as anything else, and it's the source of the traditional cuisine, which is known in particular for its bottarga and eel (see 'Orbetello's Eels', page 83).

Something keeps coming up when you talk to the locals of Orbetello about food and local products. It's the place. It's the land and the water and that particular mixture of nature and local traditions that has created something that tastes unique. Like *terroir* is to wine, the location is all-important. Even though the process for making bottarga is much the same as the one in Sardinia, Orbetello's bottarga is like no other.

Bottarga comes from an Arabic word, *botarikh*, for cured fish eggs, a technique of preserving introduced to the lagoon town by the Spanish, who ruled Orbetello more than 500 years ago. It is still made today by the fisherman's cooperative of Orbetello. Traditionally, during the months of August and September, when grey mullets are carrying eggs, the fish are caught during their natural migration at the mouth of the lagoon, then worked entirely by hand – egg sacs are removed carefully so as not to break them, cleaned, then placed under salt for brief curing, after which the egg sacs are rinsed and dried.

When I asked a fisherman from Orbetello's cooperative why Orbetello's bottarga is so remarkable, he replied quite bluntly that the difference is Orbetello. It's partly the high salinity of the lagoon, which is significantly different to the open waters of the Atlantic Ocean off the coast of West Africa (where the same fish are found). It's partly what the fish feed on in the lagoon. In short, it only tastes like this here.

The recipe for *Spaghetti alla Bottarga di Orbetello* (opposite) is the one recommended by the fishermen of Orbetello.

SPAGHETTI ALLA BOTTARGA DI ORBETELLO

SPAGHETTI WITH BOTTARGA FROM ORBETELLO

Bottarga di Orbetello is different from that of Sardinia and other places. It's stronger in flavour, salty (naturally) but with a backnote that I can't quite put my finger on – bittersweet, perhaps. It's also softer in texture, so you can slice it and eat it with just a squeeze of lemon and a splash of olive oil on *crostini*. The longer you keep it, the darker and drier it gets until you just need to grate it.

The extreme care with which the bottarga is collected, prepared and preserved in Orbetello is reflected in the price – a plate of *Spaghetti alla Bottarga di Orbetello* will easily be the most expensive plate of pasta on the menu. But, thankfully, it's very easy to reproduce this dish at home and, like other prized ingredients such as caviar or truffles, a little goes a long way. This makes a very quick and tasty dinner solution.

SERVES 4

320 g (11½ oz) dried spaghetti
50 g (1¾ oz) bottarga di Orbetello, grated
juice of 1 lemon
2 tablespoons extra-virgin olive oil
1 handful flat-leaf (Italian) parsley, finely chopped

Put the pasta in a large pot of boiling, well-salted water (see page 13). Cook until al dente (follow the recommended timing on the packet).

Drain, setting aside some of the pasta cooking liquid. Immediately toss the hot pasta with the bottarga, the lemon juice, the olive oil and a little splash of the pasta cooking liquid. Toss again quickly so that the liquids create a saucy emulsion. Garnish with the chopped parsley and serve.

NOTE
You can usually buy bottarga from good Italian delis or speciality gourmet food shops.

Bottarga needs to be peeled of its extremely thin 'skin' before grating or slicing; once you cut into it, you can easily peel off the skin of the portion you need with your hands. Leave the skin on the rest of the bottarga to help preserve it until next use. If you don't eat it very often, store the bottarga in the freezer so that it retains its freshness.

SPAGHETTI ALLE ARSELLE
SPAGHETTI WITH WEDGE CLAMS

Also known as *telline* or wedge clams, these rather small, flat and extremely tasty clams are highly regarded in the kitchen. Marco often recounts stories of family holidays on the Tuscan coast, when his father would wander off to rake through the sand for hours, coming home with buckets full of *arselle*. Unfortunately, they're not as easy to find anymore and there are many restrictions on fishing them, so this is reflected in their price at the market.

Arselle are in season from May to September, though the best season for finding them is just either side of the too-hot months of June–August, when they tend to bury themselves further into the sand to keep cool. In Monte Argentario, you can find them along the shallow, fine-sand beach of Feniglia. But there's nothing quite like enjoying a plate of pasta made with local *arselle* eaten right on the beach itself – the handful of restaurants on the Porto Ercole end of Feniglia offer this delicious dish.

SERVES 6

Rinse the clams quickly under water, weed out any with crushed shells (tiny chips or cracks are usually fine) or that are open and don't move when touched or squeezed. (Rule of thumb: if they are open *before* cooking, they're dead. If they *don't* open *after* cooking, they're dead. Throw them away). Purge the clams, if necessary, for at least 1 hour (see 'Purging Clams', page 95). And regardless of whether or not you're purging, do not skimp on step 5.

Put a large pot of well-salted water on to boil for the spaghetti (see page 13).

Put 2 tablespoons of the olive oil and the garlic in a wide frying pan over medium heat. Let it sizzle for 1 minute until pale golden, then add the clams. Toss briefly to coat the clams, then add the white wine. Turn up the heat to high, then cover and cook, giving a good shake here and there for another 90 seconds, or until all the clams have opened. Remove from the heat and set aside. Add freshly ground black pepper or chilli to taste.

When the water is boiling, add the spaghetti and cook until al dente (see the recommended time on the package). Drain, reserving about 60 ml (2 fl oz/¼ cup) of the cooking water if needed. Toss the spaghetti with the remaining olive oil, parsley, the clams and all their juice. If it needs any extra liquid to keep it all juicy, add the reserved cooking water.

Serve immediately.

1 kg (2 lb 3 oz) wedge clams (or vongole clams)
3–4 tablespoons extra-virgin olive oil
2 garlic cloves, chopped
250 ml (8½ fl oz/1 cup) dry white wine
freshly chopped red chilli or dried chilli flakes, to taste (optional)
500 g (1 lb 2 oz) dried spaghetti
1 handful flat-leaf (Italian) parsley, chopped

NOTE

In Italy, mussels and clams are often sold in plastic nets weighing either 500 g (1 lb 2 oz) or 1 kg (2 lb 3 oz), so the recipe here is for cooking 1 kg (2 lb 3 oz) of clams. It would easily feed six but if you can buy by the weight, you can pare this back to about 750 g (1 lb 11 oz) of clams and 320 g (11½ oz) pasta for four serves. You can use vongole *clams the same way, which are a little plumper and often not as sandy as* arselle.

SPAGHETTI ALLE SPERNOCCHIE
MANTIS SHRIMP SPAGHETTI

Mantis shrimp look a little like a cross between scampi and some kind of insect, with large decorative 'eyes' painted on their tails – but their sweet meat could be compared to that of lobster. They're rather difficult to get into, with hard shells and sharp thorns hidden along their armour-covered bodies, and sometimes with disappointingly little meat in proportion to the effort needed to get in – but what they do guarantee is bucket-loads of flavour. In fact, locally they're thrown into just about any mixed seafood stew, cooked whole, as their shells add incredible flavour to dishes.

I absolutely love the no-waste method here for making a rather simple pasta dish with maximum flavour. The shrimp are first boiled, then the meat fished out of their shells. The pasta is cooked in the stock left from boiling the shrimp to get double the flavour.

SERVES 4

Bring about 2 litres (68 fl oz/8 cups) of water to the boil in a large saucepan. Boil the mantis shrimp over high heat for 2 minutes, or until just cooked and opaque.

Drain the mantis shrimp, keeping the water on a simmer. When the shrimp are cool enough to handle, remove the meat from the shells. I recommend using sharp kitchen scissors to cut open the body lengthways to pull out the meat. Be careful of the thorns along the sides of the body.

In a wide frying pan, heat the olive oil, garlic and parsley over low–medium heat. Let the oil infuse for 2 minutes, stirring occasionally. Add the white wine and let it simmer for about 3 minutes. Add the mantis shrimp meat and toss to combine. Remove from the heat and set aside until needed. Taste for seasoning; it probably won't need much salt but you can add freshly ground black pepper or chilli to taste, if desired.

Add the salt to the shrimp cooking water and boil the pasta in it until al dente (refer to the packaging for timing and take it off the heat 1 minute earlier than it says). Drain, reserving about 60 ml (2 fl oz/¼ cup) of the cooking water. Add the spaghetti to the frying pan with the shrimp mixture, along with the reserved liquid. Over low heat, toss together evenly for about 1 minute to coat the pasta. Serve immediately.

1 kg (2 lb 3 oz) mantis shrimp
60 ml (2 fl oz/¼ cup) extra-virgin olive oil
2 garlic cloves
1 handful flat-leaf (Italian) parsley, finely chopped
125 ml (4 fl oz/½ cup) white wine
freshly chopped red chilli or dried chilli flakes, to taste (optional)
2 teaspoons salt
320 g (11½ oz) dried spaghetti

SUBSTITUTION
If you can't get mantis shrimp, you could use this same technique to cook scampetti *– little scampi – which are considerably less expensive than their larger, prettier counterparts. Cook them for 2 minutes, then as you're shelling them, pop their heads (the best part) back into the pot to keep simmering while you finish shelling and preparing the sauce. By the time you're ready to cook the pasta, you'll have a delicious scampi stock waiting.*

PURGING CLAMS

Clams are sold live and need to be prepared with care. To prepare clams before cooking, it's traditional in Italian kitchens to purge them of any sand that might be inside the tightly shut shells — there's nothing worse than biting into sand while eating your pasta. The idea is to filter the sand out by soaking them in water. Everyone has different advice on how to do this, much of it filtered down through family lore and a persistent series of old wives' tales.

I take the advice of lifelong clamming experts such as Hank Shaw (American journalist, forager and author of *Hunt, Gather, Cook*) and the excellent blog *Honest Food*. Both offer more in-depth advice on the subject.

The first thing to know is that most commercially available clams and mussels have already been filtered. If you've bought your clams in a supermarket, they are likely to be ready to go — just follow step 1 below for weeding out any bad ones and step 5 in case there are any closed dead ones hoarding a shellfull of sand. Trust me on step 5 — it sounds tedious but this is the most important step! If you have even one of these dead ones open in your pan while tossing, your entire dish will be ruined. If you're sourcing them from a fishmonger and you're not sure, just ask if they have already been purged.

If you need to purge the clams yourself, the best procedure is this:

1. Rinse clams quickly under water, weed out any with crushed shells or that are open and don't move when touched or squeezed. Put the clams in a large non-reactive bowl (such as glass or ceramic).

2. Cover the clams in salt water by 2–3 cm (¾–1¼ in). Actual seawater (filtered to remove any sand) is best, of course, but otherwise use sea salt (not regular table salt) and water to a salinity of about 3.5% – or 35 g (1¼ oz) to every 1 litre (34 fl oz/ 4 cups) of water. Fresh water will kill the clams. Try not to shock them to death by changing their temperature too rapidly so keep them somewhere relatively close to their current temperature. If they have been stored chilled (for example, at the fishmongers), then you can use cool water and keep them chilled in the fridge. Otherwise, set them somewhere like in a cool corner of the room.

3. Purge for at least 1 hour. I find this time sufficient for clams bought from the fishmonger. If you leave them for significantly longer than that, check on them from time to time and change the water so they don't die from loss of oxygen. When you tap or agitate them, they should close (perhaps slowly, but they should eventually completely close). The last thing you want is to forget about them and come back to a bowl of dead clams.

4. Transfer the clams to a colander using your hands or a perforated spoon (don't tip the water out directly into the colander as you'll end up pouring any purged sand back over them).

5. You'll see Italian fishmongers tapping or bouncing their clams on the counter to weed out any dead ones that look like they are closed. It's incredibly important to do this (if you've got little ones running around, they might like to help). With a plastic chopping board underneath, tap or bounce the clams one by one. Live ones will stay tightly shut. If there is a dead one in there, it will open when you do this – and will likely be full of sand that you've just saved from getting into your sauce. Now they're ready to cook.

BAVETTE AL BRANZINO
BAVETTE WITH SEA BASS RAGU

Sea bass, or *branzino* or *spigola* in Italian, is found on menus everywhere around Argentario and Orbetello – the main reason is the lagoon situated between these two places, which is the source of Italy's most famous and best-regarded farmed sea bass. The lagoon is also the source of sea bream, eels and grey mullet, which are used in a number of traditional dishes.

Farming fish has been a tradition in these parts since ancient Roman times. Just minutes away, off Giannella, the sandbar that blocks off Orbetello's lagoon to the sea to the north, there is a small beach known as Bagni di Domiziano, where you can find the ruins of a Roman villa that date to 36 BC. During low tide, you can just make out the partially submerged ruins of the stone pools used to raise sea bass and grey mullet. According to *The Twelve Caesars* – the famous biographies of twelve Roman emperors, written in AD 121 by Suetonius – the Roman Emperor Nero spent childhood summers at this villa, tending to the fish, which were fed a diet of prawns (shrimp), mussels, crabs, *corbezzoli* (fruit from the strawberry tree) and figs, to make them exceptionally tasty. Nero's was a family of noble bankers, who owned the whole of Monte Argentario – the promontory probably takes its name from this history, as *argentario* was the name for 'money lenders'.

Bavette are a typical Ligurian pasta shape – flat, narrow but thick. You can use any pasta with this, but it is nice with something long and thin like square-cut or regular spaghetti or tagliolini.

SERVES 4

Cut the fish fillets into 1.5 cm (½ in) cubes. Set aside.

Heat the olive oil in a frying pan over low heat and add the onion, garlic and parsley stalks. Season with a pinch of salt and cook gently for about 10–15 minutes, until the onion 'sweats' and is softened but not coloured (add a splash of water if needed).

Put a large pot of well-salted water on to boil for the pasta (see page 13).

Pour the white wine over the onion mixture and turn the heat up to medium. Let it simmer for 2 minutes, then add the tomato and stock and cook for a further 10 minutes. Add the diced fish and continue cooking for 5 more minutes. Remove from the heat.

When the water is boiling, add the pasta and cook until al dente (refer to the packaging for the cooking time). Drain, reserving about 60 ml (2 fl oz/

400 g (14 oz) sea bass fillets
2 tablespoons extra-virgin olive oil
1 small brown (yellow) onion, finely chopped
1 garlic clove, finely chopped
1 large handful flat-leaf (Italian) parsley, stalks separated and roughly chopped, leaves finely chopped
125 ml (4 fl oz/½ cup) dry white wine
1 tomato (or handful cherry tomatoes), chopped
250 ml (8½ fl oz/1 cup) fish stock
320 g (11½ oz) dried bavette, or 400 g (14 oz) fresh bavette (or spaghetti or tagliolini)

NOTE
If buying a whole fish to fillet yourself, you will need double the weight of the fillets. Save the heads and bones for making fish stock.

Continued overleaf >

¼ cup) of the cooking water if needed. Add the pasta and the chopped parsley leaves to the fish ragu, and toss to combine. If you need some extra liquid to bring it all together, add some of the reserved cooking water.

Serve immediately.

VARIATIONS

This dish is often made using whole fish, cooked directly in the pan with the onion, garlic, parsley and white wine. It is then removed, so the bones, head and tail can be discarded, and the meat picked over before being returned to the pan. It's a nice way of making a fish ragu, as using the entire fish adds good flavour and you don't need the stock if you do it this way. Using fillets makes this easy (and a little less messy), and if you have filleted the fish yourself, you can use the head and bones for a homemade Fish Stock (see below). *Red mullet, tub gurnard or sea bream are also good prepared this way.*

FISH STOCK

MAKES 1 LITRE (34 FL OZ/4 CUPS)

Heat the olive oil in a soup pot over medium–high heat. Sear the fish bones and head for 1–2 minutes – this will bring out extra flavour. Add the vegetables and continue cooking for 1 minute, then pour over 1.5 litres (51 fl oz/6 cups) of cold water.

Bring to the boil, then turn down to low and simmer for 30 minutes, uncovered. Remove from the heat and strain through a fine-meshed sieve.

This makes a little over 1 litre (34 fl oz/4 cups) of stock, which you can use instead of water for any fish soups, stews or pasta sauces. It also freezes well.

1 tablespoon extra-virgin olive oil
300–500 g (10½ oz–1 lb 2 oz) fish head, bones and tail
1 brown (yellow) onion, roughly chopped
1 celery stalk, roughly chopped
1 carrot, roughly chopped

MINESTRA DI PESCE
FISH SOUP WITH PASTA

Like many peasant dishes, this velvety, brothy soup is an enormously comforting and warming dish. It's like a fisherman's version of *pastina in brodo*, which is usually made with homemade chicken or beef stock, a sort of Italian chicken noodle soup. The secret behind its wonderful flavour is the use of a variety of whole, small fish – the kind you find in piles at the markets labelled *pesce da zuppa*, or 'fish for soup'.

In her classic book *Honey from a Weed* (1986), Patience Gray describes a similar dish *Zuppa di pesciolini di scoglio* ('soup of little rockfish') from Puglia's Salento, where she questions whether it is 'infanticide' to eat such tiny, immature fish: 'If left in the sea would they grow up?' Indeed, it's probably hard to find these little fish outside Italy so you can use a mixture of their adult-sized versions – the only downside to this is that you won't be able to get as much variety for this quantity (unless you are prepared to make enough for 12 portions!).

The small versions of these fish can be rather fiddly to clean and prepare, but the benefit of this recipe is that you don't need to fiddle so much as the food mill does all that work. If you don't have a food mill (a *passaverdura* or *passatutto* in Italian, or a *mouli* as some call it), I suggest getting one. You won't regret it! It'll be your best friend for every sauce, purée, jam or mash that you want to make. What makes it different from, say, a blender, is that it actually separates the things you want and those you don't want. The fish bones and head and skin? Those get filtered out through this remarkable contraption, so you're only left with all the juicy, flavourful goodness.

SERVES 4

300 g (10½ oz) small mixed fish
3 tablespoons extra-virgin olive oil
1 garlic clove, whole and unpeeled
1 brown (yellow) onion, finely chopped
1 celery stalk, finely chopped
125 ml (4 fl oz/½ cup) white wine
4 fresh large tomatoes or 400 g (14 oz) peeled tomatoes or tomato passata (puréed tomatoes)
1 handful basil leaves, chopped
1 handful flat-leaf (Italian) parsley, leaves picked and chopped
1 freshly chopped red chilli or dried chilli flakes to taste (optional)
120 g (4½ oz) dried miniature pasta, such as ditalini, risoni, stelline, quadretti, or even broken-up pieces of spaghetti

The fish need to be rinsed, scaled and gutted – make a slit underneath the fish from the head to the belly to pull out the guts. Rinse and pat dry.

Gently heat the olive oil in a saucepan and cook the whole garlic clove, onion and celery for 5 minutes over low heat, stirring occasionally. Add the fish, turn the heat up to medium and cook for a further 3 minutes. Add the wine and let it cook down for about 5 minutes.

If using fresh tomatoes, score their bottoms and blanch in boiling water for 30 seconds, then quickly remove to a bowl of ice water. They should be very easy to peel now. Remove the skins and quarter them, remove seeds and chop the rest.

Continued overleaf >

Add the tomato to the saucepan, along with the herbs and chilli, if using. Season with salt and pepper and pour over 1 litre (34 fl oz/4 cups) of cold water. Bring to the boil, then turn down the heat to a steady simmer. Cook for 10 minutes, then cover and keep on a low simmer for a further 30 minutes.

Pass the soup through a food mill to break down the solid pieces of fish and vegetables and to remove the bones (if you have particularly large pieces, you can blend the soup roughly first before passing through the food mill). Then strain the resulting soup through a fine-meshed sieve as well. If you don't have a food mill, that's fine. Blend it a little first (not too much!) and then pass it through a fine-meshed sieve.

Return the soup back to the pot and bring to a simmer. Cook the pasta directly in the soup until al dente (follow the recommended timing on the packet) and serve immediately in individual bowls.

NOTE
Typical fish for this soup include red gurnard, red mullet, scorpion fish, hake, megrim sole, stargazers and bream. If you don't have small mixed fish available to you, the best option is to use a larger one of these whole fish and combine with a couple of fillets of the other fish. Another way of adding flavour is to use the leftover fish heads and tails from other meals. Rather than throw them out when filleting fish, keep the heads/bones in the freezer for occasions like this!

ZUPPA DI SCAMPI E PATATE

SCAMPI AND POTATO SOUP

I first heard of this classic Argentario dish one beautiful day out on the near-empty beach of La Spiaggia Lunga with our friends, Umberto and Alessandra. We took their boat out to get there – a quick zip out from Porto Ercole's hushed port and just a little wading to reach the shore – and soaked up the sun while the conversation, inevitably, led to food. They recounted how there was once a family who would set up a bonfire on the beach every Ferragosto (the holiday of all holidays, it falls on 15 August, when most Italians are on a beach and a big family lunch is traditional). The family would cook up a pot of scampi and potato soup so elaborate that other beach-goers thought they were running a restaurant.

I'm pretty sure they must be the same people who are described in Enrico Bistazzoni and Vincenzo Sabatini's *Noi di Port'Ercole* (2011), a book of memories of Porto Ercole in the old days. In the book they write of Spiaggia Lunga as one of the favourites of the *portercolesi*, where you can find 'The group of thirty, forty people who pitch a tent at dawn and for lunch start with a *Caldaro* and finish with watermelon, with baked pasta and *Fritto Misto* in the middle.'

Inevitably we started discussing the recipe – Alessandra sometimes adds zucchini (courgettes) or strips of red capsicums (bell peppers), too – and I found myself salivating at the thought of this scampi soup, ladled over crisp, grilled, garlicky bread.

Usually, small scampi (*scampetti*) are used for this – but if you're looking for a cheaper (though no less flavourful) version, there's a similar traditional dish made with sardines instead of scampi, *Zuppa di Sarde e Patate*.

SERVES 4

500 g (1 lb 2 oz) scampetti
3 tablespoons extra-virgin olive oil
2 garlic cloves, 1 finely chopped, 1 whole for rubbing bread
1 handful flat-leaf (Italian) parsley, stalks and leaves separated and finely chopped
125 ml (4 fl oz/½ cup) dry white wine
400 g (14 oz) tinned peeled tomatoes
500 g (1 lb 2 oz) potatoes, peeled and diced into 2 cm (¾ in) cubes
4 slices Tuscan bread (or other crusty bread)

Remove the heads and shells of the *scampetti* and set aside the meat and tails. In a saucepan over high heat, toast the heads and shells for about 2 minutes (no oil or anything else necessary). Pour over 1 litre (34 fl oz/4 cups) of cold water, bring to the boil and turn down the heat. Let it simmer, covered, for 30 minutes, then strain. Set aside the scampi stock.

In a wide frying pan, heat the olive oil over low heat and gently cook the chopped garlic and parsley stalks for 5 minutes. Pour over the wine, turn the heat up to medium and cook for about 5 minutes. Add the tomatoes, the scampi stock and season with salt and pepper. Bring to

Continued overleaf >

the boil, then turn down the heat to low and let it simmer for 15 minutes. Add the potatoes and cook for 15 minutes or until they are just tender, then add the scampi and the parsley leaves and cook for a further 2 minutes. Season with salt and pepper.

Grill (broil) the slices of bread or put in a low oven to dry out slightly. Rub with the whole garlic clove.

To serve, place a slice of bread in the bottom of each bowl and ladle the soup over the top.

VONGOLE E POLENTA
CLAM STEW WITH POLENTA

This recipe calls for a creamy, pillowy polenta base, made with *fioretto* or fine-round cornmeal, quite different to the sturdy and firm one used in Polenta Crostini with Mushrooms (page 25). Much like fluffy mashed potatoes, this starchy, comforting staple needs love and care (and the right seasoning) for a good result. It takes a bit of time, but if you're at the stove anyway, checking on the tomato sauce and preparing these clams, you won't even notice having to give the polenta a stir every 4–5 minutes.

Polenta should be well salted, but for some good seafood flavour you can add some grated bottarga to the polenta instead of salt.

SERVES 4

- 1 kg (2 lb 3 oz) vongole clams
- 1 garlic clove, chopped
- 3 tablespoons extra-virgin olive oil
- 1 freshly chopped red chilli or dried chilli flakes to taste (optional)
- 400 g (14 oz) tomato passata (puréed tomatoes)
- 2 teaspoons salt
- 200 g (7 oz/1¼ cups) fine polenta (fioretto)
- 125 ml (4 fl oz/½ cup) dry white wine
- 1 handful flat-leaf (Italian) parsley, leaves picked and roughly chopped
- 1 handful basil, leaves picked and roughly chopped

Rinse the clams quickly under water, weed out any with crushed shells (tiny chips or cracks are usually fine) or that are open and don't move when touched or squeezed. (Rule of thumb: if they are open *before* cooking, they're dead. If they *don't* open *after* cooking, they're dead. Throw them away). Purge the clams, if necessary, for at least 1 hour (see 'Purging Clams', page 95). And regardless of whether or not you're purging, do not skimp on step 5.

In a saucepan, heat the garlic gently in 2 tablespoons of the olive oil. Add the chilli and the tomato, along with about 250 ml (8½ fl oz/1 cup) of water, and season with salt. Let it simmer for 30 minutes or until slightly reduced.

To prepare the polenta, bring 1 litre (34 fl oz/4 cups) of water to the boil in a deep, non-stick pot, add the salt (or grated bottarga) and the remaining tablespoon of olive oil. Pour in the polenta slowly while stirring (I like a wooden spoon, others like a whisk) to avoid lumps; stir for 1–2 minutes until the mixture thickens.

Turn the heat down to the lowest setting possible and cook gently, covered (but giving a vigorous stir every 4–5 minutes) until it is creamy and silky and it begins to come away from the sides of the pan. It's useful to have a small saucepan of simmering, salted water nearby to add in spoonfuls if the polenta looks too thick or lumpy when stirring. Taste it too – the polenta should be completely soft, with no bite to it, at about 45 minutes. Cover with parchment paper cut to the size of the dish or a slightly damp tea towel so that it rests against the surface of the polenta — this is to avoid developing a tough skin. Set it aside while you prepare the clams.

Continued overleaf >

Place a frying pan or saucepan with a lid over high heat. When very hot, add the drained and cleaned clams, followed by the white wine. Let them cook for 1–2 minutes, then cover and let the steam open up the clam shells. Shake the pan occasionally. After 1–2 minutes, check the clams – they should all be opened.

At this point you can choose to remove the shells – pluck the clam meat out of their shells, discard the shells but add the meat and their juices, along with the herbs, to the tomato sauce. Or you can leave the shells intact, as I do – it looks better and I don't mind getting my fingers dirty during the meal.

Portion out the warm, creamy polenta into shallow bowls and ladle the clam stew over the top. Serve immediately.

POLENTA COOKING TECHNIQUES

There are some brilliant shortcuts for cooking polenta. Italian food writer Anna del Conte has a technique where, after 10 minutes of stirring the polenta in a pot on the stove top, she transfers it to a buttered ovenproof dish and bakes it, covered, for 1 hour. While the top retains a crust (much like the crust that forms around the pot during stove top cooking), it protects the soft polenta underneath. In her book Simply Ancient Grains, *Maria Speck suggests another solution that only requires remembering to start soaking ahead of time. Pour boiling water over the dry polenta and cover. Let it sit for 8–12 hours (or even 2 days in the fridge). Then, when ready to cook, add more water, bring it to a simmer and cook, while stirring, for 10–12 minutes.*

CALDARO DELL'ARGENTARIO
ARGENTARIO FISH STEW

Every port in the Mediterranean has its version of a fish stew. Marseilles has its *bouillabaisse*, and Portugal has its *caldeirada*, which changes from town to town depending on what the fishermen usually catch. Tuscany's Monte Argentario has its *caldaro*, a traditional fisherman's soup that gets its name from the large pot (like the *caldeirada*) in which it is prepared. Like other fish soups, this has its variations, changing from household to household and dependent upon what local seafood is available at the time.

Like Livorno's famous *cacciucco*, a fundamental part of the stew is that it contains a large variety of the freshest seafood. In this area of Tuscany, you would choose flavourful, fleshy fish, such as red scorpion fish, tub gurnard, john dory and catshark (similar to flake), together with octopus, squid or calamari. Eels are also very typical of this area. You could also add a handful of crustaceans like mantis shrimp or scampi. If you can find them, *lampatelle* (a type of sea snail known as limpets in English), volcano-shaped seashells that you find stuck to the rocks around Argentario's coastline, add a strong sea flavour. It is this combination of locally found seafood that makes the *caldaro* unique.

This recipe has been adapted from the book of Paolo Petroni, *Il Grande Libro della Vera Cucina Toscana* (1996). Like *bouillabaisse*, it's difficult to make small quantities of this dish because of the sheer number of ingredients required – it's usually made for a large number of people to eat together. This should be enough for six but you could stretch it to eight if eating other dishes along with this, too.

SERVES 6

Roughly cut the octopus into smaller pieces (unless they are really small, in which case they can stay whole). The calamari's tentacles can be left as they are, but slice the body into strips, either lengthways or in rings. The fish can be filleted and only the fillets used, although it's common to see gurnard chopped into thick steaks, bones included, because they add flavour (if you're not keen on keeping an eye out for bones in the soup, you can fillet this, too). Small fillets can go in whole, but if you have large fillets, cut them into smaller chunks.

Gently cook the onion, squashed garlic, parsley and chilli in the olive oil with a pinch of salt over low heat for about 10 minutes, or until they all soften. Add the octopus and calamari, turn the heat up to medium–high

800 g (1 lb 12 oz) cleaned baby octopus and calamari
1 kg (2 lb 3 oz) combination of fish such as gurnard, scorpion fish, john dory, catshark
1 brown (yellow) onion, finely chopped
3 garlic cloves, 2 squashed, 1 whole for rubbing on bread
1 small bunch Italian (flat-leaf) parsley, stalks and leaves both chopped
1 red chilli, chopped
3 tablespoons extra-virgin olive oil
125 ml (4 fl oz/½ cup) dry white wine
400 g (14 oz) tinned peeled or chopped tomatoes
150 g (5½ oz) mantis shrimp
150 g (5½ oz) scampi, rinsed and kept whole or sliced in half lengthways
6 slices of stale or grilled (broiled) Tuscan bread (or other crusty white loaf)

Continued overleaf >

and cook for 5 minutes, browning on all sides. Pour over the white wine and let it cook over medium–high heat until nearly completely evaporated, about 5 minutes. Add the tomatoes, along with about 250 ml (8½ fl oz/ 1 cup) of water. Season with salt and pepper. Bring to a simmer and cook over low heat for a further 25–30 minutes.

Add the fish pieces, cover and cook for 15 minutes, adding water as necessary to keep it quite brothy. Finally, add the shrimp and scampi and cook for 3 minutes. Remove from the heat and pour the soup into a large bowl along with garlic-rubbed bread (some like to decorate the edges of the bowl with it; others like to place a slice in the bottom of each individual serving bowl).

NOTE
With this quantity of seafood, it's easier if you can ask your fishmonger to clean the seafood for you. The fish needs to be scaled and gutted and the octopus and calamari should be cleaned, with beaks and eyes removed. Otherwise, follow the instructions for how to clean octopus on page 87 and calamari on page 80.

MONTE ARGENTARIO

Watching waves crashing against the cliffs in slow motion from far above is a mesmerising scene from my first trip to Argentario that is burned into my memory. Our home away from home on that short Easter holiday was a cottage built on a cliff above the pretty cove of Cala Piccola, not far from Porto Santo Stefano. It had 180° views of indigo sea and Campari-coloured sunsets, which we admired every evening from the open-air kitchen. Leaning just a little from the terrace railing, you could watch the silent waves moving from deep blue to aqua as they crept closer to the tall, pale cliffs.

Monte Argentario was, in ancient times, an island. Over time two strips of sandy beach built up to tie Monte Argentario to the mainland, creating Orbetello's lagoon in the process. One of the sand bars, Giannella, is wide enough to accommodate a busy road, hotels and camp sites for holidaymakers. The other, Feniglia, is just a long, shallow sandy beach and a cool forest of umbrella pines inhabited by deer.

It still has the feel of an island, a rugged one at that, with steep, rocky cliffs and pebbly beaches surrounded by magnificent ink-blue sea and, as its name suggests, an overgrown, mountainous centre. There are just two towns, both fishing ports that are particularly noted for tuna, anchovies and sardines.

The larger of the two towns, Porto Santo Stefano, is also the younger one, dating to the sixteenth century. Today the town rambles high up the hillside and you'll notice big yachts and fishing boats surrounded by the cheerful port front. It's hard to believe it was

practically obliterated by heavy Allied bombing during the Second World War.

Porto Ercole (Port Hercules) is a small town with an ancient Etruscan past. It has an impossibly pretty but practically abandoned historic centre high up on the south side of the port. Today, most of the action happens down around the port, where the clear water, the little wooden boats and the old town make a nice backdrop for a *passeggiata* (walk) along the seafront. In the evening, the fishing boats pull in to the south side of the port to unload their catch, which makes quite a spectacle.

STOCCHETTO ALLA PORTERCOLESE
COD WITH PINE NUTS AND OLIVES

This is the dish that often gets mentioned first if you ask someone from Porto Ercole for a typical local recipe. *Stocchetto* refers to the dried and salted fish that was once a cheap, staple protein – like *stoccafisso* (air-dried cod) or baccalà (dried salted cod). But, in this case, it's not cod from Norway – it's *ficamaschia*, the local term for *melù* or blue whiting, a relative of the cod. It's abundant in the waters around Monte Argentario, and is usually eaten in fried form but often crumbed, too.

It's hard to find *stocchetto* outside Porto Ercole, where there is a long history of preparing it. Actually, you can rarely buy it even there, unless you know a local fisherman, as the fillets are traditionally prepared on-board the fishing boats while at sea. The fish are filleted, salted, then the fillets left to dry for a day or two before being consumed by the fishermen and their families – it's a sort of rustic, 'poorer' baccalà.

Because *ficamaschia a stocchetto* is so difficult to find, this recipe uses fresh cod fillets instead, but you could also use haddock or baccalà.

SERVES 4

Remove the cod or baccalà's skin (if any) and bones (they are large and should be easy to spot and pull out). Chop into chunks and set aside.

Heat the olive oil in a flameproof casserole dish and gently cook the onion, chilli (if using) and rosemary over low heat for about 10 minutes, or until the onion is very soft but not coloured (you can add a splash of water or turn down the heat if it begins to colour). Add the fish, followed by the wine, and turn the heat up to medium. Let it cook for 5 minutes.

Pour over the tomato and the potatoes, then add enough water to cover, about 250 ml (8½ fl oz/1 cup). Bring back to a simmer, then turn the heat down to low and let it cook, stirring occasionally, until the potatoes are soft and a fork easily pierces them, about 15 minutes. Taste for seasoning (and remember to taste the olives to get an idea of how much salt they'll bring to the dish) and add a pinch of salt as needed. If the sauce reduces too much during this time, top up with a little water. Add the olives and pine nuts and remove from the heat.

Serve as a main course with plenty of crusty Tuscan bread for mopping up the sauce.

800 g (1 lb 12 oz) fresh cod fillets or pre-soaked baccalà
2 tablespoons extra-virgin olive oil
1 brown (yellow) onion, finely chopped
freshly chopped red chilli or dried chilli flakes (optional)
1 rosemary sprig, leaves picked and chopped
125 ml (4 fl oz/½ cup) dry white wine
400 g (14 oz) tinned chopped tomatoes or tomato passata (puréed tomato)
3 medium-sized potatoes, peeled and cut into 2 x 2 cm (¾ x ¾ in) chunks
150 g (5½ oz) quality black olives in brine
2 tablespoons pine nuts
Tuscan bread (or other crusty white loaf), to serve

NOTE
You can find baccalà in an Italian supermarket or deli in two forms: dried or soaked. The soaked version is usually done by the same vendor who sells it dried and it simply makes things easier for you as it is ready to go. But it is nice to have it dried so you can soak it yourself to your liking. Usually it needs to be soaked for 2–4 days, changing the water three times a day, but sometimes it will need up to 10 days of soaking. Fresh cod fillets are my preference, even if the texture of baccalà is close to the real thing.

FRITTURA DI PARANZA
FISHERMAN'S FRIED FISH

If I had to bottle the sound of summer in Monte Argentario, it would be the song of cicadas whirring in the trees, the eerie echoing call of the enormous seagulls circling over the port, and the crunch of pine needles underfoot, fallen from the thick huddle of umbrella pines along the beach. If it was a scent, it would be the perfume of just-cut watermelon, combined with the waft of *fritto*, as you walk past someone's kitchen, their windows wide open in an attempt to make the smell of deep frying fish escape.

This isn't a dish that belongs strictly to this one place. You will find it anywhere along Italy's long coast. It's a dish synonymous with summer, when restaurants open along the beaches and offer one form or another of *frittura di paranza* (which is named after traditional coastal fishing boats and their nets of the same name).

The small fish used for frying can be spotted at the markets or at fishmongers labelled *pesce per fritto* (fish for frying) and seem to be simply the small, miniature versions of larger fish – no larger than the width of your palm – that might be thrown back into the water in most other places. I suggest using naturally smaller sized whole fish, such as anchovies and sardines, mixed with some fillets of larger fish such as cod, red mullet and mackerel. You can also add small, whole prawns (shrimp). When deep-fried, they become so beautifully crisp and crunchy on the outside, you can eat the whole thing – shell, head and all.

You can also use rice flour for this, instead of regular flour. Although it's not traditional, it gives the fish a light-as-air coating.

SERVES 4

Prawns can remain whole, shell and all, if using small ones. If they are very large, you may want to remove the shell but keep the head and tail on. Likewise, small fish can be kept whole, but clean their interiors as these will taste bitter – cut a small slit from their throat along their belly and pull out what's there. Rinse and pat dry. Larger fish fillets can be cut into 4–5 cm (1½–2 in) pieces for easy eating.

Put the flour in a bowl or on a plate, and dredge the prawns and fish to coat lightly but evenly in the flour – shake off any excess.

Heat a medium saucepan or deep frying pan with enough oil to allow the seafood to float – about 4 cm (1½ in) deep at least. When the oil

300 g (10½ oz) small raw prawns (shrimp), such as school prawns
500 g (1 lb 2 oz) small fish, such as whitebait, anchovies, sardines (or fillets of larger fish)
60 g (2 oz) plain (all-purpose) flour, for dusting
vegetable oil, for frying
1 lemon, cut into wedges, for serving

Continued overleaf >

reaches about 170°C (340°F), it's ready for the seafood. You can test the temperature by dipping the end of a wooden spoon in the oil – when it's surrounded immediately by many tiny bubbles, it's ready. Begin frying in batches. Do not overcrowd the pan or you will lower the temperature of the oil too much.

Fry the prawns for 1 minute and remove; drain on plenty of pieces of paper towel. Fry the fish for about 2 minutes for the fillet pieces, and 3 minutes for the whole small fish. Drain on paper towel.

Sprinkle with salt and serve immediately with lemon wedges.

ORATA AL CARTOCCIO CON I FUNGHI
PAPER-BAKED SEA BREAM WITH MUSHROOMS

I am partial to any food preparation that is low maintenance, with a high proportion of delicious eating compared to the amount of effort put into it – and fish baked *al cartoccio*, or in paper, is one of those things. You bring it home, turn on the oven, stuff it with herbs, splash it with some wine or lemon juice, wrap it in paper, and 20 minutes later dinner is ready. It's so easy and flavourful, and the fish stays moist, as it is wrapped up and cooked in all its steaming, aromatic juices.

Gilthead sea bream, a local speciality that is farmed in Orbetello's lagoon, is ideal for this sort of treatment but you could cook any whole large fish this way – sea bass and snapper are also good. I love the combination of *mare e monti*, where the sea and the mountains come together so beautifully. A mixture of earthy mushrooms, tossed with some garlic, make a nice bed for the fish. You could do the same with some thinly sliced potatoes (which, like the mushrooms, will soak up the flavours of the lemon and the herbs beautifully), cooked like the mushrooms before going under the fish – but this bream is also lovely on its own.

SERVES 4

Make sure the fish have been scaled and cleaned, and remove the fins with kitchen scissors; rinse and pat dry. Cut 3 slashes about 1.5 cm (½ in) deep along the fleshiest part of the fish, on both sides. Season with salt and pepper, rubbing it into the slices and skin. Sprinkle salt in the belly cavities, then stuff with about two-thirds of the herbs and a few slices of lemon to fill. Set aside in the fridge until needed.

Pick the leaves from the remaining herbs. Heat half the olive oil in a frying pan and cook the garlic over medium heat for 1 minute. Add the mushrooms and the rest of the herbs and cook in the oil until golden and softened, about 5–6 minutes. Allow them to cool.

Heat the oven to 200°C (400°F).

Tear a large sheet of baking paper for each fish – about double the length of the fish – and distribute the mushrooms in the middle. Place the fish on top of the mushrooms, then pour over the lemon juice and drizzle with the rest of the olive oil.

Wrap the fish in the paper – bring together the long edges of the paper, folding them down together so they overlap slightly. The short sides can

2 medium gilthead sea bream, about 500–600 g (1 lb 2 oz– 1 lb 5 oz) each, scaled and cleaned
2 handfuls fresh herbs, such as thyme, basil, oregano, calamint, mint, flat-leaf (Italian) parsley and rosemary
2 lemons, 1 sliced, 1 juiced
80 ml (2½ fl oz/⅓ cup) extra-virgin olive oil
2 garlic cloves, sliced
400 g (14 oz) mushrooms, cleaned and sliced

Continued overleaf >

be folded at the fish's tail and head, towards the middle of the fish and secured with a piece of kitchen string, like a present.

Bake for about 20–25 minutes. Remove the fish from the oven and let it sit, wrapped, for 5 minutes before serving. If using a different-sized fish, you may need to double-check if the fish is cooked properly. To check, unwrap the paper carefully (escaping steam is hot). Take a knife and see if the skin and flesh easily lifts off near the spine. Also look at the gashes – they should reveal opaque, soft meat. If not, wrap it back up and put it back in the oven to check in 5-minute increments.

To serve, you can transfer the whole fish to a long oval plate, dribbling the juices and mushrooms over the top. But I prefer to place it right on the plate, as it is, still sitting in its paper.

SOGLIOLA AL LIMONE
LEMON-MARINATED SOLE

I found this recipe in Edda Servi Machlin's fascinating cookbook, *The Classic Cuisine of the Italian Jews*. Published in 1981, the recipes and the stories recounted by Machlin are of her childhood in the heart of Jewish Pitigliano (see also her recipe for *Sfratti*, page 213). It's like time-travelling directly to this fascinating Maremman town in the 1930s.

Her original recipe is called *filetti di sogliola al limone del sabato*, where she describes this as a dish for Sabbath or Shabbat, a day set aside for rest and worship, observed between sundown on Friday until Saturday evening. It's a wonderfully simple dish that requires a full night of marinating, so it's the perfect thing to prepare the day before you want to serve it. Similar to the South American preparation for ceviche, delicate sole fillets are cured in lemon juice overnight and then eaten raw with a dressing of olive oil, parsley and olives. You can also steam these marinated fillets and it's still a delicious dish. Note that when serving raw fish, it's imperative that you freeze the fish first.

In Argentario, it's common to find four-spot megrim, similar to megrim sole, which is wonderful for this delicious, refreshing dish. This is enough for four main servings, but you can halve this and serve as part of an antipasto, too.

SERVES 4

See page 124 for instructions on preparing raw fish.

Put the sole fillets in a shallow dish or container and pour over lemon juice so they are completely covered. Leave to marinate overnight (8–12 hours) in the refrigerator.

Drain the liquid and transfer the fillets to a serving plate. Dress with olive oil and parsley, and season with salt and freshly ground black pepper to taste. Remove the pits from the olives by flattening them with the side of a kitchen knife and pulling out the pits. Chop roughly and scatter over the fish.

600 g (1 lb 5 oz) or 4 whole small soles
juice of 2–3 lemons
1–2 tablespoons extra-virgin olive oil
1 handful flat-leaf (Italian) parsley, finely chopped
4–6 good quality black olives in brine (I like taggiasche olives for this)

VARIATION
You can also do a cooked version of these. In her original recipe, Edda Servi Machlin notes that you can place the plate of marinated fish on top of a pot of boiling water to cook the fish for 5 minutes – if you put a lid over the top to steam it, even 2 minutes is long enough. (Remember, you don't want the fish to overcook and become rubbery.) To cook the fish this way, I remove it from the marinade, put it on a plate with the olive oil before placing on top of the pot of boiling water and covering. Then, I add the parsley, olives and seasoning. Be careful handling the plate for serving as it will be hot!

PREPARING RAW FISH

When eating raw fish you want to be absolutely certain of its freshness. I would recommend buying the fish whole as you can judge its freshness from seeing it whole, especially its skin and eyes. Then ask your fishmonger to fillet it for you. Alternatively, you can take it home and fillet it at home.

When preparing raw fish, use clean chopping boards (preferably not wood) and knives, and resist the temptation to wash or rinse the fillets in water.

While the acid in the lemon juice appears to 'cook' the fish, it does not kill bacteria as cooking or freezing does. To safely eat raw fish, you need to freeze the freshly prepared fillets for 7 days in a regular home freezer that measures -20°C (-4°F) and defrost in the refrigerator before marinating.

FROM THE VEGETABLE PATCH

DALL'ORTO

FETTUNTA AL LIMONE
TOASTED BREAD WITH LEMON

Let's start with *fettunta*, the most ancient form of *bruschetta* (pronounced broo-ske-ta). It's a slice of Tuscan bread, toasted and drizzled generously with extra-virgin olive oil – this is what gives it its name, *fetta unta* or, literally, 'greasy slice'. There are few things as pleasurable as warm *fettunta* when you have just the right combination of good bread and excellent olive oil. The Maremmans know this very well, and would make this with wood-fired Tuscan bread and their own olive oil, made from the olives crushed in the communal *frantoio*, where everyone in the area goes to make their own oil.

The name bruschetta comes from *bruscare* (to char), and the best *fettunta* or *bruschetta* is the one that is charred over a charcoal grill on both sides. To give it an upgrade, you can also rub it with a raw garlic clove, or sprinkle it with sea salt. A step up from this is the addition of freshly chopped, ripe tomatoes and torn basil, which is what everyone thinks of when they hear 'bruschetta', or you can simply rub it with half a cut tomato to give it the hint of tomato and top it with flavourful anchovy fillets (see *Pane e Pomodoro con le Acciughe*, page 130).

But for this refreshing, quite addictive *fettunta*, we keep it simple with just a hint of lemon, which I first heard about in a lovely little illustrated collection of recipes called *Quaderno delle ricette di Maremma* by Claudia Spargi. She calls this *'la bruschetta all'Amiatina'*, referring to Monte Amiata.

SERVES 4

Grill (broil) the slices of bread on both sides until crisp and warm. Rub the lemon half over each slice of bread, drizzle with the olive oil and sprinkle sea salt over the top. Serve immediately.

4 slices Tuscan bread (or crusty white loaf), sliced about 1 cm (½ in) thick
½ lemon
1–2 tablespoons extra-virgin olive oil
pinch of sea salt flakes

LA MERENDA

'The snack is snatched, *la merenda* is shared.' British food writer Patience Gray wrote in her cookbook-memoir *Honey from a Weed* (1986). *La merenda* is the typical mid-afternoon snack that many tend to associate with coming home from school as a child. That moment of the day, somewhere around 4 o'clock, when small stomachs growl with emptiness and a little something will help make it through to dinner time.

My husband Marco has a soft spot for mortadella folded in between some bread, or *pane al pomodoro*, the way his nonna used to prepare it for him – simply by rubbing a piece of toasted bread with tomato. Or a *zabaione*-like *uovo sbattuto*, which nonna would make to send him off to soccer practice with a burst of energy – an egg yolk, some sugar and coffee, whipped in a teacup over a bain marie. Pellegrino Artusi describes this as the antidote to a crying child. Our daughter's favourite *merenda* is gelato (in the warm weather, it's undoubtedly everybody's favourite *merenda*, whether big or small).

But it's not just little tummies that need filling up. A *merenda* can happen pretty much anywhere, and really anytime that justifies a little something to get you through to dinner.

PANE E POMODORO CON LE ACCIUGHE
TOAST WITH TOMATO AND ANCHOVIES

This is so simple it really doesn't need a recipe. It's more of an idea and it can be adjusted to your taste. A tomato, cut in half, is rubbed over the bread until it is stained pink (even toasting it is optional). It needs only a sprinkle of salt and pepper and good olive oil. If you really wanted, you could embellish it – some fresh basil, some garlic (if you don't mind the persistence of raw garlic on your breath). Instead of salt, I like to drape anchovy fillets, dripping with oil, over mine. It's a punchy *merenda* (afternoon snack) that goes well with a very cold glass of dry white wine, but it is also the perfect lunch or even dinner on those hot days when you don't feel like cooking anything or eating much at all.

SERVES 4

Grill (broil) the slices of bread on both sides until crisp and warm. If using garlic, rub once over each piece of bread. Rub the tomato half over each slice of bread until pink and drizzle with the olive oil. Drape over two anchovy fillets on each piece of bread. Some freshly ground black pepper is nice too, but I usually forego the salt. Serve immediately while still warm.

4 slices Tuscan bread (or crusty white loaf), around 1 cm (½ in) thick
1 garlic clove (optional)
1 tomato, halved
1–2 tablespoons extra-virgin olive oil
8 anchovy fillets packed in oil, drained

NOTE
Elsewhere, I usually advocate salt-packed anchovies – see the recipe for Pizza Gigliese *(page 145) and* Pizza Rossa con Salsa Verde *(page 141). But here, I prefer the soft, limp, oily versions that practically start melting when they hit the warm bread.*

PANE, VINO E ZUCCHERO
BREAD, WINE AND SUGAR

This lovely and indulgent but simple little snack is one of those things that people seem to make less often these days, so when it is mentioned, you see eyes light up with the trigger of nostalgia. Marco remembers the treat of being allowed bites of this snack of bread sprinkled with red wine and sugar as a boy at big family dinners in the countryside. A Tuscan friend once recounted to me that his farmer father used to eat this for breakfast before heading out into the fields. It was seen as a big boost of energy and an easy, cheap bite to eat.

Day-old Tuscan bread is the best bread for this, as its sturdy texture means that the liquid does not turn the bread soggy. Its unsalted neutrality and blandness also means the astringency of the wine and the sweetness of the sugar are balanced. But if you don't have stale Tuscan bread, I recommend grilling (broiling) the bread or drying it out in a low oven slightly so it doesn't get too soggy. You could even try this with a slightly sweet bread like brioche.

SERVES 4

Sprinkle the red wine over the slices of bread as evenly as you can. Sprinkle the sugar on top of the wine and serve immediately. The wine will seep a little into the bread and the sugar will give it a delightful crunch.

60 ml (2 fl oz/¼ cup) red wine

4 slices Tuscan bread (or crusty white loaf), around 1 cm (½ in) thick

1 tablespoon granulated or raw sugar, or to taste

CARCIOFINI SOTT'OLIO

BABY ARTICHOKES PRESERVED IN OIL

Set out on the table in little dishes, this is an excellent antipasto, one that you can keep popping into your mouth, like good olives. They can even be part of a simple lunch, accompanied by nice bread and a glass of wine, or even sliced and used as a sandwich filling (they're delicious with tuna and a squeeze of lemon juice or prosciutto).

These are made in the Maremma with baby artichokes that are abundant in the late spring, when you'll find them tumbling out of their huge crates at the market. Preserving – or making *sott'olio* (vegetables 'under oil') and *sott'aceti* (vegetables 'under vinegar', or pickles) – is all about making the most of cheap and plentiful produce when it is in season and keeping them for later.

MAKES 2 JARS OF 250 ML (8½ FL OZ/1 CUP) CAPACITY

juice of 1 lemon
1 kg (2 lb 3 oz) carciofini (baby artichokes), about 25
500 ml (17 fl oz/2 cups) white wine (or water)
500 ml (17 fl oz/2 cups) white wine vinegar
2 garlic cloves, sliced (optional)
4 dry or fresh bay leaves
vegetable oil, to cover (I use a mixture of half olive oil, half sunflower oil)

Put the lemon juice into a bowl of water – this will be used to stop the artichokes from oxidising. Pull off the outer leaves of the artichokes until you reach pale and tender leaves. Trim the stalks and peel the base of the artichokes. Slice the top half of the artichokes off completely. As you go, place the artichokes in the bowl of water.

Pour the white wine (or water) and the white wine vinegar in a saucepan with a pinch of salt and bring to the boil. Drain the artichokes, add them to the saucepan and cook over medium heat until tender (a knife should easily slip into the base of the artichoke). This should take about 10–15 minutes. For the last 2 minutes of cooking, add the garlic slices (if using) to the boiling artichokes.

Remove the artichokes and place them, cut side down, stalk side up, on a tea towel (dish towel) set over a wire rack. Let them drain this way for several hours or overnight. Put them in sterilised jars, slide in the slices of garlic (if using) and bay leaves, and top with the mixture of oil to cover.

Give the jar a gentle tap on the counter to let out any air bubbles (you can also run a knife around the sides of the jar to move any air pockets). If needed, top up the jar so that it is full and covers the artichokes by about 5 mm (¼ in).

Close the lid and seal (see instructions on sterilising and sealing jars, page 137). If you want to eat them right away, you can store them in the fridge without sterilising or sealing – wait at least 3 days before eating, though. They're even better after a month, so consider sealing them for the best results.

Continued overleaf >

Once sealed, keep in a cool, dark place until opened, then store in the fridge. These will keep for 3 months unopened; once opened, consume within a couple of weeks and ensure the vegetables are always covered with a layer of oil.

VARIATIONS

This same recipe can be used for eggplants (aubergines) – especially those long finger-shaped eggplants that are dark, almost black, or the baby eggplants that look like shiny ceramics, painted with streaks of pale lavender. Small mushrooms are also good prepared this way, perfect for when you have gone foraging in the woods and come back with more than you know what to do with. For the eggplants, cut into 1 cm (½ in) slices and sprinkle generously with salt. Leave them to weep, perhaps with something heavy over them, in the fridge for a few hours before draining and rinsing with fresh water. Pat dry or, better, leave to dry out on a clean tea towel (dish towel) in the fridge overnight, then continue as for the artichokes. You can also use regular artichokes for this, though you will need to cut them in half, remove the fluffy choke with a teaspoon and then cut into quarters. Ada Boni, in Il Talismano della Felicità *cookbook (1929), adds slices of lemon to the jarred artichokes.*

STERILISING AND SEALING JARS

Glass jars used for preserving should be sterilised to reduce the risk of spoiling your hard work. Sterilise jars and their lids just before you need to fill them.

There are two ways to sterilise jars for preserving. In Italy, they like to place the jars, mouths up, along with their lids (not screwed on, but left off) in a large pot, covered with water, then boil them for 10 minutes. If you live in an area with hard water, you may find that boiling the jars will leave a chalky finish on the glass – a splash of vinegar in the water will prevent this. Remove jars and lids (I do this with tongs) to air-dry on a clean tea towel (dish towel), mouths of the jars up. The water should evaporate off the hot glass quite quickly. When dry, they are ready to be filled.

The oven is another way to sterilise jars. Wash jars with warm, soapy water. Place jars, mouths up, on a baking tray and place in a low oven until dry. The lids should be boiled for 10 minutes and left to air-dry on a tea towel (dish towel).

If the jars are filled with something cold, like the preserved artichokes (page 135), boil the filled jars in a water bath. Once filled and the oil is poured in to cover by 5 mm (¼ in), screw the lids on the jars, then place in a saucepan, upright. Fill the saucepan with water to reach the lids (add a splash of vinegar if you live in an area with hard water that will leave the jars chalky). Boil for 10 minutes. Carefully (again, tongs help) remove the jars and let them cool completely on the counter.

If jars are filled with something boiling hot – just-made, bubbling hot jam, for instance – fill to about 5–10

mm (¼–½ in) from the top. Immediately screw lids on tightly (careful, the jars will be extremely hot) and leave on the counter to cool completely. As the jars cool and the pressure inside the jar changes, they will seal completely. If your lids are the ones with 'safety buttons' that 'click' when pushed, you can check they are sealed by pressing down on the button on the lid – if sealed properly, it will not 'click'. There is no need to turn the jars upside-down, as many like to do.

TORTINO DI CARCIOFI
FRIED ARTICHOKE OMELETTE

When I inevitably come home with bunches of this versatile vegetable from the market, I am tempted to use them in everything, from pasta and risotto to salad and fritattas. There are so many delicious ways to enjoy artichokes, but what makes this such a wonderful dish is the combination of two things – the fried artichokes, which become at once nutty and crisp on the outside but also meltingly soft. And the egg, which is pushed around the hot pan and cooked quickly so that it remains soft and wobbly, a little like just-cooked scrambled eggs.

The dish is inspired by a recipe from the heart of Jewish Pitigliano at the turn of the century, one that Edda Servi Machlin calls 'Tortino della Nonna Debora', or her Grandma Debora's omelette in *The Classic Cuisine of the Italian Jews*. It's also very similar to a dish at one of my favourite trattorias in Florence, where they use little frying pans for individual omelettes – just the right size for an antipasto.

SERVES 4 AS ANTIPASTO

juice of 1 lemon
4 medium artichokes
4 eggs
60 ml (2 fl oz/¼ cup) extra-virgin olive oil

Put the lemon juice into a bowl of water – this will stop the artichokes from oxidising. Pull off the outer leaves of the artichokes until you reach pale and tender leaves. Trim the stalks to about 1.5 cm (½ in) from the base and peel the base and stalk of the artichoke, like you would peel a carrot. Slice the top half of the artichoke off completely. Cut in half and remove the furry choke with a teaspoon. Thinly slice and place the artichokes in the lemon water.

Put the eggs in a bowl, add 1 tablespoon of water and a good pinch of salt and beat with a fork briefly – just enough to muddle them.

Drain the artichoke slices and pat dry with paper towels. Heat a non-stick frying pan with the olive oil over medium–high heat. When hot, add the artichoke slices. Fry them, stirring often, until they are tender and golden-brown on the thinnest edges, about 5–7 minutes.

Pour over the beaten eggs (they should sizzle immediately and set at the edges) and let them cook for about 10 seconds. Then, using a spatula, begin to move the egg around the pan a little, exposing the bottom of the pan in some places and tilting the pan to allow the uncooked egg to flow into those spaces. Continue cooking in this way for about 1 minute. When the mixture starts to thicken and firm up a little, but is still soft, slightly wobbly and glistening on top, remove from the heat. Slide onto a plate and serve immediately with plenty of freshly ground black pepper.

PIZZA ROSSA CON SALSA VERDE
PIZZA WITH TOMATO AND SALSA VERDE

In Porto Ercole there is a hole-in-the-wall pizzeria called Grano, where they sell long trays of fresh-out-of-the-oven pizza, cut into squares and sold by the slice. This particular topping is inspired by one of my favourites from Grano: anchovies and salsa verde, a zingy, bright sauce of parsley and capers. It packs quite the punch and you won't even miss the cheese.

The salsa verde recipe is adapted from a recipe from Pellegrino Artusi's *Science in the Kitchen and the Art of Eating Well* (1891). It makes about 200 g (7 oz/1 cup) of salsa, so it's much more than you'll need for this pizza – but it is so good, you'll want to have extra. It keeps well in a glass jar in the fridge and is a great sauce to have on hand for topping anything from simple grilled fish or meat to boiled eggs and boiled new potatoes. It's even good on toast.

While the parsley lends this sauce its bright colour, its name and its volume, it is really the capers that give it its distinct, punchy flavour. Go for capers packed in salt (rather than brine) for superior flavour. The same goes for the anchovies. Salt-packed anchovies are my preference, even if anchovies preserved in oil are more convenient. Just don't skimp on soaking these ingredients properly before using – and taste for seasoning before adding any extra salt.

If you're making these for a snack, this amount will serve six. As a meal, it serves two hungry people who want their own whole pizza.

MAKES 2 PIZZAS

Stir or crumble the yeast into the water in a mixing bowl and let it sit for 10 minutes to soften. Sift the flour into a wide bowl with the salt and pour over the yeast and water mixture, plus the olive oil. Mix together to create a smooth but sticky dough. Knead the dough on a lightly floured work surface until elastic and no longer sticky; this just takes a few minutes.

Place the ball of dough in a large, lightly greased bowl, cover with a clean, damp tea towel (dish towel) and let it rise in a warm place free from draughts until it has doubled in size, about 1 hour. Alternatively, keep it in the fridge and let it rise for 8–12 hours or overnight.

When ready to bake, preheat the oven to 250°C (480°F).

If using anchovies packed in salt, rinse them under running water to remove any excess salt, then place them in a bowl of fresh water to soak for 15 minutes – see page 142 for removing spines. Do the same with the

DOUGH

20 g (¾ oz) fresh yeast, or 7 g (¼ oz/2½ level teaspoons) active dry yeast
280 ml (9½ fl oz) lukewarm water
500 g (1 lb 2 oz/3⅓ cups) plain (all-purpose) flour, plus extra for dusting
1½ teaspoons salt
60 ml (2 fl oz/¼ cup) extra-virgin olive oil
1 handful semolina, for dusting

TOPPINGS

6 salt-packed anchovies (page 142) or 12 anchovy fillets in oil
100 g (3½ oz/½ cup) salsa verde (about half of the following recipe)
60 ml (2 fl oz/¼ cup) extra-virgin olive oil, extra for drizzling
240 g (8½ oz/1 cup) tomato passata (puréed tomatoes)

SALSA VERDE

1 salt-packed anchovy (or 2 anchovy fillets in oil)
2 heaped tablespoons salt-packed capers
¼ brown (yellow) onion
½ garlic clove
100 g (3½ oz) flat-leaf (Italian) parsley
10 basil leaves
juice of 1 lemon
60 ml (2 fl oz/¼ cup) extra-virgin olive oil

Continued overleaf >

capers if using capers packed in salt. If using anchovies preserved in oil, drain them on paper towel until ready to use.

For the salsa verde, blend the anchovies, capers, onion, garlic, herbs and lemon juice together thoroughly with a food processor or stick blender, and add the olive oil until you have a paste-like consistency. Season with salt and pepper. For the pizza topping, stir about half the salsa verde into about 60 ml (2 fl oz/¼ cup) of olive oil so that it is a little more fluid. Set aside.

In a small bowl, season the tomato passata with a generous pinch of salt and freshly cracked black pepper. Set aside.

Divide the dough into two even portions. Work with one at a time (keeping the rest of the dough covered) on a work surface dusted with semolina (or flour). Roll or stretch out the dough to a thickness of about 3 mm (⅛ in) in the middle (the edges can be thicker) and transfer to a rectangular baking tray or a round pizza tray.

Spoon over the tomato passata mixture to just lightly cover the base, leaving a 2 cm (¾ in) border around the edge. Place the anchovy fillets evenly here and there over the pizza and drizzle over some olive oil. You can bake the pizzas one by one, on the lowest shelf possible, but if you'd rather have them ready at the same time, position the two pizzas on two shelves in the oven, one on the lowest shelf possible and the other in the middle of the oven. Bake for a total of 12–15 minutes, swapping them around halfway. The crust should be golden and crunchy and the top should look almost dry, with the anchovies sizzling.

Remove from the oven, spread over dollops of salsa verde here and there, and serve.

NOTE
This dough can easily be frozen – place the portions in an airtight container and freeze. When you want to use it, thaw in the fridge overnight or on the kitchen bench for 2 hours. Let it come to room temperature before using as normal.

SALT-PACKED CAPERS AND ANCHOVIES
To prepare salted capers for a recipe, first rinse off any excess salt under running water, then place the capers in a bowl full of fresh water and let them soak for 15 minutes. Once a jar is opened, any remaining salt-packed capers not used for the recipe should be stored in the refrigerator. They keep very well.

Anchovies packed in salt are 'fresher' and fleshier and should always be stored in the refrigerator. They do need a little more attention and care in preparing them for dishes, but you'll find it's worth the (tiny) bit of extra effort. First, they need to be rinsed of any excess salt very well and soaked like the capers for 15 minutes. This will soften them so they are more pliable. Then their spines need to be pulled out – starting from the tail end, split them lengthways by pulling them apart. Then you can remove the spine and you will have 2 anchovy fillets ready to go.

PIZZA GIGLIESE
GIGLIO ISLAND PIZZA WITH ONIONS AND ANCHOVIES

The ferry ride from Porto Santo Stefano to the little paradise that is Giglio Island is a quick and breezy trip (in many senses of the word). As you arrive in the turquoise waters of the port and see the little shops lining the shore, you may start to feel a bit peckish. That's when you head to the nearest bakery and order a slice of pizza gigliese. It's made of two halves of pizza dough sandwiching a filling of soft, sweet, caramelised onions, fresh tomatoes and anchovy fillets that add a smack of saltiness, like a wave of sea water in your face. After tasting it for the first time, I knew I had to remake it at home. Luckily I was able to adapt a recipe from a slim, little cookbook of traditional Giglio recipes collected from the memories of the *nonne* on the island, *Antiche Ricette del Giglio*.

It reminds me of the filled pizza you find in faraway Lecce, in Puglia's far south, where onion and anchovies are a favourite combination (sometimes with the addition of more salty goodness such as black olives, capers or tinned tuna).

SERVES 4 AS A SNACK

Combine the yeast with about 60 ml (2 fl oz/¼ cup) of the water, mix gently with a spoon and let it sit for 5–10 minutes to let it soften and dissolve. The fresh yeast may need to be crumbled a little bit in your fingers and mixed with the water until creamy.

In the meantime, place the flour in a bowl, make a well in the centre, add the salt and olive oil and pour in the rest of the water, followed by the yeast mixture. Bring everything together to form a dough, either by machine or by hand. For the latter, it will take about 10 minutes of pushing, folding and pulling on a lightly floured surface until the dough is smooth and elastic (poke it – it should bounce back nicely) and no longer sticky. Place the dough in a large bowl, lightly greased with olive oil. Drizzle a bit of olive oil over the top and cover with a tea towel (dish towel). Let it rise in a warm spot until doubled in size, about 1 hour. Otherwise, let it rise overnight in the refrigerator.

To prepare the salt-packed anchovies, see page 142. If using anchovies preserved in oil, simply drain on paper towel. Chop roughly into smaller pieces.

For the filling, heat the olive oil in a wide frying pan over low heat; add the onions with a good pinch of salt. Let them sweat gently, stirring occasionally, until they begin to soften but not colour. Let them cook

DOUGH

15 g (½ oz) fresh yeast or 5 g (¼ oz) active dry yeast
250 ml (8½ fl oz/1 cup) lukewarm water
500 g (1 lb 2 oz/3⅓ cups) plain (all-purpose) flour, plus more for dusting
1 teaspoon salt
60 ml (2 fl oz/¼ cup) extra-virgin olive oil, plus extra for greasing

FILLING

4 salt-packed anchovies (or 8–10 anchovy fillets in oil)
2 tablespoons extra-virgin olive oil
500 g (1 lb 2 oz) brown (yellow) onions (about 4 medium-sized onions), finely sliced
180 g (6½ oz) cherry tomatoes (about 10; or use 1 large tomato), chopped

Continued overleaf >

slowly for about 30 minutes, adding a splash of water if you need to. The idea is to bring out the sweetness of the onions by cooking them until soft and almost jammy. Remove from the heat and let them cool completely.

Preheat the oven to 200°C (400°F).

Divide the dough into two equal parts. Take one half and roll it out or stretch it with your hands until it's about 5 mm (¼ in) thick. Place on a baking tray lined with baking paper and continue stretching gently, forming the dough roughly into a rectangular shape – about 20 x 30 cm (8 x 12 in) until it is as thin as you can get it. Spread the onion mixture evenly over the top, leaving a 1 cm (½ in) border around the edge. Lay the anchovy fillets and tomatoes over the top, distributing evenly.

Roll out or stretch the rest of the dough to roughly the same size and shape (don't worry too much about holes) and lay it over the top, pulling the edges together to meet up. Seal the edges by gently pressing down. Drizzle olive oil over the top and sprinkle with salt flakes. Let the pizza rest for 30 minutes before baking in the oven for 25–30 minutes, or until crisp and golden brown.

Remove the pizza and let it cool slightly before cutting into squares. This is also good served cold or reheated the next day, even if the dough isn't as fresh.

NOTE

Before the modern convenience of active dry yeast arrived on the island, it was traditional in Giglio to use lievito madre, *or your own homemade sourdough starter. At one time, everyone had this sitting at home, ready for baking bread in the communal woodfired ovens. By all means, use sourdough starter if you have it.*

ACQUACOTTA MAREMMANA

Acquacotta recipes will differ from kitchen to kitchen in Maremma, and partly the idea is to use what you have on hand. But when I think of acquacotta, this is what I have in mind – a thick, slow-cooked stew of vegetables, mostly tomatoes, poured over a slice of stale bread. There's also a sunken egg '*in camicia*' (as poached eggs are described in Italian, which makes me imagine the yolks, buoyant and still runny, dressed in oversized, floppy white shirts), nestled in the soup. It's this soft-yolked egg that makes the dish. Break into it with your spoon and let the creamy yolk run into the soup. It's warming, comfort food at its best.

One day I had the luck to meet and be invited into the house of Ilena Donati, an elderly woman from Capalbio who spent most of her life working in kitchens. You could see by the way her eyes lit up while talking about food that it was her passion. She told me two secrets for making the perfect *acquacotta* – one was to leave out the carrot in the soffritto. Onions (and here there are plenty) are naturally sweet, especially when slow-cooked. Carrots are even more so and adding them would upset the balance. So, no carrot. The other was to cook everything *piano, piano* (slowly, slowly).

SERVES 4

Score a cross on the bottoms of the ripe tomatoes with a sharp knife. Place them in a pot of boiling water for about 30 seconds, then remove and plunge them into a bowl of ice-cold water until cool enough to handle. Their skins should be very easy to peel now. Chop them into quarters and remove the watery seeds. Chop the rest of the tomatoes into cubes and set aside.

Heat a casserole pot with the olive oil over low heat. Add the onions and celery along with a good pinch of salt and let it cook, stirring occasionally, for about 15 minutes or until the vegetables are soft. Add a splash of water if you see the onions are sticking.

Turn the heat up to medium and add the white wine, simmering for about 3–4 minutes to reduce.

Pour over the tomatoes. If using tinned whole, peeled tomatoes, use a wooden spoon to break them up once in the pan. Add another pinch of salt and, if using, sprinkle over the chilli. Add half the stock (or water) and bring to a simmer, then turn the heat down to low and let it cook slowly, uncovered, for about 45 minutes. During this time, check on it now and

1 kg (2 lb 3 oz) fresh, ripe tomatoes, or 800 g (1 lb 12 oz) tinned whole, peeled tomatoes

3 tablespoons extra-virgin olive oil

4 large brown (yellow) onions, finely sliced

½ celery stalk, finely chopped

125 ml (4 fl oz/½ cup) dry white wine

1 freshly chopped red chilli or dried chilli flakes, to taste (optional)

1 litre (34 fl oz/4 cups) vegetable stock (see page 161) or water

4 eggs

4 slices stale Tuscan bread (or crusty white loaf)

50 g (1¼ oz/½ cup) grated parmesan or pecorino cheese (optional)

Continued overleaf >

then, and stir occasionally. The liquid should reduce to a nice, rather thick consistency, but there should still be enough liquid to be able to poach the eggs in it. Top up with the rest of the stock (or water) as necessary.

Taste for seasoning and, if necessary, add salt or freshly ground black pepper. Then crack in the eggs, one by one, not too close together. If you prefer, you can crack the eggs first into a small bowl and then carefully tip the cracked egg into the soup. Poach them until the whites are cooked and the yolks still soft and runny (this can take anywhere from 3–6 minutes, depending on the pan used and the temperature of the eggs). Remove from the heat.

Place a slice of stale bread at the bottom of each bowl. With a ladle, carefully scoop out the poached eggs one by one and place each on top of a slice of bread. Scoop out more soup and pour over the top to soak the bread. Sprinkle each dish with grated cheese (if desired) and let it sit for a minute or two to allow the bread to absorb some of the liquid adequately before serving.

NOTE
This is perfect for using up overly ripe fresh tomatoes in summer, but otherwise you can use tinned whole, peeled tomatoes as an alternative (passata or tomato purée is too smooth). Stale bread soaks up the liquid nicely and doesn't get soggy. If you don't have stale bread on hand, you can dry it out in a low oven until crisp (don't toast – this changes the flavour of the bread too much). You can prepare the soup in advance, right up to the point just before you put the eggs in; this can be kept in the refrigerator overnight or you can freeze for later use. Just reheat with a splash of water and, once simmering, add the eggs.

ACQUACOTTA: A VARIATION FOR EVERY HOUSEHOLD

Acquacotta comes in many forms, depending on the season, the town and the kitchen. In *Cucina Maremmana*, Aldo Santini suggests that centuries of Maremma's malaria-ridden marshlands are responsible for the existence of so many variations. It meant that the many little towns, although close together, remained isolated for a long time. Each town developed their own, quite specific, *acquacotta*. In turn, each household, each hand holding the wooden spoon, interpreted the dish differently.

There are some similarities – an abundant use of grated cheese, an egg per person cooked in the soup, a stale (not toasted) slice of bread in the bottom of the bowl. But personal taste dictates exactly what cheese – pecorino for the purists, parmesan for those with more delicate tastes – and whether the eggs are poached whole or beaten and poured over the *acquacotta*.

In Grosseto, you might find this classic acquacotta prepared with strips of red capsicum (bell pepper), maybe even some sausage. And the eggs are beaten with a handful of cheese before being poured over the top of the soup to cook for a few minutes.

Some like to add a bit of pancetta to the frying vegetables at the beginning. Others may add some finely chopped basil, *nepitella* (calamint, a lovely wild herb that is like a cross between oregano and mint), or celery leaves and stalks. Chilli is always a good idea.

In Pitigliano, popular additions include greens such as English spinach or Swiss chard (silverbeet), and a blob of fresh ricotta on top may take the place of the egg. Being near the mountains and the sea, you may find that freshly foraged Caesar's mushrooms find their way into the *acquacotta*, along with some baccalà.

It's more traditional to use water (it is called 'acquacotta' after all), but many will use stock and you can find recipes that call for vegetable, chicken or even beef stock. I find meat stocks tend to alter the flavour of the soup too much. Vegetable stock can give a boost of flavour, while water keeps it pure and simple.

Either way you go, the advice to cook it *piano, piano* (slowly, slowly) is right – the longer it cooks, the better it is. Some even go as far as to make this a 2-day process – cook the soup the day before and reheat the next day, adding the eggs just before serving.

For more on the history of *acquacotta*, see 'What is *Acquacotta*?', page 14.

ZUPPA MAREMMANA
MAREMMAN BEAN AND VEGETABLE SOUP

Rather like a minestrone, this simple vegetable soup of cannellini beans, leafy greens and mushrooms is the food equivalent of a comforting hug. If you can find it (literally, by foraging for it), the best green to use would be sea beet or *bietola selvatica* (*Beta vulgaris* or *Beta maritima*). This wild weed is the ancestor to beetroot (beet) and Swiss chard (silverbeet) and grows, as its name suggests, near the sea. This particular recipe is from Capalbio, but Italo Arieti (who writes on the food history of Lazio's Maremma) says the roots and young, glossy leaves of sea beet were traditionally collected for preparing the similar *Acquacotta Viterbese* (page 42). Other substitutes would be beetroot (beet) leaves or even English spinach. Use any favourite mushrooms here.

SERVES 4

Trim the base of the silverbeet stalks and wash well to ensure there is no dirt. Chop roughly and set aside.

Pour the olive oil into a medium to large soup pot and add the onion, celery and a pinch of salt. Cook on low heat, stirring occasionally, for 10 minutes. When the onion is soft and translucent, add the potatoes and mushrooms and cover with stock or water. Bring to a simmer over low–medium heat and cook for 10–15 minutes, or until the potatoes are just tender. Season with salt and pepper, and add the silverbeet and cannellini beans. Bring back to a simmer and continue cooking for 5 more minutes, or until the greens are tender but still bright. Taste for seasoning and adjust as necessary.

Grill (broil) the slices of bread (or dry out in a low oven) until crisp. Rub one side with a raw clove of garlic.

Pour the soup in bowls with freshly ground black pepper, a drizzle of olive oil and, if desired, some pecorino cheese. Serve with the garlic-rubbed bread on the side.

150 g (5½ oz/1 small bunch) silverbeet (Swiss chard) leaves
2 tablespoons extra-virgin olive oil, plus extra to serve
1 brown (yellow) onion, finely sliced
1 celery stalk, finely sliced
2 small potatoes, peeled and cut into 1.5 cm (½ in) cubes
100 g (3½ oz) mushrooms, thinly sliced
1 litre (34 fl oz/4 cups) vegetable stock (see page 161) or water
240 g (8½ oz) cooked cannellini beans
4 slices stale Tuscan bread (or other crusty white loaf)
1 whole garlic clove
1 handful grated pecorino cheese (optional), to serve

NOTE
If you want to cook your own cannellini beans, see page 186. Otherwise, a drained tin of cooked cannellini beans is just right for this, too.

STROZZAPRETI AL SUGO FINTO
STROZZAPRETI PASTA WITH 'FAKE SAUCE'

Strozzapreti are an ancient, homemade pasta, closely related to Siena's *pici*. It's a simple, rustic preparation of water and flour, rolled out by hand and cut into thin noodles (no pasta machine necessary). They are then rolled quickly and lightly in your hands until they resemble long, twisted ropes (hence the pasta's name, 'priest stranglers'). The folds in the 'ropes' are great for holding pasta sauce and the thick, resilient pasta is well-matched to hearty sauces such as *Sugo Maremmano* (page 194) – the word *sugo* is the more traditional word used to describe 'ragu' in Tuscany.

I like to pair this with *sugo finto*, an aptly named sauce that has no meat in it – hence the reference to 'fake'. The sauce is born of *cucina povera*, when meat (especially beef) was a rare and special ingredient, usually reserved for nobility. The idea is to make this vegetable ragu thick and chunky, so the usual *battuto* of vegetables are a little more abundant than in a regular tomato sauce, the pieces are a little chunkier, and the sauce is reduced to make it thicker.

SERVES 4

If using fresh tomatoes, score their bottoms with a cross using a sharp knife and blanch them in a pot of boiling water for 30 seconds or so. Remove and place them in a bowl of ice-cold water. Their skins can now be peeled easily. Chop into quarters, discard the seeds and then dice the rest of the tomatoes into 1 cm (½ in) pieces. Set aside.

Heat the olive oil gently in a large frying pan and add the finely chopped vegetables, along with the garlic and finely chopped parsley stalks. Season with a pinch of salt and let the vegetables slowly cook and soften, stirring occasionally, for about 15 minutes.

When the onions are transparent and the carrots have softened, pour over the wine. Turn the heat up to medium and continue cooking for 3–5 minutes, or until the liquid has reduced significantly. Add the chopped tomatoes and 250–500 ml (8½–17 fl oz/1–2 cups) of water, or enough to cover the vegetables (the amount of water required will also depend on how juicy the tomatoes are). If using tinned tomatoes, pour in the lot (juice and all), and break the tomatoes up with a spoon. Bring to a simmer over low–medium heat and cook, stirring occasionally, for 30–40 minutes or until the *sugo* has become thick and rich. (If needed during cooking, you can top up with water.) Taste and season with salt and pepper if

PASTA

250 g (9 oz/2 cups) semolina
250 g (9 oz/1⅔ cups) plain (all-purpose) flour
300 ml (10 fl oz) water

SAUCE

600 g (1 lb 5 oz) ripe tomatoes or 400 g (14 oz) tinned peeled tomatoes
2 tablespoons extra-virgin olive oil
1 onion, finely chopped
1 celery stalk, finely chopped
1 carrot, peeled and finely chopped
2 garlic cloves, chopped
1 handful flat-leaf (Italian) parsley, stalks separated from leaves, finely chopped
60 ml (2 fl oz/¼ cup) dry white wine
1 handful basil leaves
1 handful grated parmesan or pecorino cheese (optional)

VARIATION

If we head from Maremma to the other side of Monte Amiata and into the province of Siena, where pici were born, there is another very good sauce that you could make by simply adding sausage meat. Use gluten-free, pure pork sausages. Peel the skin off and crumble the meat in with the soffritto *of vegetables before adding the wine. It is known as* sugo bugiardo, *another aptly named ragu meaning 'liar sauce', because it is made with sausage rather than beef.*

NOTE

Both parts of the recipe can be made ahead of time. The dough can be kept in the fridge while resting, and you can keep it here for several hours, though it begins to turn dark the longer you keep it. The sauce can be made the day before, and it is even better when it's had time to sit. If making it all at once, you can make the dough first and, while that is resting, start the sauce. Then, while the sauce is simmering, finish making the pasta.

needed, then set aside. If you prefer a smoother sauce, you can pass this through a food mill. Otherwise, leave it chunky and thick.

While the sauce is cooking, make the pasta by combining the flours and water until you have a smooth dough. Place the dough in a bowl with a tea towel (dish towel) over the top. Allow it to rest for 30 minutes.

On a lightly floured surface, roll the dough out to a thickness of 2–3 mm (1/8 in) and dust lightly with flour. Roll up the sheet of dough and cut into 1 cm (½ in) thick strips. One by one, take a noodle between the palms of your hands and roll the noodle quickly and lightly, twisting them to create thick noodles.

Put the pasta in a large pot of boiling, well-salted water (see page 13). Cook until al dente, about 3–4 minutes (taste a noodle – it should be slightly resistant, even chewy, but not taste like flour). When cooked, drain the pasta, add to the sauce and toss together until well coated. Serve immediately, scattered with basil and, if desired, a handful of grated pecorino or parmesan cheese.

TAGLIOLINI AL LIMONE
LEMON TAGLIOLINI

Sometimes I am feeling particularly adventurous and energetic enough to cook something new or fiddly, and sometimes I just want something familiar, fast and guaranteed to be tasty. This dish is one of the latter – it takes almost no effort and is my ultimate quick meal.

Any pasta shape can work with this. With the silky, creamy, tangy sauce of lemon and zest, I particularly like something long and flat, like *bavette* or *tagliolini*. A dash of cream binds everything together, but Marco sometimes likes to add *caprino* (soft and tangy goat's curd) instead. The sauce can be made in the time it takes the pasta to cook. If you're in a real hurry to get food on the table, you can buy fresh pasta (as opposed to dried) and it only takes minutes to cook – and you'll still be able to make the sauce in time.

SERVES 4

Put the pasta in a large pot of boiling, well-salted water (see page 13).

Finely grate the lemons with a microplane for their zest (be careful not to use any of the white pith, as it's unpleasantly bitter). Cut the lemons in half and squeeze all the juice from them. Set the zest and juice aside.

Put the butter and olive oil in a frying pan to melt over medium heat. Once melted, add the lemon zest and let it infuse for about 1 minute, stirring (do not let the lemon burn). Add the lemon juice and let it simmer for 3 minutes. Add the cream and about half the cheese, and season with salt and pepper. Cook for a further 1–2 minutes or until thick. Remove from the heat.

Drain the pasta when al dente, but save about 125 ml (4 fl oz/½ cup) of the pasta cooking water. Toss the *tagliolini* in the frying pan with the lemon sauce to coat. Add some extra pasta water if it's looking dry. Serve with the rest of the grated cheese.

320 g (11½ oz) tagliolini (or other long pasta)
2 large organic lemons
50 g (1¾ oz) butter
1 tablespoon extra-virgin olive oil
125 ml (4 fl oz/½ cup) pouring (single/light) cream
50 g (1¾ oz) grated pecorino or parmesan cheese

NOTE
Seek out organic lemons, as they haven't been waxed or treated with pesticides, and since the flavour of this dish relies mostly on their zest, those kinds of treatments are the last thing you want to taste. Do give them a good rinse under running water and pat dry before using, though.

TORTELLI MAREMMANI
RICOTTA AND SPINACH TORTELLI

Along with *acquacotta* and wild boar in any which way, this is the southern Maremma's most famed dish. *Tortelli* are square ravioli and not to be confused with tortellini, Emilia-Romagna's little belly-button-shaped filled pasta. Maremma's *tortelli* tend to be larger than anyone else's and have a thick border around the filling, charmingly called *il marciapiede* (the footpath) or *la frangia* (the fringe), usually cut out with a ruffled-edge pastry cutter that make the edges of every square of pasta good for trapping sauce. Because of their size, the pasta for these *tortelli* is a little thicker than normal. This also makes them sturdy enough for a robust sauce.

The filling is local sheep's milk ricotta – which is firm and creamy, and has a sweet milky taste with a slight tang – speckled with blanched and finely chopped English spinach. The spinach sometimes changes seasonally with other greens such as silverbeet (Swiss chard), or even the leaves of stinging nettles or beetroot (beets). They're usually topped with a heaping serve of rich *Sugo Maremmano* (page 194), as Maremman-style ragu is called, or simply with just-melted unsalted butter and sage.

The question of how many portions this makes all comes down to how you're serving these. Fresh pasta is often used on special occasions, which also means you're serving antipasto before and a main after this dish (if the host is anything like my mother-in-law, then it's quite possible there will even be two different pasta dishes). It's highly probable there'll be dessert too, and coffee and biscuits and *digestivi* to finish. If this were the case, then this recipe would be plenty for eight people. If this is the only dish being served and those eating it are ravenous teenagers, then it would feed four. For anything in between, I would say you could serve six with this.

SERVES 6

Put the flour in a bowl and make a well in the centre. Pour the eggs, yolks and water in the well and use a fork to whisk the eggs, incorporating the flour little by little until you can no longer whisk with the fork. Use floured hands to combine the rest of the flour until you have a smooth, elastic dough. Place the dough in a bowl and cover; rest for at least 30 minutes.

If you're starting with fresh spinach, trim the stalks and cook in a large pot of rapidly boiling water for about 2 minutes. Once cooked, drain the spinach extremely well (squeezed of all its liquid) and chop very finely.

PASTA

400 g (14 oz) plain (all-purpose) flour, plus extra for dusting
2 whole eggs, plus 4 yolks
2 tablespoons water

FILLING

300 g (10½ oz) cooked English spinach, well-drained and cooled, about 1 kg (2 lb 3 oz) fresh
500 g (1 lb 2 oz) fresh, firm ricotta (sheep's milk is preferable), drained if needed (see note)
1 egg, beaten
50 g (1¾ oz) finely grated pecorino or parmesan cheese
½ teaspoon freshly ground nutmeg
¼ teaspoon salt

NOTE

If you can't get sheep's milk ricotta, regular cow's milk ricotta is fine. Just make sure to use a good quality, firm ricotta that can stand on its own. If it is a bit too soft or watery, leave it to drain in a sieve lined with some muslin (cheesecloth) or a tea towel (dish towel) over a bowl for a few hours.

Continued overleaf >

Prepare the filling by combining the spinach with the ricotta, beaten egg, grated cheese, nutmeg and salt in a bowl.

Cut the dough into four pieces and roll out one piece of dough at a time (keep the rest covered while you work), dusted with plenty of flour. Using a pasta machine or rolling pin, roll it thin enough that you can begin to see your hand through it (on a pasta machine, this is usually the third or second last setting). You may want to cut the long pieces of dough in half when they get too long to handle. With a rolling pin, you have your work cut out for you as this is a very elastic dough, but try rolling from the centre outwards for best results.

Working on strips of pasta about 14 cm (5½ in) wide and as long as you like, place balls of 2 teaspoons of filling onto the pasta sheet along one long edge, roughly 2 cm (¾ in) from the edge and 4 cm (1½ in) apart. Fold the sheet of pasta lengthways to cover the filling and line up the edges. Press the pasta sheet down carefully around each spoonful of filling, being careful not to trap too much air (work from one side to the other, one *tortello* at a time). With a frilled-edge pastry cutter, trim the *tortelli* so that you have ravioli roughly 7 x 7 cm (2¾ x 2¾ in) with a 2 cm (¾ in) border around the filling. If you don't have a pastry cutter, you can use a sharp knife to cut the *tortelli* out and a fork to press down along the edges. This has a dual purpose: to seal the edges and to create that texture that helps hold sauce. If you find folding over the pasta tricky, you can also simply layer one sheet on top of the other and trim – the remnants can be rolled back together into a ball and rolled out into a new sheet.

Continue until you finish the pasta and filling. Line a baking tray with baking paper and dust with flour. Keep the finished *tortelli* in a single layer on the tray.

Put the *tortelli* in a large pot of steadily simmering, well-salted water (see page 13). Cook until al dente, about 5 minutes. The *tortelli* will begin to float and puff up slightly. If you taste to check whether they are cooked, look especially at the edges where two sheets of pasta are overlapping.

When done, take the pot off the heat, remove the *tortelli* with a slotted spoon and place onto a clean, slightly damp tea towel (dish towel) to drain off any excess water for a moment. Then place the *tortelli* on a large oval serving plate or distribute directly into bowls. Top with your preferred sauce, a good sprinkling of grated pecorino cheese and serve immediately.

Tortelli are best made fresh and cooked right away, but if you do want to prepare them in advance, the best way to keep them is frozen. To freeze, blanch the *tortelli* in boiling, salted water with a drop of olive oil for 10 seconds. Remove, place on a damp tea towel to drain and arrange the *tortelli* flat on a sheet of foil. Fold them up well, place in a freezer bag or zip-lock plastic bag and freeze. When you are ready to serve them, boil them as you would normally.

RISOTTO CON LE ZUCCHINE
ZUCCHINI RISOTTO

In the late spring and summer when you find piles of young, sweet zucchini (courgettes) at the market, with their huge, bright yellow blossoms still attached, this risotto is a weekly fixture on our table. My absolute favourite of the many different varieties of zucchini you can find are the slightly speckled, pale green, slender heirlooms with gentle ribs along the length of the vegetable. They are tender and cook beautifully. I like to grate them, which I find quick and easy in this dish. I also love the way the grated zucchini pieces blend in with the rice. Alternatively, you can slice them thinly – because of the ribs, the slices will look like little stars.

These lovely pale vegetables are known variously as Zucchini 'Costata Romanesco' or Florentine zucchini. If you have your own vegetable garden, these heirloom seeds are easy to buy and grow yourself so you have access to these beautiful zucchini and their flowers.

The vegetable stock recipe here is double what you will need for this recipe, but it's always useful to have for soups or stews in place of water. If not using it right away, you can freeze it – an ice cube tray filled with stock is handy, so you can pull out exactly the amount you need.

SERVES 4

To make the vegetable stock, chop the vegetables into rough chunks and place in a stockpot with the herbs and 3 litres (101 fl oz/12 cups) of cold water. Bring to the boil, then turn down to a simmer and cook, uncovered, for 1 hour. Strain and set aside until needed.

Wash the zucchini and pat dry. Remove the flowers and roughly slice, then set them aside. Grate the zucchini and set aside separately.

Heat 3 tablespoons of olive oil in a wide, deep frying pan over low heat. Add the onion along with a good pinch of salt and cook for about 10 minutes, stirring occasionally, until softened but not coloured.

Add the rice and stir through the olive oil until it is glistening and thoroughly coated, about 2 minutes. Pour over the white wine and bring the heat up to medium. Let the wine simmer for about 5 minutes, then ladle over just enough warm stock to cover the rice. Cook, stirring occasionally and adding stock to cover as the liquid reduces.

VEGETABLE STOCK
1 brown (yellow) onion
1 large carrot
1 celery stalk
1 handful flat-leaf (Italian) parsley stalks
2 fresh bay leaves

RISOTTO
4 small zucchini (courgettes) and their flowers, about 250 g (9 oz)
60 ml (2 fl oz/¼ cup) extra-virgin olive oil
1 brown (yellow) onion, finely chopped
300 g (10½ oz/1½ cups) risotto rice (such as carnaroli)
125 ml (4 fl oz/½ cup) dry white wine
60 g (2 oz) grated pecorino or parmesan cheese (optional)

Continued overleaf >

After about 10 minutes, add the grated zucchini (keep the flowers for later). Continue cooking, stirring occasionally, and topping up with stock for another 7 minutes, or until the rice is al dente. With the last addition of stock, add the grated cheese (if using) and taste for seasoning (add any salt, if needed). Add the remaining 1 tablespoon of olive oil and toss the rice energetically until it becomes creamy but is still 'soupy' – this is what the Italians refer to when they say risotto should be '*al onda*', literally 'on the wave'.

Remove the risotto from the heat at this point (the rice will continue cooking and will get stiffer as it is plated). Stir through the sliced zucchini flowers so they wilt. Serve immediately on flat plates and sprinkle over some freshly ground black pepper and a little extra grated cheese if desired.

INSALATA GIGLIESE
TOMATO AND CELERY SALAD FROM GIGLIO ISLAND

This bright, refreshing salad is all I feel like eating all summer long – either just on its own or as a side dish to some simply grilled fish. The crunch of celery and the squirt of summer tomatoes are wonderful, but the thing I love most are the celery leaves, so underused and underrated in the kitchen. Here, the leaves are treated almost like a herb – so pick a nice stalk of celery that's not too large and old (which will be tough), something young and tender with healthy leaves. It's a good one to prepare in advance to give the flavours a chance to mingle.

SERVES 4 AS SIDE DISH

Put the sliced spring onions or red onion in a bowl of cold water for 10 minutes. Drain, then toss together with the celery and tomatoes. Dress with olive oil and vinegar and season with salt and pepper about 30 minutes before you want to serve it. This gives the ingredients a bit of time to get to know each other. Finally, toss through the parsley and serve.

- 2 spring onions (scallions) or ½ red onion, finely sliced
- 4 young celery stalks with leaves, finely sliced
- 4 large tomatoes, diced
- 2–3 tablespoons extra-virgin olive oil
- 1½ tablespoons red wine vinegar
- 1 handful flat-leaf (Italian) parsley, finely chopped

SCIROCCO

I'd never heard about *scirocco* until I moved to Porto Ercole and even then I only noticed it at first as a romantic name for a boat. But I was intrigued and impressed the first time I heard the check-out lady at the mini market talking about it, considering my own knowledge of the wind and the direction it was coming from was zero. And then I realised, during one particularly oppressive summer heatwave, that it was all any of the locals ever talked about – this *scirocco* and the thick blanket of foggy humidity that instantly made your skin sticky and the air unbearable.

Scirocco is a hot wind that blows from the south-east, originating in the Sahara and making its way to the Mediterranean and on to northern Europe. It has a different name in every country that it passes through, where it might even bring dust from the desert or be the culprit of stormy weather or even the *acqua alta*, which drowns Venice's streets.

It didn't take long before I realised that I, too, could tell when the winds were blowing from the south – one look out the window and you could see the haze of hot, humid African air covering the port. You can't tell where the sea ends and the sky begins on a horizon affected by *scirocco* – it blends in together, as if an artist has brushed over the lines again and again until it's all a blur.

And then, after days of seemingly endless *scirocco*, suddenly the winds change. '*Maestrale*', you hear people say, in relief, at the bakery or the fish shop as they chat incessantly about the weather. The sky looks brighter, the sea bluer and calmer, the air limpid and, for a short time, everyone breathes a little easier.

The sticky heat of the summer months in all ways affects the rituals of the day during this period. It means that turning on heat in any form in the kitchen is avoided at all costs – except, of course, to make another pot of strong coffee with the *moka*, the Italian stove-top percolator. Melons and watermelons (abundant and local) are devoured, becoming daytime meals on their own. If you're smart, you cook at night – a big pot of something that you can serve cold the next day, without having to turn on a stove or an oven. Something that's ready to serve right away so that you spend all morning cooling off at the beach and get home with a cold lunch already waiting.

The hours in the middle of the day are the quietest, when everyone retreats to the cool of their shutter-drawn apartments, hibernating until early evening. The town barely stirs and even shops remain closed for several hours in the middle of the day until 5pm – although barely anyone is about until 6pm when the *lungomare*, the esplanade along the port, becomes shady enough for comfortable strolling. And then everyone is out and about, lining up for gelato or sipping on cool drinks in one of the bars on the shores of the port. And the town, like everyone in it, is suddenly alive again.

PEPERONI E PATATE
RED PEPPERS AND POTATOES

This is a bit like a *peperonata* and a bit like a *gurguglione* – a summer vegetable stew with a pirate name from Elba Island, it's made with diced eggplant (aubergine), zucchini (courgettes), capsicums (bell peppers), tomato and potato. One day I wanted to make a *gurguglione*, but realised I was missing a few ingredients, so had to improvise. This is now a summer staple in our house. Like anything with capsicums, it just gets tastier the longer you keep it, so I like to make a big batch and eat it over the next few days. This always turns out to be a great idea, especially during hot weather when you don't want to turn on the stove very much at all. Have it as a side dish to grilled fish or meat; on its own, topping some good crusty bread rubbed with garlic and drizzled with olive oil; or cold, for lunch the next day, with some fresh mozzarella and a few slices of prosciutto.

SERVES 4 AS A SIDE DISH OR LIGHT LUNCH

2 large red capsicums (bell peppers), about 600–700 g (1 lb 5 oz–1 lb 9 oz)
2–3 ripe tomatoes, or about 125 g (4½ oz) tinned chopped tomatoes
3 tablespoons extra-virgin olive oil
1 brown (yellow) onion, finely sliced
1 garlic clove, sliced
3 medium potatoes (about 500 g/1 lb 2 oz), peeled and diced
1 handful basil, oregano and/or parsley, roughly chopped

Rinse the capsicums. Then remove the stems, cut in half, pull out the seeds and slice into strips. Set aside.

If using fresh tomatoes, score their bottoms with a sharp knife, making a cross. Blanch them in a pot of boiling water for about 30 seconds, then remove them to a bowl of ice water. The skins can now be easily peeled. Cut into quarters and remove the seeds. Chop the rest of the tomato flesh and set aside.

Heat the olive oil in a wide frying pan over low heat and cook the onion for approximately 10 minutes, stirring occasionally, until soft but not coloured. Add the garlic and the capsicums, along with about 125 ml (4 fl oz/½ cup) of water. Cover and let them cook, stirring every now and then and checking on their progress, until the capsicums have completely given way and are soft. About 30 minutes is sufficient, though I usually prefer to let them go a bit longer, about 40 minutes. Add the tomatoes, the potatoes and some more water – about 125 ml (4 fl oz/½ cup) – along with a pinch of salt. Bring to a simmer and cook, uncovered, until the potatoes are tender and the liquid has thickened to a sauce, about 15–20 minutes.

Taste for seasoning, remove from the heat and scatter over the herbs. You can serve this hot, warm or even cold.

SFORMATO DI CIPOLLOTTI
SPRING ONION GRATIN

The *sformato* is quite an old-fashioned side dish – it just takes one glance at Pellegrino Artusi's cookbook, which lists eighteen different *sformati* (four of which are desserts), to realise how popular they were on Italian tables in the nineteenth century. It's easy to see why – it's such a simple preparation and it feeds a large table effortlessly. It's the type of dish that has survived so long partly because it's so homely and comforting, much like anything soft, cheesy and creamy, if you ask me.

Sformati are often prepared with a single seasonal vegetable, which are cooked and sometimes even puréed so that the dish remains creamy. My favourites, other than this one, have English spinach, cardoons or artichoke. Sometimes they are baked in a water bath, which is why *sformato* is often translated to the English word 'flan' (much like the wobbly custard dessert, like a crème caramel). But I like the crunch of the golden-brown edges and top when baked like the French gratin.

This flan of sweet spring onions (scallions) and creamy bechamel sauce is traditionally served as a side to Wild Boar Stew (page 52) in the Maremma. It's a wonderful match, much like mashed potatoes and soft polenta are perfect alongside rich, gamey meat stews. But it's also just as nice with roast chicken or baked fish.

SERVES 4 AS A SIDE

- 25 g (1 oz) butter
- 25 g (1 oz/1½ tablespoons) plain (all-purpose) flour
- 250 ml (8½ fl oz/1 cup) milk, warmed
- 250 g (9 oz/2 bunches) spring onions (scallions)
- 3 tablespoons extra-virgin olive oil, plus extra for greasing
- 1 egg, beaten
- ½ teaspoon freshly ground nutmeg
- 60 g (2 oz) grated pecorino or parmesan cheese
- 35 g (1¼ oz/⅓ cup) fine dry breadcrumbs

Prepare the bechamel sauce by melting the butter in a small saucepan with the flour over low heat. Mix together, stirring often (I like a wooden spoon, some like silicone spatulas), and let it bubble and simmer for 1–2 minutes. Add the warm milk (do make sure it is warm, as this helps avoid lumps), stirring as you pour it all in to make a smooth mixture. Cook, stirring, until the sauce is thick, smooth and coats the back of the spoon easily, a few minutes. Remove from the heat and let it cool. You can also prepare this in advance.

Rinse the spring onions of any dirt, remove the outermost layer, cut off the roots and discard. Slice the spring onions finely using all of the white part and the pale green part. Discard the dark green tops.

Heat 2 tablespoons of olive oil in a frying pan over low–medium heat and add the spring onions, along with a good pinch of salt. Cook, stirring occasionally, for 10 minutes, until very soft but not coloured. You may want to add about 60 ml (2 fl oz/¼ cup) of water during cooking to prevent any burning or sticking. Remove from the heat and let it cool.

Preheat the oven to 180°C (350°F).

Combine the cooled bechamel and onions together in a bowl, and season with salt and pepper. Add the egg, nutmeg and half of the cheese and mix through. Pour into a lightly greased ovenproof dish – a 20 cm (8 in) square or 20 x 25 cm (8 x 10 in) rectangular one works well.

In a separate bowl, combine the rest of the grated cheese and the breadcrumbs. Sprinkle over the top of the flan and drizzle over the remaining tablespoon of olive oil. Bake until golden brown, about 25–30 minutes.

NOTE
Out of season, you can replace the spring onions with 4 leeks – these are just as good, if not better.

FROM THE FARMHOUSE

DALLA FATTORIA

CROSTINI MAREMMANI
MAREMMAN CROSTINI

Crostini are always present in a classic Tuscan antipasto and they come in many shapes and forms, but the classic toppings (and the most popular) are the *crostini di fegatini* (which you find closer to Florence and are also called *crostini neri, crostini toscani*, 'black *crostini*' and 'Tuscan *crostini*') and *crostini Maremmani*, which are a Maremman relative of the Florentine ones.

While the classic *crostini di fegatini* are topped with a smooth pâté of chicken liver, the topping for Maremman *crostini* is essentially a ragu, a mixture of minced (ground) beef and chicken liver, with the addition of anchovies and capers for some punchy savouriness. It's an excellent antipasto for a large party or gathering, as the topping can be prepared in advance. And for those who aren't keen on the richness of the pure chicken liver in classic *crostini toscani*, this is a delicious alternative.

Crostini are great as finger food, so use small, easy-to-hold, easy-to-bite slices of bread. Serve them on a large platter along with some slices of prosciutto and wedges of pecorino cheese for antipasto.

MAKES ABOUT 20 CROSTINI

Dry out the slices of baguette in a low oven until crisp but not coloured. Set aside.

If using salt-packed capers, first rinse off any excess salt under running water, then place the capers in a bowl full of fresh water and let them soak for 15 minutes. If using capers in brine, simply drain and pat dry.

Put the finely chopped onion, carrot and celery in a wide frying pan with the olive oil and a pinch of salt and cook over low heat, stirring occasionally, for about 10 minutes or until the vegetables have softened. Add the beef, chicken livers, anchovies and capers and cook, stirring, over medium heat until the meat and livers are browned, about 5–10 minutes.

Once browned, transfer the pieces of liver to a large chopping board.

Add the tomato paste to the pan and cook for 1 minute, stirring to incorporate it, then pour over the wine. Let the wine cook down until the mixture is almost dry, about 7 minutes.

In the meantime, with a sharp knife or mezzaluna, chop the livers finely. You can go as rustic as you like and leave them roughly chopped, or if you prefer a smoother topping, you can put them straight into a food processor and pulse until you have a thick paste. Return the livers back to the pan.

- 1 baguette or similar, cut into 1 cm (½ in) slices
- 4–5 capers
- 1 brown (yellow) onion, finely chopped
- 1 carrot, finely chopped
- ½ celery stalk, finely chopped
- 2 tablespoons extra-virgin olive oil
- 200 g (7 oz) minced (ground) beef
- 150 g (5½ oz) chicken livers, whole
- 2 anchovy fillets, either preserved in oil or cleaned salt-packed ones (see page 142)
- 1 tablespoon tomato paste (concentrated purée)
- 160 ml (5½ fl oz/⅔ cup) dry white wine

Add enough water to cover the ragu, about 750 ml (25½ fl oz/3 cups), and bring to a simmer. Then turn down to low heat and cook for 40 minutes, topping with water as necessary. After about 30 minutes, check for seasoning and add salt and pepper as necessary.

Place the warm ragu on top of the dried baguette slices and serve as antipasto.

NOTE
The ragu can be made in advance. When you need it, reheat with about 60 ml (2 fl oz/¼ cup) of water and bring back to a simmer before topping the crostini.

UOVA SODE CON ACCIUGATA
BOILED EGGS WITH ANCHOVY SAUCE

Salting anchovies was a method of dealing with a glut of these cheap and abundant fish in the days before refrigeration. Around the Tuscan islands and the coast, there are a million uses for them and this sauce, which is a traditional preparation on Giglio Island, is just one – but the sauce in itself has a further million uses.

I could put it on just about anything. If you're an anchovy-lover like me, you could start by putting it on toast, or tossing through steaming, boiled potatoes, or even as a quick solution to dressing some freshly boiled pasta. Anchovies and cauliflower is a match made in heaven, no matter how they're combined. The options are only limited to your imagination, though you might see the pattern – anchovies add a boost of flavour to anything that is rather neutral or even perhaps creamy in nature.

Naturally, anchovies are wonderful on eggs in any form. I grew up in the 1980s when devilled eggs were a fixture at gatherings and parties, and I am still partial to the rather old-fashioned but foolproof halved boiled eggs on a platter. Topping boiled eggs with a spoonful of this anchovy sauce is my favourite combination, but a spoonful folded through scrambled eggs makes an incredible breakfast or lunch, too.

MAKES ABOUT 125 G (4½ OZ) SAUCE

Soak the anchovies in water and clean them following the instructions on page 142.

Put the anchovy fillets and oil in a small frying pan over low heat. Let the anchovies cook for about 5 minutes (they will appear to melt down), stirring to break them up.

Add the vinegar, turn the heat up to medium and cook for 1 more minute. Remove from the heat, add the parsley and stir until incorporated. Set aside to cool completely.

Pour water into a medium saucepan until it's 3 cm (1¼ in) deep and place over medium heat. Once simmering, carefully add the eggs and cook, covered, for 7½ minutes for an almost set, not too hard or chalky boiled egg. Remove from the heat and plunge the eggs in cold water to cool down straight away. Peel and slice in half. Place the egg halves on a platter and top with about ½ teaspoon of anchovy sauce.

120 g (4½ oz) salt-packed anchovies (about 10)
60 ml (2 fl oz/¼ cup) extra-virgin olive oil
1 tablespoon red wine vinegar
1 large handful flat-leaf (Italian) parsley leaves, finely chopped
6 eggs

NOTE

Try to get salt-packed anchovies for this recipe. They are worth seeking out for this recipe as they have a different texture and a different quality to anchovies preserved in oil. Use eggs that weigh 55–60 g (2 oz).

The anchovy sauce recipe can easily be doubled and it keeps very well in a small jar in the fridge. If you find you don't use it often (which is an absurd idea in this house), you can pour a layer of olive oil over the top to help keep it longer.

VARIATIONS

In a recipe from Giglio Island from Antiche Ricette di Giglio, *a handful of chopped cherry tomatoes are combined with the anchovies in the pan, too. Although a little further afield, this is very similar to another anchovy sauce from Tuscany's Valdarno, south of Florence, where capers are a must.*

SATURNIA

This pretty, ancient Etruscan town, most famous for its nearby natural hot springs, was named for Saturn, the Roman god of time. It is said that he created the sulphurous spring by hurling a lightning bolt to earth (the Etruscan god Satre supposedly also liked hurling lightning at people). Another story claims it was Jupiter throwing a bolt of lightning at Saturn – and missing. Either way, while the Etruscan and Roman Maremmans revelled in their sacred hot springs, by the Middle Ages it was believed that the hot waters encouraged temptation and led to the gates of hell. In the meantime, the town itself was destroyed by warring states and then abandoned for several centuries.

You would never guess the town's dark history by how it looks today – a picturesque, well-kept town that can thank the beauty of the reviving, relaxing hot springs for its good fortune.

Following the winding roads towards Saturnia, if you look carefully and it's cool enough, you may be able to spot the steam rising from the warm water, which flows at body temperature out of the spring. A cool, very early autumn or winter morning is the best time to come down to the water, when you have the place all to yourself, except for maybe a deer in the nearby olive groves. The water, which seems to explode out of the side of an ancient mill, gushes into small, opaque, azure pools the colour of Peruvian opal. Set against the backdrop of the lush rolling hills of the Maremman countryside, with the heavy pounding of the gushing water, there's really nothing quite like the experience.

CIAFFAGNONI MANCIANESI
MANCIANO-STYLE CRÊPES

Humble, light and bubbly, and – most importantly – paper thin, these crêpes are made out of the bare essentials (eggs, flour and water) and cooked in a cast-iron frying pan greased with *lardo*. The locals from Manciano like to tell the story that their *ciaffagnoni* (pronounced 'chaf-an-nyoni') were brought to France by a Maremman cook in the entourage of Florentine noblewoman Catherine de' Medici when she married Henry II. For their crêpes, the French used richer milk instead of the water, and they cooked them in butter. It's the same story that the Florentines like to tell about their *crespelle*.

Regardless of their history, the *ciaffagnoni* are delicious – and worth mastering. Creating these crêpes takes a bit of practice, partly due to the high water ratio of the batter and partly because they're made so paper-thin. (They say that you should be able to make 10 crêpes with just one egg.) For more on making the perfect Manciano-style crêpe, see page 181.

This is the most traditional ratio of eggs to flour and water, and is an easy-to-remember recipe. A dash of olive oil in the mixture (which isn't traditional) can help make handling these delicate crêpes a little easier. The right pan makes every bit of difference. If you have a crêpe pan handy, that's perfect. Otherwise, use a well-seasoned cast-iron or a non-stick frying pan – if the latter, you don't need to grease the pan and you might find you don't even need to sacrifice any crêpes at the beginning.

You can eat these any way you prefer, but some favourite toppings are the simplest – a sprinkling of sugar or a blob of jam for a sweet snack, or a sprinkling of grated pecorino cheese for a savoury one. Top your warm crêpe with these as soon as you can. Another delicious topping is fresh ricotta, sweetened with some sugar and cinnamon or a drizzle of honey.

MAKES 20–25 CRÊPES (OR, IF YOU'RE REALLY GOOD, 30)

3 eggs
150 g (5½ oz/1 cup) plain (all-purpose) flour
300 ml (10 fl oz) water
1 tablespoon extra-virgin olive oil, plus more for greasing the pan

Combine the eggs and flour, beat with a fork until creamy, then add the water and oil. Continue to beat with a fork or use a whisk to combine until smooth. Let the batter rest in the fridge overnight.

When ready to cook, place a small 15 cm (6 in) frying pan (greased lightly with olive oil if needed) over high heat until very hot. Give the batter a quick stir (the flour tends to settle to the bottom), then pour a small amount of batter into the hot pan (1½ tablespoons is enough for this

Continued overleaf >

size pan) and quickly swirl to just cover the bottom of the pan. It should immediately bubble and set on the bottom. When the top looks dry (this takes about 20–30 seconds), flip over and cook the other side for a further 10–15 seconds. Don't overcook them as they will become brittle and break when folded.

Place the crêpe on a plate, add your choice of topping while warm, then fold into quarters (fold in half, then halve again). Continue making crêpes until you've used all the batter.

VARIATIONS

In other parts of Maremma, where similar crêpes are made, they're called migliacci *or* fregnacce. *Maremma-born food writer Edda Servi Machlin (see page 212) writes of* migliaccini con tonno, *where small crêpes are filled with a sauce made of tinned tuna, anchovies in oil and parsley, then folded in half and piled onto a baking tray to be warmed briefly in the oven. She recalls that they were a favourite appetiser for Hannukah in her native Pitigliano, and were usually served at lunch with stewed cannellini beans.*

THE SECRET TO MANCIANO'S CRÊPES

The first time I tried making *ciaffagnoni*, or Manciano-style crêpes, I found myself scraping most of the crêpes off the bottom of the pan. I was nowhere near. After my third attempt, still only producing a few decent crêpes with each batch of batter, I went to see an expert, Valentina Di Virginio. She's the chef at her family's beautiful estate, Villa Acquaviva, which is run by her son Fabrizio D'Ascenzi. It's between the gushing natural hot springs of Saturnia and the town of Manciano, a 10-minute drive to each. They are well known for their *ciaffagnoni*, which they produce in the thousands for their signature dishes.

'The first ten will break', she warned me. She was exaggerating a little, of course. It's more like three, but it's part of the preparation. The pan (especially a cast-iron one) needs to *fare la faccia*, as they say: as soon as it reaches that perfect temperature they will – as if by magic – no longer stick or break. I was relieved to hear those first few are sacrificial.

She soon revealed other secrets. The pan – cast iron, greased lightly with olive oil (or, traditionally, a block of *lardo*), needs to be burning hot. You need to hear that *chhhhhhhhhh* as soon as you pour in the batter, which will begin to bubble immediately. This is what gives them their light and bubbly texture – and helps them not stick.

The batter needs to be well rested – overnight if possible. This is vital. When you first make the batter, it might look like water. But give it overnight for the flour to absorb the liquid and the next day you have a completely different batter – beautifully creamy and much better behaved.

There were other things I noticed. To flip the crêpes, Valentina used a wooden skewer stick to first run around the edge of the crêpe to loosen it. Then, poking the stick through, she flipped it with her fingers. She used no other utensils with these delicate things (though a silicone spatula is pretty useful, too).

At Villa Acquaviva, *ciaffagnoni* are made with a miniature pan and are used instead of pasta sheets for layering individual lasagne with cheese, artichokes and sausage. 'After all, they're eggs and flour, like pasta', Valentina points out.

ZUPPA DI FARRO
FARRO SOUP

This soup is quite different to the famous farro soup of Lucca that most Tuscans know so well, in which the beans are blended into a creamy purée, making a very thick, hearty soup to warm you to the core in cold weather. Better suited to the warmer months, this farro soup can be served as a cold dish. It's refreshing, light and nourishing, just perfect for summer eating. However, when served hot, this soup is brothy and warming, ideal for inter-seasonal weather, such as a chilly spring evening. It's versatile that way. Overnight, the farro soaks up all the broth, and the resulting cold mixture becomes more like a farro salad, delicious eaten just as is with a swirl of olive oil and an extra grind of black pepper over the top.

SERVES 4

- 1 brown (yellow) onion, finely chopped
- 1 carrot, finely chopped
- 1 celery stalk, finely chopped
- 60 ml (2 fl oz/¼ cup) extra-virgin olive oil, plus more for serving
- 160 g (5½ oz/¾ cup) dried, semi-pearled or pearled farro
- 1 litre (34 fl oz/4 cups) vegetable stock (see page 161)
- 200 g (7 oz) cooked cannellini beans, drained
- 200 g (7 oz) cooked borlotti beans, drained
- 1 handful finely grated pecorino or parmesan cheese (optional)

Combine the chopped vegetables with the olive oil and a pinch of salt in a saucepan and put over the gentlest heat you have. Cover and cook slowly for about 20 minutes, stirring and checking occasionally. If you find the vegetables are sticking rather than sweating, you can add a splash of water.

Add the farro and toss through the vegetables. Let the farro toast, stirring, for 1 minute, then add the vegetable stock. Bring to the boil, then simmer on medium heat until the farro is tender, usually about 35 minutes. (Check the instructions on the packet; different kinds of farro have different cooking times.) Add the drained beans (if you find it's not brothy enough at this point, you can add some more water) and continue cooking for 5 minutes. Check for seasoning, and add salt and pepper to taste.

When served warm, it's very good with freshly grated pecorino cheese over the top (if desired), along with the obligatory drizzle of extra-virgin olive oil and plenty of freshly cracked black pepper.

NOTE

Farro (emmer) is a confusing ingredient outside Italy, as there are several different varieties, names and sizes. The naming of grains differs from country to country, so look for farro imported from Italy – Tuscany is a particularly important producer. And try to get farro that is semi-pearled or pearled. This means that the husk is partially or fully removed, which reduces the cooking time greatly. Pearled farro does not require soaking before use and has the quickest cooking time; if you have semi-pearled farro, you can soak it overnight to reduce the cooking time if you prefer (without soaking, it may take up to 35–40 minutes to cook).

ZUPPA LOMBARDA
CANNELLINI BEAN SOUP

The name of this dish, which translates to 'Lombard soup', is a little misleading. It's neither from Lombardy, nor really a 'soup' – though technically it is still a *zuppa*. Supposedly, it was the dish fed to the workers who were brought into the Maremma from northern Italy to dredge and fill the malaria-ridden wetlands towards the end of the 1700s. In fact, this recipe should really be called *zuppa per i lombardi* ('soup for the Lombards').

This typical Maremman peasant dish is made of locally grown cannellini beans cooked slowly in water with onion, garlic and herbs. Once cooked, the beans, along with some of their delicious liquid, are scooped over a slice of grilled or perhaps stale Tuscan bread. Like the most efficient sponge, Tuscan bread soaks up everything. It is one of my favourite dishes.

Good beans are essential for this recipe, and I would recommend using dried cannellini beans – the liquid produced from cooking the dried beans from scratch is what makes this so special. Another important tip is not to add any salt to the cooking beans until right at the end – the salt keeps the beans stubbornly tough and you will need to cook them for much longer.

SERVES 4–6 (WITH LEFTOVERS)

Rinse the beans and put them in a large bowl of cold water (they need plenty of space). Let them soak for 12 hours or overnight.

Drain the beans, then put them in a large, heavy-bottomed saucepan (or flameproof terracotta pot if you have one) with the onion, garlic, herbs and olive oil. If you don't like rosemary sprigs floating through your beans, simply tie the sprigs of rosemary together.

Pour over about 1.5 litres (51 fl oz/6 cups) of water to cover. Place on the lowest, gentlest heat you have and bring to a simmer (a rolling boil can damage the beans), then cover and cook for 1½–2 hours (some beans may need even longer), or until the beans are tender but not falling apart. Check occasionally to make sure there is still plenty of liquid and scoop off any scum from the surface. Top up with water if needed. Right towards the end, add the salt, and once the beans are tender, remove from the heat.

Serve a scoop of warm (not hot) beans over grilled slices of bread. If you like, you can also rub these with a clove of raw garlic. Drizzle over some extra-virgin olive oil and add pepper to taste.

300 g (10½ oz/1½ cups) dried cannellini beans
1 onion, finely sliced
4 garlic cloves, whole, plus 1 for serving (optional)
4 sage sprigs
2 rosemary sprigs
3 tablespoons extra-virgin olive oil, plus more for serving
½ teaspoon salt
4 slices Tuscan bread (or other crusty white loaf), grilled (broiled)

NOTE
The general rule with cooking dried beans is that you'll get triple the amount you started with. You can halve this recipe easily and it would be just enough for 4 light servings (suitable if you've got a main to follow or other dishes on the table), but I like having some leftovers as it is such a versatile preparation. These beans make a classic side dish (just drain and drizzle with good extra-virgin olive oil), stir through soup such as the Zuppa di farro (page 184) or the Zuppa maremmana (page 151), or blend them and spread on top of crostini.

TAGLIOLINI CON CECI
TAGLIOLINI WITH CHICKPEAS

This is a version of *pasta e ceci*, which is, in turn, a relative of *pasta e fagioli* (pasta with beans). Pasta and legumes are a classic, wonderfully starchy and comforting combination that you can find in many regions, from Tuscany going southwards. As with many home-cooked favourites, *pasta e ceci* can take on many different guises: there are versions stained with tomato; others with chickpeas kept whole, such as *alla romana*; others with a portion of the chickpeas puréed (a third, half or three-quarters); those that are more like soup with a little pasta floating in it; and those made with short pasta.

This version cooks the pasta directly in the sauce. It does not involve the usual *soffritto* of chopped carrot, celery and onion, but is very simply flavoured with some garlic (a must) and rosemary. You could also add some anchovies, melted down in a little olive oil with the garlic, for some extra savouriness. I like making this with fresh egg pasta, such as *tagliolini*, because it cooks quickly, which works nicely with this sauce. But you could use regular dried pasta, too.

It goes without saying that with any dish as simple as this one, the quality of the ingredients is paramount – I cannot stress how important this is for the chickpeas (dried or tinned) and the final touch of olive oil, especially.

SERVES 4

- 200 g (7 oz) dried chickpeas, or 600 g (1 lb 5 oz) pre-cooked, tinned chickpeas
- 1 garlic clove
- 1 rosemary sprig
- 2 tablespoons extra-virgin olive oil (if using tinned chickpeas), plus extra for serving
- 400 g (14 oz) fresh tagliolini, or 320 g (11½ oz) dried pasta such as linguine
- 1 handful finely grated pecorino or parmesan (optional)

If you're using dried chickpeas, put them in a bowl covered with plenty of fresh cold water the night before and leave them to soak in the fridge. The next day, drain the soaked chickpeas and put them in a saucepan, cover with at least 3 cm (1¼ in) of fresh water, add the garlic and rosemary, and simmer until the chickpeas are soft. Keep an eye on the chickpeas – scoop off any scum that rises to the top of the water, and top up with water if needed. Add salt to taste at the end.

If using tinned chickpeas, pour the extra-virgin olive oil into a flameproof casserole dish or deep frying pan with the garlic clove and rosemary and let the oil infuse over low heat. Cook for about 10 minutes, turning the garlic and ensuring it doesn't burn or colour too deeply. Add the chickpeas and enough water to cover by 3 cm (1¼ in), add a good pinch of salt and bring to a simmer. Cook for 10 minutes.

Remove the rosemary sprig and blend the chickpeas and the cooking liquid to make a smooth purée (if you prefer a bit of texture, you can set aside a third of the whole chickpeas before you do this). Pour back into

Continued overleaf >

the pan, season to taste and heat. Add enough extra water for it to be a creamy, quite fluid, but not too thick sauce – 500 ml (17 fl oz/2 cups) should suffice.

Once simmering, cook the *tagliolini* directly in the sauce until al dente. If using fresh pasta, this will only take about 5 minutes. If using dried pasta, cook it separately in a pot of water until half-cooked (use the packet instructions for timing), then add it to the sauce to finish cooking. If you need to top the sauce up with any water, you can use the pasta cooking water. Stir occasionally to ensure the pasta isn't sticking to the bottom of the pan.

Let the pasta sit for a moment or two before serving as it will be piping hot. Allow it to cool just a little for the flavour to be at its best. Season with salt and plenty of freshly ground black pepper, then pour over your very best extra-virgin olive oil – a bright, peppery, green olive oil is the thing you need. If you like (I do), add a handful of grated pecorino or parmesan over the top.

RIGATONI ALLA BUTTERA
COWBOY-STYLE RIGATONI

Once, at a *sagra* (see page 202) in Capalbio, we ordered *rigatoni alla buttera*. It's a popular dish in southern Maremma, where *butteri* (cowboys – or in this case, their wives) are local icons. It arrived, steaming, in a flimsy plastic bowl, with a plastic fork, and we sat under fluorescent lights on the long, communal table with a cheap, cold bottle of Bianco di Pitigliano. The mosquitoes were out in full force and every now and then the breeze brought over a waft of smoke from the nearby grills, where cooks charred thick pork sausages and meat of all kinds.

A blanket of pecorino cheese covered the pasta, and I swirled it in a little bit before taking a bite. I can still remember the incredible flavour. I gave a forkful to Marco and watched his eyes light up. 'What do you think is in this?!' I asked him. With every bite we tried guessing the possible combination of ingredients that made it so good. It was something salty. Something rich. Something umami. It was quite possibly the tastiest plate of pasta I have ever eaten, and every plate of *rigatoni alla buttera* eaten since has had to try to match that one.

Afterwards, we found the list of ingredients of the dishes (it's always posted somewhere at a *sagra*) and we realised our guesses were, for the most part, wrong. Marco was convinced its tastiness was due to chicken livers, but it was actually something so simple. Pork sausages, pancetta, the usual *battuto* of onion, celery and carrot. Wine. Tomato. I had to try this at home.

SERVES 4

Pour the olive oil into a wide frying pan and add the onion, carrot, celery, garlic, prosciutto, pancetta and herbs with a pinch of salt. Cover the pan with a lid and cook over low heat, stirring occasionally, for about 10 minutes or until the vegetables have softened and the fat is transparent. Add the sausages, crumbling the meat into the pan. Cook over medium heat for about 10 minutes, stirring to brown all sides.

Pour over the white wine and let it cook down for about 5–7 minutes.

Add the tomato passata and 500 ml (17 fl oz/2 cups) of water and bring to a simmer. Cook on low for about 30 minutes, stirring occasionally. Check for seasoning and add salt and pepper as necessary (this is a fairly robust sauce with lots of flavour from the prosciutto, pancetta and sausage, so you may not need any extra salt), then continue cooking for

2 tablespoons extra-virgin olive oil
1 brown (yellow) onion, finely chopped
1 carrot, finely chopped
½ celery stalk, finely chopped
1 garlic clove, chopped
30 g (1 oz) prosciutto, cut into thin strips
60 g (2 oz) pancetta, cut into thin strips or diced
a few sage leaves
1 rosemary sprig, leaves chopped
300 g (10½ oz) pork sausages, casings removed
125 ml (4 fl oz/½ cup) dry white wine
200 g (7 oz) tomato passata (puréed tomatoes)
320 g (11½ oz) dried rigatoni (large tube-shaped pasta) or penne pasta
finely grated pecorino or parmesan cheese, for serving

NOTE
In Tuscany, sausages are always pork, have natural casings and are only flavoured with a few fennel seeds. Choose good quality sausages. Go for fresher sausages over aged ones (they will be softer, so easier to crumble and incorporate into the sauce). Make sure there is no gluten or anything else added that might affect the texture of the cooked sausages in the ragu. If you can't find rigatoni, go for penne pasta.

Continued overleaf >

a further 10 minutes or so. You should have a well-reduced, thick, rich sauce. Set aside.

Put the pasta in a large pot of boiling, well-salted water (see page 13). Boil until al dente, then drain and toss with the sauce.

Serve with plenty of finely grated pecorino or parmesan cheese.

ANYTHING BUT BEEF
Like most peasant dishes, there are multiple versions of rigatoni alla buttera. *Once I started trying out the various recipes, the thing that struck me most was that each version was completely different to the next. Just like the many Tuscan recipes that are named 'alla contadina' (the farmer's wife), the cowboy's wife was simply using what she had on hand. Leftovers like prosciutto, pancetta, sausage, chicken livers – anything to add and 'beef up' a ragu that may not actually have had any beef in it. The irony is that although the* butteri *were raising beautiful Maremmana cattle – an ancient breed with long horns in the shape of a lyre and a greyish coat that looks like it has been rubbed with charcoal – they didn't actually get the chance to eat beef themselves. These cattle (see overleaf) were tended for nobility, the only ones who could afford to eat beef.*

SUGO MAREMMANO

MAREMMAN BEEF, PORK AND SAUSAGE RAGU

The Italian word 'ragu' is borrowed from the French ragoût, which refers to a stew more than a meat sauce and derives from a term that means 'to awaken the appetite'. The main thing these two different preparations share, other than the name, is slow cooking. And it is, indeed, a not-so-secret secret that the longer you cook a ragu, the better it will be.

In southern Tuscany, the more traditional word *sugo* (literally, 'sauce') is preferred to describe ragu or any vegetable sauce that is destined for coating pasta, whether *sugo al pomodoro* (tomato sauce) or *sugo finto* ('fake' sauce, see page 152). *Sugo maremmano* is the best sauce for *Tortelli maremmani* (page 156), large ravioli of ricotta and spinach; but it's also a classic for eating with pasta, long or short. It's made of a mixture of meats, such as sausage meat and minced (ground) pork and beef. Traditionally, using less expensive, homegrown pork and sausage was a way to add volume to the ragu. It is also an extra tasty combination that Maremmans love.

It's a good idea to prepare this sauce the day before you want to serve it. The extra resting time, with flavours mingling, means it tastes even better the next day.

SERVES 4 (WITH PASTA)

- 1 brown (yellow) onion, finely chopped
- 1 carrot, finely chopped
- 1 celery stalk, finely chopped
- 1 small bunch Italian (flat-leaf) parsley, stalks and stems separated and chopped
- 2 tablespoons extra-virgin olive oil
- 250 g (9 oz) minced (ground) beef
- 250 g (9 oz) minced (ground) pork
- 1 pork sausage, casing removed and meat crumbled
- 250 ml (8½ fl oz/1 cup) dry red wine
- 700 g (1 lb 9 oz) tomato passata (puréed tomatoes)

Combine the onion, carrot, celery and parsley stalks in a wide frying pan with the olive oil and a pinch of salt. Cook over low heat, stirring occasionally, for about 10 minutes, or until the vegetables have softened. Transfer the vegetables to a bowl and set aside.

Turn the heat up to medium–high and add the beef, pork and sausage meat. Cook, stirring regularly, until the meat has roasted and browned. There are a few stages to this process. First, the meat will colour on all sides but remain pale. Then you will start to see some liquid coming out of the meat. Then the real browning starts to happen. The bottom of the pan may get sticky and browned, too – all of this adds a lot of flavour.

Return the vegetables to the pan and pour over the red wine. Let the wine cook down for about 5–7 minutes, then add the tomato passata, along with about 500 ml (17 fl oz/2 cups) to cover. Bring to a simmer, then turn down to low heat and cook for at least 40 minutes, topping up with water as necessary. After about 30 minutes, check for seasoning and add salt and pepper as necessary. The parsley leaves can be stirred through right before serving or saved for sprinkling over the top (I prefer the previous).

CONIGLIO RIPIENO
RABBIT STUFFED WITH POTATOES

I heard about this recipe through the chatty and wonderful Ilena in Capalbio, whose Wild Boar Stew (page 52) is etched into my memory. She briefly mentioned a traditional recipe where a deboned rabbit is stuffed and roasted with *patatine* (little potato pieces), but could also mean potato chips. I couldn't get this idea out of my head, which seemed all at once practical, appealing and delicious. It turned out to be the best roast rabbit I've ever had.

Not far away, in Lazio's province of Viterbo, they make a similar roast rabbit, which is stuffed with potatoes, pork sausage and black olives, the whole thing scented with wild fennel.

SERVES 4–6

Quarter the potatoes lengthways and slice thinly. In a wide frying pan, heat 60 ml (2 fl oz/¼ cup) of the oil over medium–high heat. Add the potatoes with 1 rosemary sprig and fry, stirring here and there to prevent sticking and to help them cook evenly. Cook the potato slices for 10 minutes, or until they're browned and cooked through. Remove, drain on paper towel, season with salt and allow to cool.

Preheat the oven to 180°C (350°F).

Open up the rabbit and lay the prosciutto over the inside. Distribute the potatoes in an even layer down the middle of the rabbit. Carefully roll it up and tie with kitchen string to hold it in place (an extra pair of hands helps here). Weave the remaining rosemary sprigs through the string here and there.

Place the rabbit on a large, lightly greased baking tray. Pour over the wine and season the rabbit all over with salt and pepper. Pour over the remaining 2 tablespoons of olive oil and cover with aluminium foil.

Roast for 30 minutes, then remove the foil and continue roasting for 15 more minutes. If you have a meat thermometer, the internal temperature should reach 65–71°C (150–160°F). Remove from the oven, cover with the foil again and rest for 10 minutes. Serve in thick slices.

---

2 medium potatoes
80 ml (2½ fl oz/⅓ cup) extra-virgin olive oil, plus extra 2 tablespoons
3–4 fresh rosemary sprigs
1 kg (2 lb 3 oz) rabbit, deboned
100 g (3½ oz) thinly sliced prosciutto
160 ml (5½ fl oz/⅔ cup) dry white wine

NOTE

Deboning a rabbit is a skill I have yet to master fully. If you are in the same boat, I suggest asking your butcher to prepare it for you.

This can be made ahead of time; keep the stuffed, cooked rabbit whole until needed, then remove the string and cut into thick slices. Heat in a pan with the juices and serve. This is actually easier to slice when it has been able to rest and cool completely as the stuffing doesn't fall out this way.

POLLO ALL'ACETO
VINEGAR CHICKEN

This is an intriguing dish I came across while reading Aldo Santini's *Cucina Maremmana*, a collection of recipes from around Maremma. This book is a wonderful resource of traditional dishes recounted by chefs, home cooks and others, where many recipes of oral tradition have finally been written down.

Santini describes this dish as an ancient one, derived from a method commonly used to cook game, such as wild boar or guinea fowl (the vinegar was not only for flavour, but also preserved the meat). In fact, along with the vinegar, the use of juniper, bay leaves and so many herbs is reminiscent of many traditional wild boar dishes (see *Cinghiale in dolce-forte*, page 55), and they all help to make this sauce so very special. It has become one of my favourite dishes.

The recipe that Santini recounts comes from Igino and Eloge Niccolucci from a hotel and restaurant in Pitigliano called Guastini, where you can dine while overlooking a stunning view of the valley and Pitigliano itself. After the vegetables are cooked, they're puréed to create a creamy sauce to serve over the chicken. It's a more elegant way to have this, but I quite like it rustic and simple, as it is.

1 whole chicken, about 1–1.2 kg (2 lb 3 oz–2 lb 10 oz), chopped into large pieces
3 tablespoons extra-virgin olive oil
1 brown (yellow) onion, finely chopped
1 carrot, finely chopped
½ celery stalk, finely chopped
1 handful fresh herbs such as basil, sage, parsley, oregano, calamint and fennel pollen
3–4 juniper berries
2 bay leaves
80 ml (2½ fl oz/⅓ cup) white wine vinegar
juice of 1 lemon
125 ml (4 fl oz/½ cup) dry white wine

SERVES 4

In a deep casserole pot, brown the chicken pieces (in batches if necessary) in the olive oil over high heat until evenly coloured, about 5–7 minutes. Remove the chicken from the dish and set aside.

To the same dish, add the onion, carrot and celery with a pinch of salt and turn the heat down to low. Cook, stirring occasionally, for about 10 minutes or until the vegetables have softened. Add the herbs, juniper berries and bay leaves, then pour over the vinegar, lemon juice and wine. The liquid will deglaze the pan, so scrape up any wonderful juicy brown bits from the bottom of the pan.

Return the chicken to the pan with the vegetables, add about 500 ml (17 fl oz/2 cups) of water and season with salt and freshly ground black pepper to taste. Bring to a simmer and cook, covered, for 1 hour. Check occasionally, and top up with a little splash of water if needed. Towards the end, check for seasoning.

Serve the chicken with its lovely sauce and any form of bread, potatoes or polenta (for a soft, creamy polenta, see page 106) to soak up the sauce.

SCOTTIGLIA

CHICKEN, GUINEA FOWL AND PORK STEW

The wonderful flavour of *scottiglia* comes from its medley of meats, but also from the bone-in cuts used. There are many versions to be found in Maremma, many of which involve cooking these in a tomato sauce – sometimes just enough for adding a hint of colour, sometimes enough to swim in, a little like a *cacciatora* 'hunter's' stew. But I adore this version *in bianco*, without tomato, and I imagine this is what it would have been like before the sixteenth century, when tomatoes found their way into Italian kitchens.

This is my favourite combination – chicken, guinea fowl and pork – but you can use any meat for *scottiglia*. It's usually made with white meat, which might also include rabbit or turkey, but you'll see it with lamb or even wild boar.

Tuscan gastronome Aldo Santini likens *scottiglia* to Livorno's *cacciucco* (much like Argentario's *Caldaro*, page 110) in that it's an economical miscellany of meats aimed at bulking out the meal with what's available (possibly also leftovers). It was once cooked out in the open, in a large cauldron – not unlike the *caldaro*, where the meat was cooked in order of toughest to most delicate. It was a main meal. The only meal. Where bread was used to sop up the delicious juices and to help fill hungry bellies, and glasses of red wine were obligatory accompaniments.

SERVES 4

- 1 kg (2 lb 3 oz) mixed meat (such as chicken, guinea fowl and pork neck)
- 3 tablespoons extra-virgin olive oil
- 3 whole garlic cloves
- 3 rosemary sprigs
- 1 handful sage leaves
- 2 bay leaves
- 750 ml (25½ fl oz/3 cups) dry white wine
- chilli flakes or chopped fresh red chilli (optional)

Chop the meat into large chunks and season them with salt and pepper.

Heat the olive oil in a wide, deep casserole pot over high heat and brown the meat, in batches, until evenly coloured on all sides. This should take about 5 minutes for each batch.

With the last batch, return the rest of the meat to the pan and add the garlic and herbs, along with a pinch of salt. Pour over the wine and add the chilli (if using). Bring to a simmer, then turn the heat down to low. Cook for 1 hour, turning the meat every 10 minutes or so. The meat should be tender and the wine reduced to a thick sauce. You can top up with a splash of water, or even vegetable stock (see page 161), if needed during cooking.

Serve on top of polenta (see page 106 for a soft, creamy polenta) or with grilled (broiled) crusty bread, possibly rubbed with garlic, along with plenty of the pan juices.

BUGLIONE

LAMB AND TOMATO STEW

The unusual name of this dish makes even Tuscans from outside Maremma respond with an inflective 'Eh?' when they hear it. It seems related to the French word *bouillon*, which means broth, and comes in turn from the word *bouillir* (to boil), both of which could refer to the cooking method of this southern Tuscan dish. But an explanation I like better is that *buglione* (pronounced with a silent g) is also a forgotten Italian word that means a 'confusing mixture' or 'a muddle' – you could use it to describe a dish made with too many unnecessary ingredients or a chaotic situation that involves too many people, for example. From the same root, you have the word *ingarbuglione*, which describes a person who is something of a blunderer. This makes me wonder if the name came about because this dish was a mixture of whatever was at hand (much like *Scottiglia*, page 198). In the case of *buglione*, this is particularly about the herbs and spices added – some like to add at least three different herbs, plus a bit of heat from some chilli. Or was it named for the fact that it's so easy that even the clumsiest person can fumble their way through the recipe? Perhaps it's a bit of both.

SERVES 4

In a deep casserole dish, brown the lamb (in batches if necessary) in the olive oil over high heat until evenly coloured. Don't overcrowd the pan. Brown for approximately 5–10 minutes for each batch.

Add the garlic, chilli and herbs to the meat, and turn the heat to medium. Continue cooking for 1–2 minutes, then add the wine. Let it simmer for about 5–7 minutes, stirring occasionally, then add the tomato. Season with salt and pour over enough water to cover, about 1 litre (34 fl oz/4 cups). Bring to a simmer, then turn the heat down to low. Cook, covered, for 1 hour. Uncover and cook for a further 30 minutes, or until the meat is tender and falling off the bone and the liquid has reduced slightly – it is meant to be quite soupy.

Serve with grilled bread (rubbed with garlic, if you wish) to soak up the sauce.

1 kg (2 lb 3 oz) lamb leg or shoulder, chopped into large chunks
extra-virgin olive oil
3 whole garlic cloves, plus 1 extra garlic clove for rubbing bread (optional)
chilli flakes or sliced fresh red chilli (optional)
2 fresh bay leaves
2 rosemary sprigs
250 ml (8½ fl oz/1 cup) dry red wine
400 g (14 oz) tinned whole tomatoes
thick slices Tuscan bread (or other crusty white loaf), grilled (broiled), for serving

NOTE

In Tuscany, it's uncommon to find conveniently packaged, diced lamb; it's easier to get a leg or shoulder of young lamb. If you don't have a heavy cleaver at home to chop this into large chunks, ask your butcher to do this for you. Alternatively, you can use diced lamb without bones, but as the bone will add flavour to the dish, you could try lamb shanks (1 per person), which is perfect for this type of long, slow cooking.

LA SAGRA

The *sagra* is a proud celebration of local food, traditions and community. It's often run by a local association over a short period, a weekend or two, and it's a whole family (from nonna to grandchild) and neighbourhood effort. Food is the main theme, be it a local ingredient (cherries, bonito, wild boar, porcini mushrooms, chestnuts) or a special dish (polenta, *zuppa di funghi*, *buglione*, *tortelli maremmani*). Quite often there's live music or other entertainment, too.

Sometimes it's just a place to eat, elbow to elbow with others at long communal tables – quite like a temporary, no-frills, outdoor restaurant. Sometimes it involves little stalls of fresh or prepared food along with knick-knacks and souvenirs. Some even have historical events tied to their *sagre*, so that food and tradition come together in unusual ways. In Paganico, near the Ombrone river, they not only have the *sagra della granocchia* (dedicated to the frog), where the gastronomic delights of this traditional speciality of Maremma are enjoyed, but there's also a *palio*, where the quarters of the medieval town race each other while dressed in historic costumes and with live frogs on their wheelbarrows. Whoever gets to the end with the healthiest amphibian still clinging on is the winner.

Between spring and autumn, it seems nearly every little village or town in the Maremma is holding a *sagra*, many of them overlapping each other. In summer, when most of them take place, a visit to a Maremman *sagra* is an obligatory outing. It may not always be perfect food – I've had some of the best and some of the worst meals at *sagre* – and there may be plastic plates, fluorescent lights and mosquitoes, but it's a symbol of summer holidays. There's that festive atmosphere, you can eat outdoors (which in summer means there's more chance of a breeze than eating in your own house), you can meet up with a group of friends or family and no-one has to spend a fortune on a restaurant or wash up afterwards. Many happy memories have been made at *sagre* – here are a couple of my favourites:

Having grown up in Australia, where lamb is an iconic Sunday family dinner, I missed it when I moved to Florence, where you don't often see it on a menu or at the butchers, except at Easter time. But in Maremma, a land of shepherds and cowboys, it's a favourite dish – so much so that they dedicate an annual food festival to it. The *Sagra del Buglione*, on the outskirts of Capalbio, has been around for more than 30 years. There's live music, bouncy castles for the kids, and a smoky outdoor barbecue armed with a group of men in white aprons with hot, glistening faces and a kitchen full of just as many women guarding enormous simmering pots. A marquee houses plenty of long, communal tables to fit everyone in the long queue forming at the ordering counter, and there's cheap local wine and good food representing the best of traditional home cooking from the area. Other than *Buglione* (see page 200), the menu features other classics like *Tortelli maremmani* (page 156), *Rigatoni alla buttera* (page 189), polenta with mushrooms, *Acquacotta* (page 147), grilled sausages and ribs and stewed beans (see page 186). The desserts are all strictly *casalinghi*, or home-made – on offer are things like slices of *Crostata di ricotta* (page 223), tiramisu, *Tozzetti* (page 209) and *Tronco* (page 236).

Capalbio also has a *Sagra di Cinghiale*, held in September every year. It's one of the best known around and is over fifty years old. Wild boar is the main feature and you'll find specialities such as *ammazzafegati* ('liver killers' – charmingly named spicy, wild boar and liver sausages), wild boar *alla cacciatora*, polenta with wild boar stew, and *acquacotta*.

In Porto Ercole on Monte Argentario, the *Sagra della Ficamaschia* is held, as is often the case, at the local football field. It's as no-frills as you can get, but this *sagra* is one of the only occasions when you get to try the speciality of blue whiting, which has such a long history in this little fishing village.

SWEETS

DOLCI

COROLLI ROSSI
RED CROWN BISCUITS

These pretty pink cookies are made in the local bakery at Porto Ercole. When my temperamental oven was short-circuiting the apartment, I'd buy these to have on hand for serving with coffee to visiting friends. Soft and crumbly and smelling of spices, they're always a hit. Traditionally made with lard and lots of eggs, and perfumed with citrus zest, the special ingredient – that bright pink pop of colour – comes from Alchermes, a Florentine liqueur (see page 238).

The name *corollo* comes from the Latin *coronula*, which refers to a crown of flowers. These little crowns are also the name of a similar, ancient Sienese pastry, which had the distinct fragrance of aniseed. It was common for *corolli* or other similar, ring-shaped biscuits, to be strung up with a piece of string and hung like an edible garland across the counter, tempting customers to pluck them off to have with their coffee.

MAKES ABOUT 36 BISCUITS

400 g (14 oz/2⅔ cups) plain (all-purpose) flour
200 g (7 oz/1 cup) sugar
zest of 1 lemon
1 teaspoon baking powder
3 eggs, beaten
60 g (2 oz/¼ cup) melted butter

TOPPING
125 ml (4 fl oz/½ cup) Alchermes
200 g (7 oz/1 cup) sugar

Combine the flour, sugar, lemon zest and baking powder in a large bowl. Add the eggs and (cooled) melted butter and mix to make a firm dough. If you find it's a little crumbly, add a splash of the Alchermes (or some water).

Preheat the oven to 180°C (350°F) and line 1–2 baking trays with baking paper, depending on size.

Take 1 tablespoon of dough and roll into a log about 14 cm (5½ in) long. Bring the ends to meet and, overlapping slightly, press gently together to seal the ring. Continue making rings until you have used all the dough.

Put them on the baking tray (or trays) about 4–5 cm (1½–2 in) apart from each other (they will puff and rise) and bake for 20 minutes, or until they are puffed and pale golden. Remove from the oven and let them cool on a wire rack.

Pour the Alchermes in a small, shallow bowl. Put about a quarter of the sugar in another small, shallow bowl. Dip each cooled *corollo* face down first in the Alchermes (just halfway), then directly into the sugar. (The drips of liqueur will create an even finish on the cookies.) Place them on a tray to dry. As the sugar gets used up, top with fresh sugar.

These will keep several weeks when stored in an airtight container in a cool, dark place.

CIAMBELLINE AL VINO
RED WINE BISCUITS

Delicate and simple, these lovely biscuits are made for dunking into wine, but go just as well dunked into coffee or tea. They're really perfect anytime and seeing as they're made with just a few pantry staples – flour, sugar, olive oil and wine – they can be whipped up at any moment.

They can be made with red or white wine or, if you don't like wine, you can replace with milk. If you have it, a splash of aniseed-scented liqueur is commonly used, too.

MAKES ABOUT 40 BISCUITS

500 g (1 lb 2 oz/3⅓ cups) plain (all-purpose) flour
150 g (5½ oz/¾ cup) sugar, plus extra for topping
½ teaspoon baking soda
125 ml (4 fl oz/½ cup) extra-virgin olive oil
125 ml (4 fl oz/½ cup) red wine

Use your hands to make a soft dough by combining the flour, sugar, baking soda, olive oil and wine together until smooth.

Preheat the oven to 180°C (350°F) and line 1–2 baking trays with baking paper, depending on size.

Take 1 tablespoon of dough and roll into a log a little wider than your palm – about 12 cm (4¾ in) long and 1 cm (½ in) thick. Bring the ends to meet and, overlapping slightly, press gently together to seal the rings.

Put a few tablespoons of sugar in a small shallow bowl or plate and press each ring, face down into the sugar. Place on the baking tray about 2 cm (¾ in) apart from each other.

Bake for 20 minutes or until pale golden and dry to the touch. Remove from the oven and let them cool on a wire rack.

These will keep several weeks when stored in an airtight container in a cool, dark place.

TOZZETTI EBRAICI
JEWISH CINNAMON BISCOTTI

'My aunt made these. My father's family is from Pitigliano. My grandfather was born there. He came to America in 1904.' An American woman called Kathleen Dickey wrote to me when she saw me write about these intensely cinnamon-scented biscotti, 'They all made those *tozzetti* and every Sunday I could smell the cinnamon as I walked in the door for our family dinner.'

I love knowing that this tradition that is holding on by a thread in the ancient place where it was born is alive somewhere else, reviving someone's family memories through that scent of cinnamon wafting through the air.

I've found it difficult to track down any recipes that are even remotely similar to the delicious *tozzetti ebraici* or 'Jewish *tozzetti*' that I picked up one day at the Forno del Ghetto, a bakery at the mouth of the old ghetto in Pitigliano. I was relieved to know that they did indeed exist outside that bakery – but then the thought dawned on me that perhaps, when the last Jewish families left Pitigliano after the Second World War, they took this recipe with them. Though there is no longer a Jewish community in Pitigliano, a handful of Jewish traditions have survived here. There are still *Sfratti* (page 213), Pitigliano's best-known baked good; *pane azzimo* (unleavened matzo or mahtza bread); and these biscotti.

In the biscotti world, almond-studded *cantuccini* are the best known, especially in northern Tuscany around Florence and in Prato, the town where they were born. In southern Maremma, they are *tozzetti*, no doubt a tradition that has seeped over the nearby borders of Lazio and Umbria, where they are also common. They're all similar, of course, but *tozzetti* are usually made with hazelnuts instead of almonds because they are more commonly available. And then there are *mandelbrot* (meaning 'almond bread') – they're Jewish cookies that look remarkably similar to classic Tuscan *cantuccini*, so much so they could be cousins. I can't help but imagine that *tozzetti ebraici* are the result of *mandelbrot* and rustic Maremman *tozzetti* coming together within the ancient stone walls of Pitigliano. The main feature of *tozzetti ebraici* is the cinnamon – there's enough to give these biscotti that hint of coppery brown colour and to perfume the whole house when you pull them out of the oven.

MAKES ABOUT 50 BISCOTTI

3 eggs
250 g (9 oz/1¼ cups) sugar
125 ml (4 fl oz/½ cup) extra-virgin olive oil
470 g (1 lb 1 oz/3 cups) plain (all-purpose) flour, plus extra for dusting
1 teaspoon baking powder
2 teaspoons Dutch (unsweetened) cocoa powder
2 tablespoons ground cinnamon
zest of 1 lemon
200 g (7 oz) whole, peeled hazelnuts

Continued overleaf >

Beat together the eggs and sugar. Add the oil and blend until creamy. Add the flour, baking powder, cocoa powder and cinnamon, and combine to form a dough. If it's too sticky to handle, carefully add a little more flour. You should have a soft dough. Add the lemon zest and nuts towards the end.

Preheat the oven to 180°C (350°F) and line two baking trays with baking paper.

With floured hands, divide the dough into six portions and roll these into thin logs, about 2.5 cm (1 in) in width. Place them on the baking trays with plenty of space between them.

Bake in the oven for 20 minutes. They should appear dry and firm, usually cracked along the top but not browned. Remove from the oven, let them cool for several minutes until you can handle them, and slice with a heavy, sharp knife (not a serrated knife) into biscotti, about 1.5–2 cm (½–¾ in) thick. Return the sliced biscotti to the oven to dry out ever so slightly, about 5 minutes.

Thick and chunky, these are just the thing for dunking into a cup of tea, coffee or dessert wine.

EDDA SERVI MACHLIN AND JEWISH PITIGLIANO

Edda Servi Machlin's cookbook, *The Classic Cuisine of the Italian Jews* (1981), quite simply put, moved me. It's hard to find now as it's out of print and the only second-hand copies that exist are in the US. For interested readers, this book is a goldmine, a snapshot of a culture that no longer exists – in regional Italian cuisine or in Jewish cuisine. Edda's writing and her recipes (many a mixture of Roman or Tuscan Maremman specialities) are the main reason I wanted to visit Pitigliano, where she was born and grew up. Her description of the now 'vanished way of life' that she knew in the 1930s and 1940s – before the Second World War forced Jewish families to escape or go into hiding – is simply wonderful. It's worth seeking out the book for this alone.

Pitigliano is, quite simply, a breathtaking town. When you turn the corner and suddenly see this remarkable city seemingly carved right out of the cliff of tuff rock, like an enormous sculpture rising out of the valley, you will lose your words, mouth open, nothing coming out. As you wander the meandering stone streets down to the tip of the town, where there's nothing but a sheer drop hundreds of metres down towards the valley, you will continue to be lost for words. It's like some kind of fairytale town, beautiful and unreal.

It was, up until Edda's time and the Second World War, one of the most renowned centres of Jewish culture in Europe. In this Maremman town, just 4 kilometres from the border of Lazio, Jewish families had found a safe refuge since the seventeenth century.

Edda was born into an influential Jewish family in Pitigliano in 1926 (her father was the last acting rabbi of the town). When the Second World War broke out, she and her family narrowly escaped the extermination camps by hiding in the hills with partisans. They briefly moved to Florence before settling in America in the 1950s. Edda was encouraged to write her first cookbook by friends and family, and it was published in 1981. Not only does it include a delightful and

fascinating account of growing up in the heart of 'The Little Jerusalem' of Tuscany in the 1930s, but it has a wonderful selection of traditional family recipes – a mix of Tuscan, Roman (her mother was from Rome) and Jewish specialities, such as ricotta-filled pizza, fried artichokes, *pappa al pomodoro pitiglianese*, deep-fried mozzarella sandwiches, gnocchi *alla romana* (baked semolina gnocchi) and the famous Italian-Jewish *cuscussù* (couscous with meatballs and stuffed vegetables).

A number of recipes in this book are inspired by her, including the *Tortino di carciofi* (page 140) and lemon-marinated fillets of sole (page 123). You can also make her *migliaccini*, which are described as a variation in the recipe for *Ciaffagnoni* (page 179).

SFRATTI
HONEY AND NUT PASTRIES

There are still a handful of bakeries and little shops in Pitigliano that sell these stick-shaped, hardy rolls of pastry filled with walnuts and honey. These delicious pastries are the town's most famous gastronomic tradition, and have survived despite their origins in the Jewish community, which no longer exists in Pitigliano.

The pastry's name comes from the Italian word for eviction, *sfratto*, and it is no coincidence that their stick-like appearance matches that of the batons once used by authorities attempting to evict Jews from their community.

Edda Servi Machlin writes, 'Much of Jewish food lore is based on reproducing, in a sweet form, some symbolic item of unhappy events of the past as a reminder of the constant and dreadful danger of their recurrence and also to ward off such a possibility.' Almost like a good luck charm. In fact, even the non-Jewish Pitiglianesi adopted this idea, and *sfratti* became a must-have to serve at weddings and other special occasions, for good fortune.

This recipe is adapted from Edda Servi Machlin's in *The Classic Cuisine of the Italian Jews*. Sometimes you'll find the pastry made like a shortcrust pastry, which would be crumblier and softer and some like to brush the *sfratti* with beaten egg yolk for a shiny glaze. But I like this one of Edda's, which is hard (almost brittle), but thin and so basic. It is more like the ones I've tried from Pitigliano.

MAKES 6 SFRATTI

PASTRY

350 g (12½ oz/2⅓ cups) plain (all-purpose) flour
150 g (5½ oz/¾ cup) sugar
pinch of salt
125 ml (4 fl oz/½ cup) dry white wine
80 ml (2½ fl oz/⅓ cup) olive oil

FILLING

350 g (12½ oz/1 cup) honey
½ teaspoon ground cinnamon
¼ teaspoon ground cloves
¼ teaspoon ground black pepper
¼ teaspoon ground nutmeg
finely grated zest of 1 orange
350 g (12½ oz) shelled walnuts, chopped very finely
2 tablespoons fine breadcrumbs

For the pastry, combine the flour, sugar and salt in a bowl and make a well in the centre. Add the wine and the oil into the well and whisk the mixture together with a fork, moving from the centre outwards, gradually incorporating more dry ingredients. You want a smooth but quite firm dough. Knead for a few minutes, then roll into a disc shape (with a flattened top), cover and set aside to rest for 30 minutes.

To make the filling, put the honey in a saucepan and melt over high heat (watch carefully that it doesn't bubble over). Add the spices, orange zest and nuts, and cook for 3 minutes. Remove the saucepan from the heat and add the breadcrumbs, then transfer to a bowl to let the mixture cool, turning occasionally to speed up the cooling process – it will be very thick and sticky. When cool enough to handle, divide the honey and nut mixture into six portions. I find a knife works best for this. With wet hands, shape the filling into logs about 2.5 cm (1 in) thick.

Continued overleaf >

Preheat the oven to 190ºC (375ºF) and line a baking tray with baking paper.

Divide the dough into six portions. With a rolling pin, roll out strips about 10 x 25 cm (4 x 10 in). Put a honey and nut log in the middle of the strip (make sure there is a little space for both ends of the 'log' to be sealed) and wrap the dough around it, overlapping slightly, to cover all the filling completely. Roll the entire pastry with both hands to seal and even out the dough, then place on the baking tray, seal side down. Press down on the ends to seal and tuck the extra pastry underneath.

Continue with the rest of the dough and filling.

Bake in the oven for 20 minutes or until the dough is still quite pale but dry to the touch. Let it cool completely.

Wrap the cooled *sfratti* in aluminium foil; they keep well like this for weeks without refrigeration (there are no eggs or dairy in this recipe). If you can wait, they taste better a day or two later. Cut into 1 cm (½ in) thick rounds and serve with coffee, but more traditional would be with a glass of vin santo or other dessert wine.

CASTAGNACCIO
CHESTNUT FLOUR CAKE

Castagnaccio is often called a 'cake' in English translations but it's really somewhere between a slice and a dense, thick crêpe (for a real 'chestnut cake', I would see the one on page 232). The smooth, dense texture of this ancient, rustic Tuscan delicacy is quite difficult to describe to those who have never come across it before. I can only compare it to Japanese sweets, such as *yokan* (which is made of azuki bean paste), which I gobbled up at any opportunity when I was a child (and I still do).

This is one of those dishes that you either love or hate. The flavour of chestnuts seems to be intensified in flour form, so you must love chestnuts to enjoy this. Most of the sweetness comes from the natural flavour of the ground, dried chestnuts and the sultanas, so it is not overly sweet. Ancient versions of this recipe don't even include sugar (it would have been too much of a luxury for a peasant dish like this one), but today a few spoonfuls usually make their way in there and it is still, quite pleasingly, subtle.

On its own, *castagnaccio* is in its most rustic state, and eaten in small slices is perfect with a glass of vin santo (Tuscan dessert wine) or young red wine. You can transform it into a dessert by topping it with slightly sweetened whipped cream or some very fresh, slightly sweetened ricotta, whipped to make it fluffier – the ricotta version is my absolute favourite way to have it.

MAKES 1 CAKE, SERVES 8

Combine the chestnut flour, sugar (if using) and salt in a bowl. Add the water, bit by bit, stirring with a wooden spoon or whisk to avoid lumps. You are looking for a batter that will run off the back of a spoon, much like pancake batter. Depending on the quality of the flour, you may need a little more or a little less water than called for to obtain this consistency.

When smooth, add 2 tablespoons of olive oil and the orange zest to the batter and mix it in. Allow the mixture to rest at least 30 minutes (or overnight).

Preheat the oven to 180ºC (350ºF) and line a 30 cm (12 in) round pizza tray with baking paper. Alternatively, you can use a rectangular baking tray of similar dimensions.

Soak the sultanas, nuts and rosemary in cold water for 15 minutes. Drain.

Pour the batter into the round pizza tray (or rectangular baking tray). The

CASTAGNACCIO
300 g (10½ oz/3 cups) chestnut flour, sifted
2 tablespoons sugar (optional)
pinch of salt
500 ml (17 fl oz/2 cups) cold water
3 tablespoons olive oil
60 g (2 oz/½ cup) sultanas (golden raisins)
40 g (1½ oz/¼ cup) pine nuts (or walnuts)
1 rosemary sprig, leaves picked
zest of 1 orange

RICOTTA CREAM
250 g (9 oz/1 cup) ricotta
2 tablespoons sugar
finely grated zest of 1 lemon

Continued overleaf >

batter should be not much more than 1 cm (½ in) high. Evenly scatter over the sultanas and nuts, the rosemary leaves and the rest of the olive oil.

Bake in the oven for about 30 minutes, or until you begin to see little cracks appear all over the top. Do not over-bake or it will become very dry. Let it cool in the pan, then cut it into wedges.

To make the ricotta cream, whisk the ricotta, sugar and lemon zest together in a bowl. Chill until needed.

Serve the *castagnaccio* on its own or with a dollop of ricotta cream. This is best on the day it is baked, so share it around. However, it does keep for a day in an airtight container at room temperature. It's best not to store it in the refrigerator as it tends to get hard and rubbery when chilled.

NOTE
Try to use a tray similar to the dimensions given in the recipe. Otherwise, just be aware of the thickness as you are pouring the batter into the pan. If it's too thin, it can come out too dry; too thick and it will be dense and, dare I say, claggy. (In Livorno they have a thicker version, which is known as toppone *and is generally considered less refined than proper* castagnaccio*).*

PAGNOTELLA
FIG AND CHOCOLATE BREAD

This wonderful speciality of Porto Santo Stefano on Monte Argentario is halfway between a fruit cake and something dense and chocolatey, like brownies. It's the kind of thing that you can't find in shops or restaurants or even in cookbooks – it's made at home by those who know the tradition best: *nonna*.

I asked a few friends from Porto Santo Stefano if they had a good recipe for *pagnotella* that I could try and they all came back to me with cherished, handwritten family recipes from their mother or *nonna*, each of them slightly different. Alessandra's *nonna* makes this with some grated apple for moisture and keeps the chocolate in huge square-inch sized cubes, resulting in decadent pockets of melted chocolate like molten lava. Orestina makes a version with bread dough and insists on using homemade plum jam (very typical of Argentario, she notes). Valeria's mother, Filomena, cooks dried figs in vermouth for her *pagnotella*, which otherwise is very similar to Alessandra's *nonna*'s. The one thing most recipes have in common is that the amount of flour called for is *quanto basta*, or as much as is needed. This means enough to bring the sticky mixture together into a soft dough.

This recipe is inspired mostly by Alessandra's *nonna*'s recipe. It's quite soft, decadent and fruity – not to mention chocolatey. You only need a very thin slice of this, served with some dessert wine. It's traditionally made around Christmas time (these flavours and scents are particularly loved at this time of year) and, much like *panforte* or fruit cake, would make a nice gift for friends and family, too.

Pagnotella is either made as one large loaf or a few buns, dusted in flour before being baked to set. A variation is to mix all the ingredients into bread dough instead of just flour so that you have a rather hard, dense fruit and nut loaf. All versions keep a very long time and just get better as they age.

MAKES 1 LOAF, SERVES 12

Soak the figs in the wine overnight. Put the soaked figs with all the liquid in a small saucepan and add the grated apple. Bring to a simmer and cook over low–medium heat until the fruit is soft and the liquid has reduced slightly, about 15 minutes. Blend in a food processor or with a hand-held blender until paste-like. Let it cool.

Transfer the fig mixture to a large bowl and add the rest of the ingredients

250 g (9 oz/1⅔ cups) dried figs, roughly chopped
500 ml (17 fl oz/2 cups) white wine
¼ apple, peeled, cored and grated
zest of 1 orange
50 g (1¾ oz/⅓ cup) sultanas (golden raisins)
50 g (1¾ oz/⅓ cup) pine nuts
50 g (1¾ oz/½ cup) walnut kernels
50 g (1¾ oz/⅓ cup) whole almonds
50 g (1¾ oz) hazelnuts, peeled but whole
2 tablespoons Dutch (unsweetened) cocoa powder
100 g (3½ oz/⅔ cup) dark chocolate (70% cocoa), chopped roughly
2 tablespoons plum jam
¼ teaspoon ground cinnamon
¼ teaspoon ground nutmeg
100 g (3½ oz/⅔ cup) plain (all-purpose) flour, plus more for dusting

NOTE
I find 100 g (3½ oz) of flour is enough, but all flours are different, and all figs will likely be different too, so use this as a guideline. You might find that your dough can take a lot more.

Continued overleaf >

except for the flour and combine. Add the flour in a few stages until you have a soft and sticky mixture that has the consistency of bread dough – you may need to add a bit more or a bit less.

Preheat the oven to 160°C (320°F), line a baking tray with baking paper and dust the top with flour.

Directly on the baking tray, use floured hands to shape the dough into a round loaf around 20 cm (8 in) wide and flatten it until it's about 5 cm (2 in) tall in the centre. Dust liberally with flour on the top and blow off the excess. Bake in the oven for 25–30 minutes, or until the flour on the tray turns a cappuccino-coloured brown and the bread feels firm.

This delicious bread lasts ages and ages and ages. It's best to keep it in an airtight container, and stored somewhere cool and dry.

SUBSTITUTIONS
If you don't have plum jam, you can use another dark jam such as grape or fig, or even substitute completely with honey. I like this even mixture of different nuts, but you could cut it down to one or two kinds. Just choose 200 g (7 oz) of any nuts – my friend Orestina likes to use just almonds, for example. You can also use red wine for cooking the figs. Sometimes you'll see this bread in a stick shape – a long loaf rather than a round one.

FIGS AND BREAD

I first tasted *panficato*, the little brother to *pagnotella*, on Giglio Island, which you can reach by a short ferry ride from Porto Santo Stefano. I was instantly hooked. *Panficato* (literally, 'fig bread') is sold in the form of heavy little buns, speckled with fig seeds and sporting smooth, shiny tops, perhaps with some blanched almonds pushed into the top for decoration.

One bakery in Giglio's port, Panificio Di Cristina, proudly displays the speciality's history on a sign out the front. It claims its origins date to 1544, when the powerful Ottoman admiral, Hayreddin Barbarossa – who is always referred to as a pirate in Italian (his nickname Barbarossa means 'Red Beard') – sacked the island and took the inhabitants of Giglio away as slaves. The Medici, the sign continues, later repopulated the island with Sienese who began the tradition of making panficato much like Siena's panforte, but with the ingredients that were available on the island.

It is quite clear that *panficato* and Porto Santo Stefano's *pagnotella* are related to each other and are connected to Siena's *panforte*, a rich, dense treat with medieval roots. With a similar texture, *panforte* is also made quite simply with whole nuts, plenty of spices, honey and candied fruit (rather than dried fruit), all held together with some flour. Both *panficato* and *pagnotella* are made with dried figs, soaked or cooked in wine (traditionally local ansonica wine), mashed or blended to a paste, then mixed with flour, sultanas, cocoa or chocolate, whole nuts like almonds, walnuts, hazelnuts and pine nuts, honey or homemade jam and spices.

CROSTATA DI RICOTTA E PERE COSCIA
RICOTTA AND BABY PEAR TART

In the summertime you find baby pears (known as *pere coscia* in Italian) all over the local farmers markets around Argentario. Yellow-skinned, a little firmer and crunchier than regular pears, they make great toddler-sized snacks that cause minimal mess, which is one of the reasons we love them. I've also been looking for a way to cook with them, for those occasions when we don't eat them fast enough (fruit ripens so quickly in a warm, summer kitchen). So along came this tart.

Ricotta *crostata* is a favourite dessert in these parts – perhaps dotted with chocolate chips (page 228) or layered with lip-smacking sour cherry jam or compote made from visciole cherries (*Prunus cerasus*). It's from a tradition more notably found in Lazio and, especially Rome, where it is a well-known dessert of the Jewish Ghetto. In this part of the Maremma – which is closer to Rome than Florence, and is home to villages with a strong Jewish history, such as Pitigliano – it's easy to find these influences.

This very simple dessert is not overly sweet and is pretty enough to present to guests. The pears are briefly poached in water with a squeeze of lemon juice until just tender but not too soft. The pie dish is layered with the shortcrust pastry dough and smooth ricotta filling and the poached pears are carefully pushed one by one into the filling. Once baked, the tart is best when left to settle overnight in the fridge and eaten the next day – chilled if it's summer, and room temperature otherwise.

MAKES 1 TART, SERVES 8

Peel the baby pears. Leave the stems on (I don't core them, as they are so small and tender they don't need it). Slice about 5 mm (¼ in) off the bottom of the pear, so that they have flat bottoms to sit on. Roughly chop the pear offcuts and leave aside to add to the ricotta mixture. If you're making this dish with regular sized pears, peel and slice them into quarters and remove the core (if they are particularly large pears, you can slice into eighths).

Slide the pears into a saucepan of simmering water with the sugar to add a touch of sweetness to them. Cook for 15 minutes, or until they are just tender. Remove the pears, drain and let them cool.

To make the pastry, combine the flour, sugar and butter together in a bowl. Using your fingers, rub together until there are no more visible

icing (confectioners') sugar,
    to serve (optional)

POACHED PEARS
7–9 baby pears
55 g (2 oz/¼ cup) sugar

PASTRY
250 g (9 oz/1⅔ cups) plain
    (all-purpose) flour
100 g (3½ oz/½ cup) caster
    (superfine) sugar
125 g (4½ oz/½ cup) cold
    butter, chopped
pinch of salt
1 egg, plus 1 egg yolk

FILLING
500 g (1 lb 2 oz/2 cups) ricotta
100 g (3½ oz/½ cup) caster
    (superfine) sugar
zest of 1 lemon
1 teaspoon vanilla extract
    (or scraped seeds of
    ½ vanilla pod)
2 eggs

NOTE
If you can't find baby pears, you can make this with regular pears. Choose firm rather than ripe pears, which hold their shape better. This tart would work nicely with halved and seeded apricots or plums (though these would not need to be poached).

Continued overleaf >

pieces of butter (or you can pulse in a food processor). Add the salt and egg plus yolk and combine until it comes together into a smooth ball. Cover and put in fridge to chill for 30 minutes, then roll out on a lightly floured surface to about 3 mm (⅛ in) thick. Lay over a 22–25 cm (8¾–10 in) round pie dish and trim the borders. Prick the surface gently all over with the tines of a fork.

Preheat the oven to 180°C (350°F).

To make the filling, combine the ricotta, caster sugar, lemon zest, vanilla and eggs, and mix until smooth. Pour over the pastry-lined pie dish and smooth over. Carefully push the pears into the ricotta filling, then bake in the oven for 45 minutes, or until the top is firm and slightly coloured golden brown and the pastry crust is golden.

Let it cool completely before serving and, if you like, just at the last moment sprinkle over some icing sugar – this will mostly sink into the surface of the ricotta and the pears, so you won't see much of it, but it will add a hint of sticky sweetness.

Store this tart in the refrigerator and eat within 2–3 days.

HOT WEATHER PASTRY MAKING
If you're trying to roll out pastry in the hot, sweltering summer, and find that it's melting before your eyes, try placing a couple of bags of frozen peas (or similar, even ice packs) directly onto the surface where you plan to roll the pastry out for about 10 minutes to chill it. Always chill your pastry before using it (letting it rest in the fridge for 1 hour is ideal). You might even go so far as to put the rolling pin in the freezer to give it some chill. The idea is to keep the pastry (and the butter in it) cold so that you can work with it more easily.

NOTE
If you have some leftover pastry, roll out to make mini tart bases that you can blind bake in a muffin tin or cut out cookies with it that you can decorate with icing or layer with jam. It's a versatile dough that also freezes very well – nice to have for a rainy day baking project.

CROSTATA DI RICOTTA E CIOCCOLATO
RICOTTA AND CHOCOLATE TART

Dotted with chocolate pieces, this classic ricotta tart is almost like stracciatella gelato, and scented with just a hint of rum. It's a simple tart, but you could easily make little adjustments to tailor-make it to your taste. You can substitute the chocolate with raisins and soak them in the rum for a while before adding to the ricotta, or you could add a thick layer of sour cherry jam to the base before smoothing the chocolate-speckled ricotta on top. Another option for fellow chocolate lovers is to add some cocoa powder – about 50 g (1¾ oz) – to the pastry to make this tart base a chocolate one.

MAKES 1 TART, SERVES 8

To make the pastry, combine the flour, sugar and butter together in a bowl. Using your fingers, rub together until there are no more visible pieces of butter (or you can pulse in a food processor). Add the salt and egg plus yolk and combine until it comes together into a smooth ball. Cover and put in the fridge to chill for 30 minutes, then roll out on a lightly floured surface to about 3 mm (⅛ in) thick. See page 225 for tips on pastry making in hot weather.

Press the dough into a 22 cm (8¾ in) round springform cake tin, leaving the sides about 4 cm (1½ in) high. Prick the surface gently all over with the tines of a fork. Roll out the rest of the dough into a rectangular shape, 3 mm (⅛ in) thick, and cut long strips with a fluted pastry roller or sharp knife. Set aside.

Preheat the oven to 180°C (350°F).

To make the filling, combine the ricotta, sugar, eggs, rum and citrus zest, and mix until smooth. Add the chopped chocolate, then fill the dough-lined cake tin with the mixture and smooth over. Use the long strips of dough to make a criss-cross lattice top. Trim the edges with a sharp knife so that you have an even border and where the lattice meets the sides of the tart, press the edges down well to seal.

Bake in the oven for about 45 minutes, or until the top is firm and well-browned and the pastry crust golden. Let it cool completely before serving. In fact, I like this best when it has even had a bit of time to be chilled. If you like, just before serving, dust the top of the tart with icing sugar.

Store this tart in the refrigerator and eat within 2–3 days.

icing (confectioners') sugar, to serve (optional)

PASTRY
250 g (9 oz/1⅔ cups) plain (all-purpose) flour
100 g (3½ oz/½ cup) caster (superfine) sugar
125 g (4½ oz/½ cup) cold butter, chopped
pinch of salt
1 egg, plus 1 egg yolk

FILLING
500 g (1 lb 2 oz/2 cups) ricotta
170 g (6 oz/¾ cup) caster (superfine) sugar
2 eggs
2 tablespoons rum
finely grated zest of 1 lemon or orange
80 g (2¾ oz/½ cup) dark chocolate, finely chopped (or chocolate chips)

TORTA DI LIMONE E RICOTTA
LEMON AND RICOTTA CAKE

This is a *dolce casalingo*, the kind of homemade cake you would find sitting on someone's kitchen counter. It's a sturdy cake with a good crumb, not too sweet or showy, with a subtle hint of lemon. It's the perfect vehicle for dunking, and plain enough to make an ideal Italian breakfast, together with a deep, oversized mug of caffe latte.

Also known as the *torta del tre*, or the 'cake of three', it's a recipe I make a lot because it's quick and so very simple to remember (once you learn the main ingredients, you never really need to look at it again). It's also an extremely forgiving cake, so whether you make it round, rectangular or decide to add something new to it (a drizzle of lemon or rosemary icing, perhaps, see page 232), it's a nice one to have lying around at home, inviting children and adults alike to take thick slices of it with its simple, homely look.

MAKES 1 CAKE, SERVES 8

Preheat the oven to 180°C (350°F). Grease a 22 cm (8¾ in) round cake tin or an 11 x 26 cm (4¼ x 10¼ in) loaf (bar) tin and line it with baking paper.

In a clean, large bowl (preferably glass or ceramic), beat the egg whites with an electric beater until soft peaks form.

In a separate bowl, beat the egg yolks with the sugar and ricotta for 1–2 minutes, until creamy. Add the lemon juice and zest. Fold in the flour and baking powder and finally the whites.

Fold in the milk. Depending on the quality and firmness of your ricotta, you may find it is quite a dense batter – you may wish to add a splash more milk to loosen it.

Pour into the tin and bake for approximately 45–55 minutes, or until golden and springy on top. A skewer poked through the middle should come out clean.

Serve just as is with tea or coffee, for breakfast or as a snack. Store any leftovers in an airtight container in the fridge, it will keep for 3-4 days.

3 eggs, separated
300 g (10½ oz/1½ cups) caster (superfine) sugar
300 g (10½ oz/1¼ cups) ricotta
juice and zest of 1 lemon
300 g (10½ oz/2 cups) plain (all-purpose) flour
1½ teaspoons baking powder
3 tablespoons milk, or as needed

NOTE
Because this cake uses ricotta as the fat, rather than butter or oil, it's a good idea to choose a full-fat ricotta for flavour and texture. If you can, sheep's milk ricotta is preferable – it's a little richer, has more flavour and is more traditional than cow's milk ricotta in the Maremma. Try to buy the kind of ricotta that is very fresh, made as traditionally as possible (in other words, from whey) and that could stand on its own.

TORTA DI MELE E MARMELLATA
APPLE AND JAM CAKE

This soft, buttery loaf cake, with chopped apple and apricot jam swirled through the top, is essentially a dressed-up pound cake (Italians charmingly call it a 'plum cake', using the English words but pronouncing the 'u' as 'oo'.) It's inspired by a cake that I succumbed to more than once at Il Forno del Porto, my local bakery in Porto Ercole, especially during times when the oven at home was off limits. As we made the rounds of the port on our daily ritual, picking up groceries from the *fruttivendolo* (fruit and vegetable shop) or the *pescheria* (fish shop), my toddler, usually dressed in a tutu of some kind, would always be given something from shop owners – in the *forno* it was one of their little pink or white meringues, as fluffy and light as a cloud.

Highly adaptable, this cake can be made in many different ways. I often combined polenta with the regular flour for a rustic cake with a good crumb. You can leave out the apple or exchange it for another fruit (pear, apricots, berries or plums would all be nice). Just don't skimp on whipping the eggs – it's what makes this cake so soft and fluffy without any other rising agents.

MAKES 1 CAKE, SERVES 8

Preheat the oven to 170°C (340°F). Grease an 11 x 26 cm (4¼ x 10¼ in) loaf (bar) tin and line with baking paper.

Use an electric beater to cream the butter and sugar with the lemon zest until pale and creamy. Add the eggs one by one, beating well after each. Once all the eggs are in, beat continuously until very, very pale and fluffy. This takes about 7 minutes with electric beaters.

Fold in the flour carefully until it is just combined. Pour into the loaf tin, drop in the diced apple and use a butter knife to swirl through the mixture gently to distribute. Smooth over the top, then dollop the jam down the middle of the cake. Using a (clean!) knife, pointing vertically down about 2–3 cm (¾–1¼ in) into the batter, swirl the jam in a zigzag pattern.

Bake for approximately 1 hour, or until golden on top and a wooden skewer inserted in the middle comes out clean. If the jam on top begins to look like it's darkening or cooking too quickly, you can cover the cake loosely with some aluminium foil. When cool, dust with icing sugar, if desired.

Serve in thick slices. Store any leftovers in an airtight container in the fridge, it will keep for 3-4 days.

---

250 g (9 oz/1 cup) butter, at room temperature
250 g (9 oz/1¼ cups) sugar
zest of 1 lemon
4 eggs, at room temperature
250 g (9 oz/1⅔ cups) plain (all-purpose) flour
1 apple, cored, peeled and diced
3 tablespoons apricot jam
icing (confectioners') sugar, for garnish (optional)

NOTE

To bring your eggs and butter to room temperature, sit them out on the kitchen counter for at least 30 minutes. I like to chop the butter first to help it along. If you forget to do this (I am guilty of this all the time), do not just use them cold. Put the eggs in a stainless steel bowl full of very warm water for 5 minutes. Instead of chopping the butter, grate it with a cheese grater and leave it spread out on a tray for 5 minutes.

CIAMBELLONE ALLE CASTAGNE
CHESTNUT FLOUR BUNDT CAKE

Where there are chestnut trees, there are chestnuts prepared and eaten in all manner of ways. Chestnut flour has always been a good way to make chestnuts last through the winter months and beyond, and while *Castagnaccio* (page 216) is the most well-known and traditional way to use it in Tuscany, chestnut flour is also used in cakes and pasta, just like regular flour. In the case of cakes, it's best when mixed with regular plain flour as it doesn't have gluten and has a rather dense texture when cooked. But even a little is enough to lend the cake that distinct smell and flavour of chestnuts, and a pastel caffe-latte colour.

This ring-shaped cake is known as *Ciambellone dell'Amiata*, referring to the use of chestnut flour from the volcanic Mount Amiata. It's an area well known for its chestnuts, which even have IGP (Protected Geographical Indication) status, meaning they are recognised for their quality. The rosemary icing is my addition to this otherwise traditional cake. It gives the cake a pretty finish and I love the flavour of rosemary in Tuscan cakes and breads.

MAKES 1 CAKE, SERVES 10

Preheat the oven to 170ºC (340ºF). Grease a 25 cm (10 in) ring (bundt) tin with melted butter or olive oil. Tip in some flour and tap the tin to distribute a very fine, even layer all over the inside of the tin. Set aside.

Use an electric mixer to cream the butter and sugar with the orange zest until pale and creamy. Add the eggs one by one, beating well after each.

Combine the flours and baking powder in a bowl and fold these dry ingredients into the batter carefully, alternating with the milk, until just combined. Add the rum (if using) and fold through carefully. Pour the batter into the tin.

Bake in the oven for about 30 minutes, or until golden on top and a wooden skewer inserted in the middle comes out clean. Remove and let the cake cool in the tin before turning out onto a plate. You can eat it simply like this or, for a non-traditional addition, you can try adding my light, runny rosemary-scented glaze. Simply rub the rosemary into the icing sugar, then stir through just enough warm water to make it quite runny, about 2 teaspoons. Drizzle over the cake.

150 g (5½ oz/⅔ cup) butter, at room temperature
200 g (7 oz/1 cup) sugar
zest of 1 orange
4 eggs, at room temperature
150 g (5½ oz/1½ cups) chestnut flour, sifted
250 g (9 oz/1⅔ cups) plain (all-purpose) flour
1½ teaspoons baking powder
125 ml (4 fl oz/½ cup) milk
2 tablespoons rum (optional)

ICING

1 tablespoon rosemary, leaves picked
50 g (1¾ oz) icing (confectioners') sugar, sifted
2 teaspoons warm water

VARIATIONS

You can use 125 ml (4 fl oz/½ cup) of olive oil in place of the butter, or lemon zest instead of the orange zest. The milk can be replaced with water, so if you wanted to, this recipe could easily be dairy-free. Instead of the rum, you can use brandy or any aniseed-scented liqueur, or leave it out altogether.

TRONCO AL CIOCCOLATO
CHOCOLATE-FILLED SPONGE ROLL

Tronco is a favourite cake along the Tuscan coast and you find it all the way to the very top part of the Maremma, the Etruscan coast, in Cecina. It literally means 'log' or 'trunk', and is almost always stained pink with Alchermes and filled with a rich chocolate cream or even chocolate-hazelnut spread. I find the latter too sweet and rich, and prefer it with a dark chocolate pastry cream.

The sponge recipe, one of my favourites, is slightly adapted from my friend Emma Gardner's recipe – she is much more technical than me in the pastry department and I have simplified it somewhat, but it's the recipe I use most. I even make this *tronco* for Christmas. I double the recipe for two rolls and turn them into a yule log, decorating with a thick, chocolate icing, crumbled meringue for snow and candied rosemary.

MAKES 1 SPONGE ROLL, SERVES 6

For the pastry cream, melt the dark chocolate either in a microwave or over a bain marie (double broiler).

Use an electric mixer to whisk the yolks and sugar together until pale. Stir in the cornflour. Put the mixture in a saucepan over low heat and slowly add the milk, little by little. (If your lowest burner is still quite aggressive, do this over a bain marie or double broiler so the eggs don't curdle from being heated too rapidly.) Stir continuously with a wooden spoon or silicone spatula until the mixture becomes smooth and thick and coats the back of a spoon, about 10 minutes. Remove from the heat and stir through the melted chocolate. When it is smooth and well combined, cool quickly by spreading the pastry cream out into a shallow, flat container such as a glass lasagne dish or baking tray. Place a layer of parchment paper right over the top of the pastry cream, so the entire surface is in contact with the paper. This will ensure the pastry cream doesn't develop a skin. Keep in the refrigerator until needed.

Preheat the oven to 160°C (320°F) and line a 23 x 33 cm (9 x 13 in) baking tray with baking paper.

To make the sponge, sift the cornflour and flour together. Put the separated eggs in two clean metal or glass mixing bowls, yolks in one and whites in the other. Whisk the egg yolks and the sugar with an electric mixer or electric egg beaters for up to 10 minutes, or until the yolks become very pale and creamy. Clean the beaters very well, then whisk the whites until stiff peaks form. To the creamy egg yolks, gently fold in half

2 tablespoons caster (superfine) sugar for dusting
125 ml (4 fl oz/½ cup) Alchermes
icing (confectioners') sugar for dusting

CHOCOLATE PASTRY CREAM
100 g (3½ oz/⅔ cup) 70% cocoa dark chocolate
2 egg yolks
60 g (2 oz/¼ cup) caster (superfine) sugar
1 tablespoon cornflour (corn starch), sifted
250 ml (8½ fl oz/1 cup) warm milk

SPONGE
50 g (1¾ oz/⅓ cup) cornflour (corn starch) or potato starch
50 g (1¾ oz/⅓ cup) plain (all-purpose) flour
3 eggs, separated
100 g (3½ oz/½ cup) caster (superfine) sugar

TIP
If at any point you start to see lumps appearing in the pastry cream, remove the pan from the heat and stir vigorously. You can also strain out the lumps using a fine mesh sieve.

Continued overleaf >

of the whites and then half of the flours, and repeat with the remaining whites and flours until they are all combined.

Pour the batter into the lined baking tray – the batter should be about 1 cm (½ in) high. (You can also use a flat tray and spread the batter out to the size you like with a palette knife.) Bake in the oven for about 10–12 minutes, or until the top is very pale golden and springy in the middle.

Remove the sponge from the oven and let it cool ever so slightly so you can handle it easily – you still want to work with it while it's warm. Spread out a sheet of parchment paper or a clean tea towel (dish towel) and scatter it evenly with the caster sugar (this helps to stop the sponge from sticking to the paper or tea towel). Gently turn the sponge upside down onto the parchment paper or tea towel. Remove the baking paper to reveal a spongy soft cake. With a bread knife, trim the edges – this will stop the sides from cracking as they roll. Then, with a pastry brush, stain this side of the sponge evenly with Alchermes (see note for non-alcoholic version). You may have to do a couple of 'coats' for a bright pink. Take the cooled pastry cream out of the refrigerator and generously spread it over the top of the pink sponge so that it is about 1.5 cm (½ in) thick, smoothing out evenly and leaving a 1 cm (½ in) border around the edges.

The rolling part is rather like rolling sushi, if you've done it. The tricky part is really in starting the roll – the rest is all about the right amount of pressure (not too tight, but not too loose). Picking up the short end of the sponge with the help of the parchment paper or tea towel, carefully roll the entire thing up firmly and then secure by wrapping completely in the parchment paper or tea towel. Keep in the fridge to chill for 1 hour or overnight.

Remove the parchment paper or tea towel carefully, dust the top with icing sugar and serve in thick slices.

ALCHERMES
Alchermes is a scarlet-tinged alcohol that dates back to the Renaissance and is almost exclusively used for staining desserts the same vivid pink colour, such as in the Corolli rossi *(red crown biscuits, page 206),* zuccotto *or the trifle-like* zuppa inglese. *The best version is one that you can find in the pharmacy of Florence's Santa Maria Novella church. Here it has been made for centuries by the monks and was once touted as a long life elixir, used to cure palpitations of the heart, measles and, supposedly, revive 'weary spirits'. Flavoured with spices such as cinnamon, vanilla, cloves and nutmeg, it also has a strong balsamic and medicinal character. It is turned scarlet by a natural red dye, made from the infusion of dried insects, kermes (hence the name) or cochineal.*

NOTE
If you don't have Alchermes, you can make a rum (or other liqueur) syrup by bringing 125 ml (4 fl oz/½ cup) of water and 125 g (4½ oz) of sugar to a boil. Turn down to low and let simmer for 10 minutes, remove from the heat and add 2 tablespoons of rum. This is rather nice with a twist of orange peel added to the boiling syrup, too. For a non-boozy version, leave out the rum and just use the simple syrup to add moisture to the sponge – this will help it take and hold shape.

FICHI CANDITI
CARAMELISED FIGS

This is a delicious and elegant way to preserve fresh figs whole, in syrup. It's a little like fig jam, only with less sugar and rather than a mush of figs, here they are barely touched, so they are beautifully and perfectly whole.

As they cook, the figs begin to give way entirely, becoming soft and very malleable. The sugar begins to melt and the figs release their own juices, so that eventually the figs become covered in syrup. Then the figs themselves change colour as the syrup permeates them. The skin becomes glossy and transparent, the figs take on a slightly darker, caramel colour. When you cut into one of these plump, soft, syrupy figs, out pours the jam.

Caramelised figs are rather special with soft cheeses as part of a cheese platter, or with good fresh ricotta, natural yoghurt or just stolen right out of the jar, as is. You can also make them a tiny bit boozy by adding a splash of cognac or brandy to the syrup once taken off the heat.

In southern Tuscany, green figs (which seem to grow everywhere and anywhere, rising out of stone walls or cracks in the concrete) are most common, but you could use any fig for this. Just make sure they aren't bruised, split or overly ripe. In fact, this is a good recipe for slightly under-ripe figs – they hold their shape very well when cooked this way.

MAKES 2 X 250 ML (8½ FL OZ/1 CUP) JARS

1 kg (2 lb 3 oz) figs
1 lemon (organic or unwaxed)
200 g (7 oz/1 cup) sugar
splash of cognac or brandy (optional)

The night before, rinse the figs carefully and place them tightly together, bottoms down, in an even layer in a heavy-bottomed pot (one that you would use for jamming). If you need to make two layers, just make sure the figs are still carefully sitting upright. With a vegetable peeler, peel the lemon into long strips and add to the pot. Pour over the sugar and leave it overnight in a cool place.

The next day, place the pot over gentle heat and let them cook slowly, uncovered, and without stirring. After about 20 minutes of simmering, the figs will begin to soften. At this stage, try to carefully nudge them into one layer, still upright. I use a large spoon for this; be quite careful so as not to accidentally pierce them.

Continue simmering until the figs are covered in syrup. When cooked, they should be entirely soft (including their stems) and evenly caramel

Continued overleaf >

coloured, and the syrup should be producing big bubbles as it boils. The timing depends entirely on the figs themselves – what kind they are, the thickness of their skins, their level of maturity. It can take about 1 hour, but keep an eye on them.

Carefully lift out each boiling hot fig and place in clean, sterilised jars (see page 137 for more on sterilising and sealing jars). If you want to make them boozy, add a splash of cognac or brandy to the syrup now. Then pour the syrup over to cover the fruit completely, until 5 mm (¼ in) from the top. Seal the lids tightly – but don't turn them over or reboil them to seal. Just let them sit on the counter until thoroughly cooled. Store in the refrigerator.

When sealed properly, the unopened jars of figs last for several months. Once opened, store in the refrigerator and consume within a week. (They never last that long though!)

RICOTTA AL CAFFE
COFFEE-LACED RICOTTA

In the middle of a sweltering Tuscan summer, with no working oven and a two-year-old requesting attention, I had to come up with some kind of simple dessert to end a meal for some friends staying over. I found a lovely little recipe in Elizabeth David's *Italian Food* for slightly sweet ricotta with a splash of rum and a spoonful of fine coffee grounds stirred through it. She also suggests serving it with some fresh cream and thin wafer biscuits (I quite like *lingua di gatto*, or cat's tongue biscuits for this). Together with the booziness from the rum and the uplifting hit of caffeine, it's rather like a lazy idea for a tiramisu. Served well chilled in little glasses, it is a refreshing, elegant and surprisingly light way to end a meal.

I've made it many times since and it has morphed a little from the original. I prefer it with a shot of espresso rather than the coffee grounds. It's a subtler coffee flavour and doesn't seem to make your head spin as the straight coffee grounds do. Sometimes I like to fold the whipped cream directly into the ricotta, which makes it light as a cloud. And, when I want to make it a little more substantial to serve as a dessert, I crumble biscuits into the glasses and layer them with the ricotta, whipped cream and chocolate.

SERVES 4

Whip the ricotta with a whisk (if you prefer to remove all of the ricotta's characteristic lumps, you can make it perfectly smooth by passing it through a fine-meshed sieve with a silicone spatula to help you). Add the sugar, espresso and rum (if using) and whisk until smooth and well combined.

Crumble the biscuits and divide half of the crumble among the glasses. Distribute half of the ricotta mixture over the top. Add a layer of the remaining crumbled biscuits, then a layer of the rest of the ricotta mixture. Allow to chill for 1 hour before serving, then dollop whipped cream on the top and sprinkle with the dark chocolate.

250 g (9 oz/1 cup) fresh ricotta
80 g (2¾ oz/⅓ cup) caster (superfine) sugar
2 tablespoons strong espresso
splash of rum (optional)
100 g (3½ oz) soft, plain biscuits (about 8), such as savoiardi (lady fingers) or cat's tongue biscuits
100 ml (3½ fl oz) pouring (single/light) cream, whipped to soft peaks
20 g (¾ oz) dark chocolate, shaved or grated for serving

NOTE
This dessert should sit for at least 1 hour in the fridge to chill before serving, but if you want to prepare this well ahead of time, such as the night before, leave out the whipped cream until just before serving.

VARIATION
You could also serve this ricotta cream with Ciaffagnoni *(page 179), where dollops are folded inside the cooled crêpes.*

GRANITA AL MELONE
MELON GRANITA

The Tuscan summer means long days, the hot sun scorching the ancient stone towns and the crackling, dry fields of the countryside. The Italians tackle it by either staying high in the hills or spending time very close to the sea, where the evening air is more likely to bring a little relief in the form of a breeze.

Another remedy for the summer heat is to consume plenty of gelato and granita, which becomes almost an obligatory pastime in the warm afternoons and evenings. Having moved temporarily to Porto Ercole and living without any fancy kitchen equipment, I found myself making granita quite a bit. It's so unbelievably simple to make at home – you don't need any special equipment and it literally takes a few minutes (getting a little one to understand they have to wait hours until they can try it is the only tricky part).

Melone (rockmelon or cantaloupe) grows locally in Capalbio and it is possibly the sweetest, most fragrant and delicious melon I've ever tasted. I eat it all summer long and keep chilled slices in the fridge to drape over slices of salty prosciutto toscano that makes lunch or antipasto in just minutes. This refreshing granita, something between a sorbet and a slushie, is another favourite use for *melone*, much loved in our household. It's also surprisingly wonderful with a hint of chilli, which you only sense a few moments after each mouthful – a version I first experienced at a restaurant on Elba Island. Add a pinch of dried chilli powder to the mixture before freezing.

SERVES 6

Dissolve the sugar in about 125 ml (4 fl oz/½ cup) of water in a small saucepan over low–medium heat and bring to the boil for a few minutes. Remove from the heat and set aside to cool completely.

Chop the melon roughly into pieces. Pulse in a blender or pass through a food mill and reduce to a smooth pulp. Pour the melon pulp into a container that will fit in the freezer (preferably one that has a lid) and stir through the lemon juice and cooled sugar syrup. Put the container flat in the freezer and allow 4–6 hours or so to set. Stir every hour with a fork, particularly around the edges where it will freeze first, until you have a creamy, but icy consistency. Serve in little glasses with a spoon or straw.

150 g (5½ oz/¾ cup) sugar
500–600 g (1 lb 2 oz–1 lb 5 oz) rockmelon (cantaloupe), rind and seeds removed
juice of 1 lemon

NOTE

Choose your container well. You might be left with little choice depending on the shape of your freezer, but consider that if you have the mixture in a wide, shallow dish such as a glass or ceramic lasagne tray or similar, it will freeze quicker than if you have it in a deep, narrow dish like a loaf tin.

If you've left the granita too long (such as overnight) and end up with quite a solid block, simply use a fork to 'fluff' and grate the granita into icy flakes, place into glasses and give it a little stir before serving. You can also make a strawberry or cherry version by substituting the fruit.

GIGLIO ISLAND

Giglio Island, just a hop, skip and a jump (16 kilometres or 10 miles and a breezy 1 hour ferry ride) from Monte Argentario, is a rugged, pint-sized granite island surrounded by crystalline waters. With the misfortune of being in a desirable position, it has an ancient and turbulent history, suffering centuries of pillaging by pirates and changing hands of owners – from the Pisans to the Neopolitans, then to noble families like the Piccolomini from Siena, who sold the island to Eleonora di Toledo, the wife of Cosimo de' Medici I. Today it's a sleepy island for most of the year, until summer time, when beach-goers arrive, seeking the smooth sand and turquoise waters.

Giglio is also known for its white wine, Ansonaco. The first time I tasted it was during an unforgettable visit to Altura winery, with its breathtaking historic terraces of rambling vines that seem to just drop right into the sea. Almost 20 years ago, this abandoned, historic vineyard was rescued and restored by Francesco Carfagna. We visited during a scorching hot day, under deep blue skies, during the *vendemmia*. The grape bunches are picked by hand and the crates carried up steep, rocky pathways on strong shoulders, loaded into the car and brought to the Carfagna home and winery, a short drive away, to be pressed immediately.

It's here, with a 270° view of the archipelago, where they make their Ansonaco in the most natural of ways, orange and sometimes fizzy, a beautiful accident.

MARMELLATA DI UVA ANSONICA
ANSONICA GRAPE JAM

In September, you can find crates spilling over with dusty, pale, copper-tinged grapes – ansonica (also written 'ansonaco') grapes to be precise. When the fruit and vegetable shop down the road starts practically giving them away for a euro a kilo, it's a sign that it's *vendemmia* (or grape harvest) season.

When I saw the huge crates of grapes piling up at the fruit shop, I couldn't help but buy a few kilograms. I may not be able to make wine, but I can always make jam – and I found that these grapes make a wonderful, firm and intensely fragrant jam, rather reminiscent of quince paste, with an unexpectedly intense, rusty colour. It is lovely with cheese, especially something fresh like goat's curd, or sharp and bitey like a blue cheese. Not far from Orbetello, there is a beautiful farm and winery called La Parrina, where they make a range of delicious sheep's milk and cow's milk cheeses, including a unique gooey blue cheese called Guttus, which is exactly what I like to eat with this jam.

Making jam with grapes alone is a traditional way to use up excess fruit in central Italy, and it is my preference for this recipe. However, it requires an eagle eye and it is much easier to make this jam with a little sugar in it to help it set (you will, of course, end up with more jam this way, too), so I offer both methods below. Cooking the juice down is the tricky part and reminds me a little of melting sugar down into caramel – you really don't want to stray too far away from the pot, because it will easily misbehave and go too far. Once, while my back was turned, the jam turned so solid that I couldn't even cut into it. You could have bounced it off the walls.

MAKES APPROXIMATELY 2 X 250 ML (8½ FL OZ) JARS OF JAM

Rinse the grapes and pull most of the grapes off the bunch and off their stems (if some remain, you can always strain them out later). Without patting dry, transfer them to a large, heavy-bottomed pot and place over low heat. As they heat they will begin to release their own juice, and will soon be covered in liquid. But before this happens, you will need to keep an eye on the pot and stir regularly to make sure the grapes at the very bottom don't stay there too long and burn. Once the liquid is released, you can leave them and let them simmer gently for about 20 minutes, or until they are all soft.

1 kg (2 lb 3 oz) ansonica grapes (or other white grape)
100 g (3½ oz/½ cup) sugar

Continued overleaf >

Pour the grapes and their juice into a fine-meshed sieve set over a large bowl. Squash the grapes in the sieve to release the juice/flesh (I do this with a wooden spoon) and make your way through all the grapes this way to separate the juice from the skins and seeds. It can be a little laborious, but a food mill could help you (as long as it doesn't squash the seeds too – this would create bitterness) and doing it in a few stages is easier.

Pour the juice back into the pot, add the sugar and raise the heat level to high, bringing the mixture to a rolling boil. Cook until the colour of the juice turns a shiny, copper tone – this may be as little as 10–15 minutes for a soft set. Test the jam set by having a saucer in the freezer and placing a teaspoon or so of the cooking jam onto the cold saucer. Turn the saucer around to cool down the jam and see how it behaves – if it's thick, slides slowly and wrinkles when you poke it, it is perfect.

Remove the jam from the heat and pour carefully into sterilised jam jars (see page 137 on how to sterilise and seal jars).

When sealed properly, the unopened jars of jam can last for several months. Once opened, store in the refrigerator and consume within 2 weeks.

SECOND (SUGAR-FREE) METHOD

You can serve this intense, fragrant jam as you would any regular jam – but I love this especially on a cheese board.

MAKES APPROXIMATELY 1 X 150 ML (5 FL OZ) JAR OF JAM

1 kg (2 lb 3 oz) ansonica grapes (or other white grape)

Follow the instructions for the first method, except do not add sugar.

After straining, place the juice back into the pot and bring to a rolling boil. Cook down until the jam is set. This takes longer than the first method. The best guide to understanding whether the jam is ready is the colour. When it goes back in the pot, it's an opaque, pastel peach with a hint of green – rather like cloudy apple juice. Then, as it cooks, you'll watch it turn into the colour of a rusty sunset. It will slowly get darker but you want it to hover around this rosy-rusty, almost honey-toned shade. If it starts heading towards mahogany, it's gone too far. Use the saucer test as described in the first method to check when the jam is ready.

Remove the jam from the heat and pour carefully into a sterilised jam jar (see page 137 on how to sterilise and seal jars).

When sealed properly, the unopened jar of jam can last for several months. Once opened, store in the refrigerator and consume within 2 weeks.

VARIATIONS
You can use this sugar-free grape recipe with practically any white grape, although you will probably get different tones and colours with different varieties. It's even easier to make with red grapes, as you don't need to strain out the skins or even the seeds (Italians think of grape seeds as adding texture – they give crunch). In that case, you end up with a rather pulpy, fleshy jam.

THE WINES OF SOUTHERN MAREMMA

ANSONICA COSTA DELL'ARGENTARIO DOC
Ansonica, or Ansonaco as it is known in Tuscany, is perhaps better known elsewhere as a native Sicilian grape called Inzolia, which is used in western Sicily to make Marsala. The grape made its way to Tuscany via some island hopping (as was so often the case with places that have access to the sea), from Sicily to Sardinia to Tuscany's Elba Island and then to Giglio Island and Monte Argentario. It is the principal component (making up 85%) of Ansonica Costa dell'Argentario DOC, a dry, slightly aromatic, golden-hued white wine with bright acidity, made on Giglio Island and Monte Argentario. As you might imagine, this white wine is ideal for drinking with the unfussy, traditional seafood dishes of the area. This grape is also used in Parrina bianco.

BIANCO DI PITIGLIANO DOC
A large wine-making area that includes the areas of Pitigliano, Sorano and as far up as Manciano and Scansano, this white wine was one of the first in Italy to receive DOC status in 1966. It is made mostly of Tuscan Trebbiano grapes (50%–80%), with the rest a mixture of other grapes, including Malvasia Bianco, Verdello, Greco, Riesling, Sauvignon Blanc and Chardonnay. It makes a nice *aperitivo*, to drink before a meal or to drink alongside antipasti and with uncomplicated dishes of seafood or white meat. In Pitigliano, kosher wine is also made by the town's historic wine cooperative, La Cantina Cooperativa di Pitigliano. A white and red are available under the label La Piccola Gerusalemme (little Jerusalem).

CAPALBIO DOC

Wine has been made in this area since Etruscan and Roman times. Capalbio DOC is made around Capalbio towards Orbetello and up to Manciano and Magliano. It includes a number of wines, including Capalbio Rosso and Rosé (both made with 50% Sangiovese), Capalbio Bianco and a deep, honey-coloured Vin Santo (dessert wine), which are both made with 50% Trebbiano. There are also varietal wines Capalbio Sangiovese, Capalbio Cabernet Sauvignon and Capalbio Vermentino, which are made with at least 85% of their namesake grape. The Capalbio Bianco, made with Trebbiano, would be ideal to wash down with some wild mushrooms, such as in the *Pappardelle sui funghi* (page 30).

MORELLINO DI SCANSANO DOC

Originating between the Ombrone and Albegna rivers, this Maremman wine is made not only in Scansano but also in the areas of Grosseto and Magliano in Toscana, close to the coast, and the internal areas of Roccalbegna, Semproniano, Campagnatico and Manciano. Morellino is the local name for Sangiovese, which is used as a minimum of 85% in this robust red wine. Some say the name comes from *morello* (dark, slightly sour cherries that are reminiscent of Sangiovese grapes). Morellino di Scansano (particularly a young one that isn't aged in wood at all) is well matched with a hearty seafood stew such as Argentario's *Caldaro* (page 110). In the case of the Riserva, which is aged in wood, it would be good with a gamey dish like *Cinghiale in umido* (page 52).

PARRINA DOC

Not far from Orbetello is La Parrina, the area where this wine is produced, largely by a beautiful, organic estate of the same name. Parrina Bianco is this DOC's best-known wine, which is made with 30–50% Trebbiano, 30–50% Ansonica and Chardonnay. It's an aromatic, dry white, which is perfect for drinking all summer long (we certainly can attest to this), paired with cold dishes, seafood, cheese and even dishes like the *Minestra di pesce* (page 101). Meanwhile, Parrina Rosso and Rosé are both made with 70–100% Sangiovese. When young, Parrina Rosso (slightly chilled, even) is a good one for drinking with antipasto or even white meat.

SOVANA DOC

Produced in the areas of Pitigliano, Sorano and Manciano, this red wine is made with at least 50% Sangiovese, plus a mixture of other red grapes, such as Aleatico, Merlot and Cabernet Sauvignon. It's ideal for eating with wild boar (such as the *Cinghiale in umido*, page 52) or other game.

REFERENCES

There are many wonderful books that I came across while researching recipes and that have further information on this cuisine that may interest others. I wanted to share a little more about them because those that are only available in Italian are virtually unknown outside of Tuscany, and there are some treasures only available in English that are unknown to Italians.

I am constantly on the lookout for cookbooks about Maremman cuisine. There aren't many, and the ones that are around are in Italian and are often small, local publications, (some could best be described as a pamphlet) that have no photographs. They can be hard to find outside of Maremman town centres and the best place to look for them (if they have them) is in a local newsagent or bookshop. One of the first things I did when I moved to Porto Ercole was to head to the newsagent on the main street and ask about a cookbook on local cuisine. The shopkeeper pulled down a book titled *Cucina Italiana*, Italian cuisine. This happened in other places too. There was clearly something missing.

Cucina Maremmana by Tuscan journalist Aldo Santini is one of the best collections of well-researched Maremman recipes, particularly to see the differences from town to town (or indeed kitchen to kitchen) of certain dishes – it is only available in Italian.

A more general book on Tuscan cuisine that includes many Maremman dishes amongst its 1000 recipes is Paolo Petroni's wonderful *Il Grande Libro della Vera Cucina Toscana*. A small version of it can be found in English too, though it only has about a quarter of the recipes in it.

One of the most fascinating books of recipes from this area is Edda Servi Machlin's *The Classic Cuisine of The Italian Jews* (1981). Born and bred in the thriving heart of the Jewish quarter of Pitigliano, her cookbook is a wonderful mixture of Italian Jewish, Roman and Maremman specialties. Her story of the now 'vanished way of life' of Jewish Pitigliano that she knew in the 1930s and 1940s before fleeing and moving to US is, simply put, moving. It is only available in English (and is out of print), which I find very unfortunate for Italians who are missing out on this important collection of traditional recipes.

Anyone interested in foraging for wild mushrooms should purchase a good illustrated guide of mushrooms. I use one in Italian called *Atlante Illustrato dei Funghi*, which covers mushrooms found in Europe. Specific to Tuscany, Andrea Gamannossi has written a charming little paperback book on practical tips for foraging and preparing mushrooms, *La Toscana dal bosco alla cucina*. A very useful recourse on foraging and hunting in general in the US (particularly west coast) is Hank Shaw's cookbook *Hunt, Gather, Cook* and his blog, Honest Food. And for more on foraging flowers, *The Forager Handbook* by Miles Irving.

For seafood, I found Alan Davidson's *Mediterranean Seafood* indispensable. Also very useful when talking about mediterranean seafood species and treatment is Elizabeth David's *Italian Food* and Patience Gray's *Honey from a Weed*. All of them make a very good read too.

For more general reference books on traditional Italian cooking available in English, there is Ada Boni's *The Talisman* cookbook, albeit an extremely abridged version. The original Italian one, printed in 1929, is a doorstop of a book with an enormous collection of recipes, on par with Pellegrino Artusi's 1891 cookbook *Science in the Kitchen and the Art of Eating Well* (which is available in a complete version in English). Both books live in my kitchen, and while they are historic books not always practical for a modern kitchen, they are excellent resources that I cook from often.

OTHER COOKBOOKS ON MAREMMAN CUISINE:

Baffigi, Lucia and Lucia Brizzi. *Antiche Ricette del Giglio: La mi' nonna mi diceva....* Arcidosso: Editore Effigi, 2010.

Barontini, Corrado, Margherita Innocenti and Morbello Vergari. *Maremma a Tavola*. Pitigliano: Editrice Laurum, 2013.

Cantore, Susanna. *Cinghiale: Dalle Stalle alle Stelle ai Tegami*. Orbetello: Editrice Effequ, 2013.

Claudi, Alvaro and Sergio Rossi. *Zuppe e Stornelli*. Italia: Editori del Grifo, 1991.

Djoković, Milena. *Diverse Sfumature d'Anguilla*. Orbetello: Editrice Effequ, 2014.

Piazzesi, Paolo. *Cucina di Maremma*. Firenze: Libri Liberi, 2003.

Quatraro, Federico. *Il Testamento del Marinario*. Orbetello: Editrice Effequ, 2014.

Rangoni, Laura. *La Cucina Toscana di Mare*. Roma:Newton Compton, 2015.

Spargi, Claudia. *Quaderno delle ricette di Maremma Raccolte alla Tavola dei Butteri*. Verona: Edizioni del Baldo, 2009.

INDEX

VEGAN RECIPES
(or simple substitutes)

Funghi fritti (fried mushrooms) 24
Crostini di polenta con funghi (polenta crostini with mushrooms) 25
Zuppa di funghi (mushroom soup) 28
Fiori di acacia fritti (fried Robinia flowers) 34
Liquore all'alloro e rosmarino (bay leaf and rosemary liqueur) 44
Zuppa di ceci e castagne (chickpea and chestnut soup) 46
Fettunta al limone (toasted bread with lemon) 128
Pane, vino e zucchero (bread, wine and sugar) 132
Carciofini sott'olio (pickled baby artichokes) 135
Zuppa maremmana (Maremma bean and vegetable soup) 151
Strozzapreti al sugo finto (handmade pasta with 'fake' sugo) 152
Risotto con le zucchine (zucchini risotto) 161
Insalata gigliese (tomato and celery salad from Giglio Island) 164
Peperone e patate (red peppers and potatoes) 167
Zuppa di farro (farro soup) 184
Zuppa lombarda (cannellini bean soup) 186
Tagliolini con ceci (chickpea tagliolini) 187
Ciambelline al vino (ring cookies with wine) 208
Pagnotella (fig and chocolate bread) 219
Fichi canditi (candied figs) 239
Granita al melone (melon granita) 246
Marmellata di uva ansonica (grape jam) 251

Simple substitutes to make vegan
Pappardelle sui funghi (mushroom pappardelle) – *substitute vegan pasta such as a dried semola pasta or the fresh strozzapreti on page 152* 30
L'acquacotta viterbese (Acquacotta Viterbo style) – *leave out egg* 42
Pizza rosa con salsa verde (red pizza with salsa verde) – *leave out anchovies* 141
Pizza gigliese (Giglio Island pizza with onions and anchovies) – *leave out anchovies* 145
Acquacotta maremmana – *leave out egg* 147
Castagnaccio (chestnut cake) – *serve without ricotta cream* 216

GLUTEN-FREE RECIPES
(or simple substitutes to make gluten-free)

Crostini di polenta con funghi (polenta crostini with mushrooms) 25
Liquore all'alloro e rosmarino (bay leaf and rosemary liqueur) 44
Gnocchi di castagne (chestnut gnocchi) 47
Palamita sott'olio (preserved bonito) 69
Insalata di pesce alla grossetana (Grosseto-style fish salad) 72
Calamari e funghi (calamari and mushroom stew) 80
Scaveccio di sgombro (fried and marinated mackerel) 82
Polpo e patate (octopus and potato salad) 86
Vongole e polenta (clams with polenta) 106
Orata al cartoccio con i funghi (sea bream baked in paper with mushrooms) 120
Sogliola al limone (lemon-marinated sole) 123
Carciofini sott'olio (pickled baby artichokes) 135
Tortino di carciofi (fried artichoke omelette) 140
Risotto con le zucchine (zucchini risotto) 161
Insalata gigliese (tomato and celery salad from Giglio island) 164
Peperone e patate (red peppers and potatoes) 167
Uova sode con acciugata (boiled eggs with anchovy sauce) 174
Zuppa di farro (farro soup) 184
Sugo Maremmano (Maremman beef, pork and sausage ragu) 194
Coniglio ripieno (rabbit stuffed with potatoes) 195
Pollo all'aceto (vinegar chicken) 196
Scottiglia (chicken, guinea fowl and pork stew) 198
Castagnaccio (chestnut cake) 216
Fichi canditi (caramelised figs) 239
Granite al melon (melon granita) 246
Marmellata di uva ansonica (grape jam) 251

Simple substitutes (use gluten-free alternative to bread or pasta for serving)
Zuppa di funghi (mushroom soup) 28
Pappardelle sui funghi (mushroom pappardelle) 30
Fiori di acacia fritti (fried Robinia flowers) – *substitute plain flour with rice flour* 34
L'acquacotta viterbese (acquacotta Viterbo style) 42
Zuppa di ceci e castagne (chickpea and chestnut soup) 46
Cinghiale dolce-forte (sweet and sour wild boar) – *substitute plain flour with cornstarch* 55
Acciughe e carciofi gratinati (anchovies and artichokes gratin) – *use gluten-free breadcrumbs* 68
Alice dorate (fried anchovies) – *substitute plain flour with gluten-free flour* 74
Acquacotta del pescatore (fisherman's acquacotta) 88
Spaghetti alla bottarga 91
Spaghetti alle arselle (spaghetti with clams) 92
Spaghetti alle spernocchie (spaghetti with mantis shrimp) 93
Bavette al branzino (bavette pasta with sea bass) 99
Minestra di pesce (fish soup) 101
Zuppa scampi e patate (scampi and potato soup) 103

Caldaro (seafood stew) 110
Stocchetto alle portecolese (Porto Ercole style cod) 114
Frittura di paranza (fried fisherman's basket) – *substitute plain flour with rice flour* 115
Fettunta al limone (toasted bread with lemon) 128
Pane e pomodoro al limone (toast with tomato and anchovies) 130
Pane, vino e zucchero (bread, wine and sugar) 132
Acquacotta maremmana 147
Zuppa maremmana (Maremma bean and vegetable soup) 151
Tagliolini al limone (lemon tagliolini) 154
Sformato di cipolotti (spring onion gratin) – *substitute breadcrumbs and plain flour with gluten-free breadcrumbs and cornstarch* 168
Crostini Maremmani (Maremman crostini) 172
Zuppa lombarda (cannellini bean soup) 186
Tagliolini con ceci (tagliolini with chickpeas) 187
Rigatoni alla buttera (cowboy style rigatoni) 189
Buglione (lamb and tomato stew) 200
Pagnotella (fig and chocolate bread) – *use gluten-free flour* 219
Tronco (chocolate-filled sponge roll) – *substitute plain flour with cornstarch* 236
Ricotta al caffe (coffee-laced ricotta) – *use gluten-free biscuits* 242

A
acacia (black locust) blossoms
　foraging and preparing 35
　fried 34–6
acciughe 61
acciughe e carciofi gratinati 68
acquacotta 14–15
　Acquacotta Maremmana 147–9
　Fisherman's acquacotta 88–9
　variations 150
acquacotta del pescatore 88–9
Alchermes 206, 236, 238
alici 61
alici dorate 74–5
almonds, Fig and chocolate bread 219–21
anchovies 61
　Anchovy and artichoke gratin 68
　Boiled eggs with anchovy sauce 174–5
　cleaning fresh 75–6
　Deep-fried anchovies 74–5
　Giglio Island pizza with onions and anchovies 145–6
　Maremman crostini 172
　Salsa verde 141
　salt-packed 142
　Toast with tomato and anchovies 130–1
anguilla 62
anguilla sfumata 83
Ansonica (Ansonaco) 250, 256
Ansonica Costa dell'Argentario DOC 266
Ansonica grape jam 251–3
Antiche Ricette del Giglio (book) 145, 174
antipasto 34, 38, 69, 74, 80, 123, 135, 140, 172, 173, 246
Apple and jam cake 230–1
apricot jam, Apple and jam cake 230–1
Argentario fish stew 110–12
arselle 61
artichokes
　Anchovy and artichoke gratin 68
　Baby artichokes preserved in oil 135–6
　Fried artichoke omelette 140
Artusi, Pellegrino 24, 38, 50, 55, 56, 129, 141, 168
asparagus, Wild asparagus tart 38–9

B
Baby artichokes preserved in oil 135–6
baccalà 114
bavette al branzino 99–100
Bavette with sea bass ragu 99–100
bay leaves
　Bay leaf and rosemary liqueur 44
　Wild boar stew 52–3
bechamel sauce 168
beef, Maremman crostini 172–3
Bianco do Pitigliano DOC 266
biscotti, Jewish cinnamon biscotti 209–11
biscuits
　Cat's tongue biscuits 242
　Red crown biscuits 206–7
　Red wine biscuits 208
black locust blossoms, fried 34–6
boga 64
Boiled eggs with anchovy sauce 174–5
bonito 61
　Bonito preserved in oil 69–71
borlotti beans, Farro soup 184–5
bottarga 63, 82, 90
　Spaghetti with bottarga from Orbetello 91
branzino 64
Bread, wine and sugar 132–3
bubbola 23
buglione 200–1

C
Caesar's mushrooms 22
cakes
　Apple and jam cake 230–1
　Chestnut flour bundt cake 232–3
　Chestnut flour cake 216–18
　Chocolate-filled sponge roll 236
　Fig and chocolate bread 219–21
　Lemon and ricotta cake 229
calamaretti 65
calamari 65
　Calamari and mushrooms 80–1
calamari e funghi 80–1
caldaro 29
caldaro dell'Argentario 110–12
cannellini beans
　Cannellini bean soup 186
　Farro soup 184–5
　Maremman bean and vegetable soup 151
cannochie 63
cantaloupe, Melon granita 246–7
Capalbio 9, 45, 50, 51, 54, 203
Capalbio DOC 267
capers
　Grosseto-style fish salad 72–3
　Maremman crostini 172–3
　Salsa verde 141–2
　salt-packed 142
capone 62
capsicums, Red peppers and potatoes 167
Caramelised figs 239–41
carciofini sott'olio 135–6
cardarelle 22
castagnaccio 216–18
Cat's tongue biscuits 242
catshark 62
Cecina 16
cefalo 63

INDEX 263

celery, Tomato and celery salad from Giglio Island 164–5
chanterelle mushrooms 22
chestnuts
  Chestnut flour bundt cake 232–3
  Chestnut flour cake 216–18
  Chestnut gnocchi 47–9
  Chickpea and chestnut soup 46
chicken
  Scottiglia 198–9
  Vinegar chicken 196–7
chicken livers, Maremman crostini 172–3
chickpeas
  Chickpea and chestnut soup 46
  Tagliolini with chickpeas 187–8
chicory, wild, Viterbo-style acquacotta 42–3
chocolate
  Chocolate pastry cream 236
  Chocolate-filled sponge roll 236–8
  Fig and chocolate bread 219–21
  Ricotta and chocolate tart 228
  Wild boar in chocolate sauce 55
ciaffagnoni mancianesi 179–80, 181
ciambelline al vino 208
ciambellone alle castagne 232–3
cicale di mare 63
cimballo 22
cinghiale in dolce-forte 55
cinghiale in umido 52–3
clams 61
  Clam stew with polenta 106–9
  Fisherman's acquacotta 88–9
  purging clams 95
  Spaghetti with wedge clams 92
The Classic Cuisine of the Italian Jews (Machlin) 123, 140, 212, 213
cod 61
  Cod with pine nuts and olives 114
Coffee-laced ricotta 242–3
conger eels 62
coniglio ripieno 195
cooking practicalities 13
corolli rossi 206–7
Cowboy-style rigatoni 189–91
crema 29
crêpes, Manciano-style crêpes 179–80
crostata di ricotta e cioccolato 228
crostata di ricotta e pere coscia 223–5
crostini
  Maremman crostini 172–3
  Polenta crostini with mushrooms 25–7
crostini di polenta con i funghi 25–7
Crostini maremmani 172–3

Cucina Maremmana (Santini) 15, 196
cuttlefish 61

D

Deep-fried anchovies 74–5
Di Virginio, Valentina 181
digestivo 44
dogfish 62
dolce-forte sauce 55
Donati, Ilena 51, 52, 149, 195
dory, John 62
Dublin Bay prawns 64

E

eel 62
  Orbetello eels 82, 83
eggs
  Boiled eggs with anchovy sauce 174–5
  Fried artichoke omelette 140
  Manciano-style crêpes 179–80

F

Farro soup 184–5
Feniglia 21, 90, 92, 113
fettunta al limone 128
ficamaschia 61
fichi canditi 239–41
figs
  Caramelised figs 239–41
  Fig and chocolate bread 219–21
  Figs and bread 222
fiori di acacia fritti 34–6
fish 61–5
  Anchovy and artichoke gratin 68
  Argentario fish stew 110–12
  Bavette with sea bass ragu 99–100
  Boiled eggs with anchovy sauce 174–5
  Bonito preserved in oil 69–71
  Cod with pine nuts and olives 114
  Deep-fried anchovies 74–5
  Fish soup with pasta 101–2
  Fish stock 100
  Fisherman's fried fish 115–17
  Giglio Island pizza with onions and anchovies 145–6
  Grosseto-style fish salad 72–3
  Lemon-marinated sole 123
  Paper-baked sea bream with mushrooms 120–2
  Pizza with tomato and salsa verde 141–3

  preparing raw fish 124
  Salsa verde 141–2
  Fisherman's acquacotta 88–9
  Fisherman's fried fish 115–17
food mill 101
Fried acacia (black locust) blossoms 34–6
Fried artichoke omelette 140
Fried mushrooms 24
frittura di paranza 115–17
funghi 21–3
funghi di san Martino 22
funghi fritti 24

G

galletti 22
gallinella 62
gambero imperiale 63
gattuccio 62
Giannella 21, 90, 113
Giglio Island 68, 145, 174, 222, 250, 256
Giglio Island pizza with onions and anchovies 145–6
gnocchi, Chestnut gnocchi 47–9
Gnocchi di castagne 47–9
granita, Melon granita 246–7
granita al melone 246–7
grey mullet 63
gronco 62
Grosseto 16
Grosseto-style fish salad 72–3
guinea fowl, *Scottiglia* 198–9
gurnard, tub 62

H

haddock 61
hare, Pappardelle with hare sauce 56–7
hazelnuts, Fig and chocolate bread 219–21
Honey and nut pastries 213–15
Honey from a Weed (Gray) 39, 101, 129
horse mackerel 62

I

il cinghiale 50
Il Grande Libro della Vera Cucina Toscana (Petroni) 15, 110
insalata di pesce alla grossetana 72–3
insalata gigliese 164–5
Italian Food (David) 242

J

jams
  Ansonica grape jam 251–3
  Apple and jam cake 230–1
jars, sterilising and sealing 137
Jewish cinnamon biscotti 209–11
Jewish Pitigliano 123, 140, 212
John dory 62

L

la Costa d'Argento 9
La Cucina Toscana di Mare (Rangoni) 72, 88
la merenda 129
la sagra 202–3
L'acquacotta viterbese 42–3
Lamb and tomato stew 200–1
lampatelle 110
langoustines 64
L'art du Cuisinier (Beauvillier) 50
Lazio 9, 16, 42, 54, 195, 212, 223
Lemon and ricotta cake 229
Lemon-marinated sole 123
Lemon tagliolini 154–5
limpet 62, 110
liqueurs 45
  Bay leaf and rosemary liqueur 44
liquore all'alloro e rosmarino 44

M

Machlin, Edda Servi 123, 140, 180, 212, 213
mackerel 62
  horse mackerel 62
  Mackerel scaveccio 82–3
Manciano-style crêpes 179–80
  secret to 181
mantis shrimp 63
  Argentario fish stew 110–12
  Mantis shrimp spaghetti 93
Maremma 9, 16–17, 54, 202–3
  seafood 61–5
  southern wines 256–7
  wild boar as symbol of 50
Maremma Amara (song) 17
Maremman bean and vegetable soup 151
Maremman beef, pork and sausage ragu 194
Maremman crostini 172–3
marmellata di uva ansonica 251–3
mazza di tamburo 23

mazzancolle 63
Mediterranean seafood (Davidson) 64
Melon granita 246–7
merenda 129, 130
merluzzo 61
minestra 29
minestra di pesce 101–2
mirto 44
Monk's head 22
Monte Argentario 9, 21, 92, 99, 110, 113, 203, 219, 250
moray eels 62
Morellino di Scansano DOC 267
moscardini 63
muggine 63
mullet
  grey mullet 63
  red mullet 63
murena 62
mushrooms
  Calamari and mushrooms 80–1
  foraging for 21–3
  Fried mushrooms 24
  Maremman bean and vegetable soup 151
  Paper-baked sea bream with mushrooms 120–2
  Pappardelle pasta with wild mushrooms 30–3
  Polenta crostini with mushrooms 25–7
  Wild mushroom sauce 30–1
  Wild mushroom soup 28
mussels, Fisherman's acquacotta 88–9

N

nanbanzuke 82
nasello 61
Norway lobster 64

O

octopus 63
  Argentario fish stew 110–12
  Octopus and potato braise 86–7
olives
  Cod with pine nuts and olives 114
  Grosseto-style fish salad 72–3
  Lemon-marinated sole 123
onions
  Acquacotta Maremmana 147–9
  Giglio Island pizza with onions and anchovies 145–6
orata 64

orata al cartoccio con i funghi 120–2
Orbetello 12, 90
  eels 82, 83
  farmed fish 62, 63, 64
ordinali 22
ovoli 22
Oxford Companion to Italian Food (Riley) 29

P

pagnotella 219–21
palamita 61
palamita sott'olio 69–71
pancetta
  Cowboy-style rigatoni 189–91
  Pappardelle with hare sauce 56–7
pane e pomodoro con le acciughe 130–1
pane, vino e zucchero 132–3
panficato 222
panforte 55
Panificio Di Cristina 222
pannocchie 63
Paper-baked sea bream with mushrooms 120–2
pappa al pomodoro 29
pappardelle
  Pappardelle with hare sauce 56–7
  Pappardelle pasta with wild mushrooms 30–3
pappardelle sui funghi 30–3
pappardelle sulla lepre 56–7
parasol mushroom 23
Parrina DOC 267
passatutto 101
passaverdura 101
pasta
  Bavette with sea bass ragu 99–100
  Cowboy-style rigatoni 189–91
  Fish soup with pasta 101–2
  Lemon tagliolini 154–5
  Mantis shrimp spaghetti 93
  Pappardelle with hare sauce 56–7
  Pappardelle pasta with wild mushrooms 30–3
  Ricotta and spinach tortelli 156–60
  Spaghetti with bottarga from Orbetello 91
  Spaghetti with wedge clams 92
  Strozzapreti pasta with 'fake sauce' 152–3
  Tagliolini with chickpeas 187–8
pastries, Honey and nut pastries 213–15

pastry
   hot weather pastry making 225
   Ricotta and baby pear tart 223–5
   Ricotta and chocolate tart 228
   Shortcrust pastry 38–9
   Wild asparagus tart 38–9
patella 62
pears
   Poached pears 223
   Ricotta and baby pear tart 223–5
Peperoni e patate 167
pesce da zuppa 101
pesce per fritto 115
pesce prete 64
pesce sciabola 64
pesco azzuro 61
pinaioli/pinaroli 23
pine nuts
   Chestnut flour cake 216–18
   Cod with pine nuts and olives 114
   Fig and chocolate bread 219–21
   Wild boar in chocolate sauce 55
pipis 61
Pitigliano 9, 123, 140, 150, 180, 196, 209, 212, 213, 256
pizza
   Giglio Island pizza with onions and anchovies 145–6
   Pizza with tomato and salsa verde 141–3
pizza gigliese 145–6
pizza rossa con salsa verde 141–3
polenta
   Clam stew with polenta 106–9
   cooking techniques 109
   Polenta crostini with mushrooms 25–7
pollo all'aceto 196–7
polpo 63
polpo di scoglio 63
polpo e patate 86–7
porcini 23
pork
   Maremman beef, pork and sausage ragu 194
   Scottiglia 198–9
pork sausages
   Cowboy-style rigatoni 189–91
   Maremman beef, pork and sausage ragu 194
Porto Ercole 9, 113, 114, 203
Porto Santo Stefano 113, 219, 222
potatoes
   Chestnut gnocchi 47
   Cod with pine nuts and olives 114
   Maremman bean and vegetable soup 151
   Octopus and potato braise 86–7
   Rabbit stuffed with potatoes 195
   Red peppers and potatoes 167
   Scampi and potato soup 103–5
   Viterbo-style acquacotta 42–3
prawns 63
   Fisherman's acquacotta 88–9
   Fisherman's fried fish 115–17
proscuitto, Rabbit stuffed with potatoes 195

Q
Quaderno delle ricette di Maremma (Spargi) 128

R
Rabbit stuffed with potatoes 195
raw fish, preparing 124
Red crown biscuits 206–7
red mullet 63
Red peppers and potatoes 167
red scorpion fish 64
Red wine biscuits 208
ribollita 29
ricciola 62
ricotta
   Coffee-laced ricotta 242–3
   Lemon and ricotta cake 229
   Ricotta and baby pear tart 223–5
   Ricotta and chocolate tart 228
   Ricotta cream 216–18
   Ricotta and spinach tortelli 156–60
ricotta al caffe 242–3
rigatoni, Cowboy-style rigatoni 189–91
rigatoni alla buttera 189–91
risotto, Zucchini risotto 161–3
risotto con le zucchine 161–3
rockmelon, Melon granita 246–7
rombo quattrocchi 64
rosemary
   Bay leaf and rosemary liqueur 44
   Wild boar stew 52

S
sagre 202–3
salads
   Grosseto-style fish salad 72–3
   Tomato and celery salad from Giglio Island 164–5

Salsa verde 141–2
Santini, Aldo 15, 50, 150, 196, 198
sardines, Grosseto-style fish salad 72–3
Saturnia 9, 178
sauces
   Anchovy sauce 174–5
   bechamel sauce 168
   dolce-forte sauce 55
   'fake sauce' 152–3
   hare sauce 56–7
   wild mushroom sauce 30–1
scabbardfish, silver 64
scampi 64
   Argentario fish stew 110–12
   Scampi and potato soup 103–5
scaveccio 82
scaveccio di sgombro 82–5
Science in the Kitchen and the Art of Eating Well (Artusi) 24, 141
scirocco 166
scofano 64
scorpion fish, red 64
scottiglia 198–9
sea bass
   Bavette with sea bass ragu 99–100
   European 64
sea bream 64
   Paper-baked sea bream with mushrooms 120–2
seafood 61–5
see also calamari; clams; fish; mantis shrimp; octopus; prawns; scampi
seppia 62
sformato di cipolotti 168–9
sfratti 213–15
sgmobro 63
Shortcrust pastry 38–9
shrimp 63
   mantis shrimp 63
Silver Coast 9
silver eels 62
silver scabbardfish 65
silverbeet
   Maremman bean and vegetable soup 151
   Viterbo-style acquacotta 42–3
Simply Ancient Grains (Speck) 109
smoked eels 83
soffritto 147, 153, 187
sogliola 65
sogliola al limone 123
sole 65
   Lemon-marinated sole 123

soup 29
  Cannellini bean soup 186
  Chickpea and chestnut soup 46
  Farro soup 184–5
  Fish soup with pasta 101–2
  Maremman bean and vegetable soup 151
  Scampi and potato soup 103–5
  Wild mushroom soup 28
Sovana DOC 267
spaghetti
  Mantis shrimp spaghetti 93
  Spaghetti with bottarga from Orbetello 91
  Spaghetti with wedge clams 92
spaghetti alla bottarga di Orbetello 91
spaghetti alle arselle 92
spaghetti alle spernocchie 93
sparnocchie 63
spernocchie 63
spigola 64
spinach, Ricotta and spinach tortelli 156–60
Spring onion gratin 168–9
squid 65
stargazer 65
sterilising and sealing jars 137
stoccafisso 61, 114
stocchetto 61
stocchetto alla portercolese 114
strozzapreti al sugo finto 152–3
Strozzapreti pasta with 'fake sauce' 152–3
suaci 64
sugarello 62
sugo finto 152–3
sugo maremmano 194
sultanas
  Chestnut flour cake 216–18
  Fig and chocolate bread 219–21
  Wild boar in chocolate sauce 55
Swiss chard *see* silverbeet

T
tagliolini
  Lemon tagliolini 154–5
  Tagliolini with chickpeas 187–8
tagliolini al limone 154–5
tagliolini con ceci 187–8
tarts
  Ricotta and baby pear tart 223–5
  Ricotta and chocolate tart 228
  Wild asparagus tart 38–9

telline 61
Tiburzi, Domenico 45
Toast with tomato and anchovies 130–1
Toasted bread with lemon 128
tomato passata
  Clam stew with polenta 106–9
  Cod with pine nuts and olives 114
  Cowboy-style rigatoni 189–91
  Fish soup with pasta 101–2
  Fisherman's acquacotta 88–9
  Maremman beef, pork and sausage ragu 194
  Pappardelle with hare sauce 56–7
  Pizza with tomato and salsa verde 141–3
  Wild mushroom soup 28
tomatoes
  Acquacotta Maremmana 147–9
  Argentario fish stew 110–12
  Cod with pine nuts and olives 114
  'fake sauce' 152–3
  Giglio Island pizza with onions and anchoves 145–6
  Grosseto-style fish salad 72–3
  Lamb and tomato stew 200–1
  Red peppers and potatoes 167
  Scampi and potato soup 103–5
  Toast with tomato and anchovies 130–1
  Tomato and celery salad from Giglio Island 164–5
  Viterbo-style acquacotta 42–3
  Wild boar stew 52–3
torta del tre 229
torta di limone e ricotta 229
torta di mele e marmellata 230–1
torta salata con asparagi selvatica 38–9
tortelli, Ricotta and spinach tortelli 156–60
tortelli maremmani 156–60
tortino di carciofi 140
totani 64
tozzetti ebraici 209–11
triglie di fango 63
triglie di scoglio 63
tronco al cioccolato 236–8
trooping funnell 22
tub gurnard 62
Tuscan bread
  Acquacotta Maremmana 147–9
  Argentario fish stew 110–12
  Bread, wine and sugar 132–3
  Cannellini bean soup 186

  Cod with pine nuts and olives 114
  Fisherman's acquacotta 88–9
  Lamb and tomato stew 200–1
  Maremman bean and vegetable soup 151
  Scampi and potato soup 103–5
  Toast with tomato and anchovies 130–1
  Toasted bread with lemon 128

U
uova sode con acciugata 174–5

V
Vegetable stock 161–3
vellutata 29
Vinegar chicken 196–7
Viterbo 16, 42, 195
Viterbo-style acquacotta 42–3
vongole e polenta 106–9
vongole verace 61

W
walnuts
  Fig and chocolate bread 219–21
  Honey and nut pastries 213–15
wedge clams 61
  Spaghetti with wedge clams 92
weeping bolete 23
whiting 61
Wild asparagus tart 38–9
wild boar 50
  Wild boar in chocolate sauce 55
  Wild boar stew 52–3
wild chicory, Viterbo-style acquacotta 42–3
Wild mushroom soup 28
wines of southern Maremma 256–7

Z
Zucchini risotto 161–3
zuppa 29
zuppa di ceci e castagne 46
zuppa di farro 184–5
zuppa di funghi 28
zuppa di sarde e patate 103
zuppa di scampi e patate 103–5
zuppa lombarda 186
zuppa maremmana 151
Zuppe e Stornelli (Claudi and Sergio) 69

GRAZIE

I still pinch myself when I think about the fact that it was through this cookbook and the beautiful Tuscan Maremma that I got to know the great Stephanie Alexander – thank you Stephanie for lending your words to the foreword, it is a true honour.

I am so grateful for the help and inspiration of so many people that led to the creation of this book.

To Alessandra Olivari and Umberto Fanteria, for their friendship and generosity, for their stories of mushroom hunting and fishing, and for Alessandra's Nonna Quinta's recipe for pagnotella.

To le santostefanesi, Orestina Capozzi and Valeria Palombo, for sharing their family recipes.

To the wonderful Ilena Donati who I met randomly one day while at Gianni's roadside fruit and vegetable stand near Capalbio. Her knowledge of local dishes is a book in itself. Thank you to Giulia Scarpaleggia for coming back to get me.

To Elisa Costagliola and her family fish shop, Da Ledo, in Porto Ercole and to the Forno del Porto for always supplying us with fresh anchovies, meringhe and pizzette bianche to keep a two year old happy.

To Francesco Carfagna and his family on Giglio Island.

To Katja Meyer, a friend and fellow Maremma lover and expatriate, whose stories about Saturnia and advice on visiting Giglio all proved extremely valuable.

To Marie Louis Scio and her beautiful resort, Il Pellicano.

To Valentina Di Virginio and Fabrizio D'Ascenzi from Acquaviva who spent an entire afternoon showing me the art of making crepes. No, not crepes, *ciaffagnoni*.

To Clelia Andreini and Andrea Temperani, who hosted us while we cooked and photographed the recipes for this book at their beautiful B&B, Il Baciarino in Vetulonia. It is, for me, a wonderful representation of the beauty of the Maremma – the peaceful hills covered in olive trees, oak, prickly pears and wild fennel, and the sea not far off. Thank you to Andrea's family for having us on the fishing boat and for the fresh fish.

Thank you to the wonderful team who helped put this cookbook together. To Lauren Bamford, who I met for the first time when shooting the recipes of my first cookbook, *Florentine*, and who, while visiting me in Porto Ercole a few months later on her first trip to Italy said, 'We need to shoot your next cookbook here.' To the hardworking, fun, talented group who travelled all the way to Maremma, you made shooting this cookbook one of the best weeks of my life! (Pictured above from left to right: Alice Adams, Helen Johnson, Emily Weaving, Sam Emery, Lauren Bamford, Deb Kaloper, Kathy Kaloper (with my daughter on her lap!). To the Hardie Grant team, especially Emma Marijewycz in London and Susie Ashworth, Jane Willson, Andrea O'Connor, Mark Campbell and Allison Colpoys in Melbourne.

I don't know where I'd be without a gang of willing recipe testers – thank you to Jill Bernadini, Simon Bian, Becky Bishop, Julia Busuttil, Mark Davies, Sumie Davies, Lexi Earl, Helen Farrell, Camilla Ferraro, Caroline Hamilton, Francesca Lami, Carmen Pricone, Gabrielle Schaffner, Carly Slater and Kirsteen Travers.

To my family – to my parents in Australia, and my mother in law, Angela, in Tuscany.

And most of all to my husband and my daughter, for all your support and endless patience while you let me do the thing I've dreamed most of doing.

ABOUT THE AUTHOR

Emiko Davies is an Australian–Japanese food writer and photographer who spent her childhood and adolescence between Asia and Australia. She has a background in Fine Art, which took her to the US, but after falling in love with Florence, she has called Tuscany home since 2005. Emiko has written five cookbooks, *Florentine*, *Tortellini at Midnight*, *Torta della Nonna*, *Cinnamon & Salt* and *Acquacotta*. Originally published in 2017, *Acquacotta* was inspired by the rustic food and wild landscape of the Maremma. It was written while she was living in Porto Ercole on Monte Argentario when her husband, Marco Lami, was the head sommelier of Il Pellicano. They have a soft spot for this corner of southern Tuscany with its rocky islands and shimmering coastline and still spend time here whenever they can. An authority on home cooking and regional Italian cuisine, Emiko continues writing the blog she started in 2010 and contributes to publications such as *Corriere della Sera*, Italy's leading newspaper, *Financial Times*, *Saveur* and *Food52* to name a few. Emiko and Marco live in San Miniato, Tuscany, with their two children.

This edition published in 2023 by Hardie Grant Books,
an imprint of Hardie Grant Publishing
First published in 2017

Hardie Grant Books (Melbourne)
Wurundjeri Country
Building 1, 658 Church Street
Richmond, Victoria 3121

Hardie Grant Books (London)
5th & 6th Floors
52–54 Southwark Street
London SE1 1UN

hardiegrant.com/au/books

All rights reserved. No part of this publication may be reproduced, stored in a retrieval system or transmitted in any form by any means, electronic, mechanical, photocopying, recording or otherwise, without the prior written permission of the publishers and copyright holders.

The moral rights of the author have been asserted.

Copyright text, illustrations and photography © Emiko Davies 2017
Copyright photography © Lauren Bamford 2017
Copyright design © Hardie Grant Publishing 2017

A Cataloguing-in-Publication entry is available from the catalogue of the National Library of Australia at www.nla.gov.au

Acquacotta
978 1 74379 925 3

10 9 8 7 6 5 4 3 2 1

Publishing Director: Jane Willson
Managing Editor: Marg Bowman
Project Editor: Andrea O'Connor
Editor: Susie Ashworth
Design Manager: Mark Campbell
Designer: Allison Colpoys
Illustrator: Emiko Davies
Food Photography: Lauren Bamford
Location Photography: Emiko Davies
Stylist: Deb Kaloper
Home Economist: Alice Adams
Production Manager: Todd Rechner

Colour reproduction by Splitting Image Colour Studio
Printed in China by Leo Paper Products LTD.

Hardie Grant acknowledges the Traditional Owners of the country on which we work, the Wurundjeri people of the Kulin nation and the Gadigal people of the Eora nation, and recognises their continuing connection to the land, waters and culture. We pay our respects to their Elders past and present.